Case Studies for Inclusive Educators & Leaders

Darrin Griffiths & James Ryan
Editors

Word & Deed Publishing Incorporated & Edphil Books
1860 Appleby Line, Suite #778
Burlington, Ontario, Canada, L7L 7H7
(Toll Free) 1-866-601-1213

Copyright © 2018 Word & Deed Publishing Incorporated

Case Studies for Inclusive Educators & Leaders

All rights reserved. Except as permitted under (U.S. Copyright Act of 1976), or (Canadian Copyright Act of 2012), no part of this publication may be reproduced, distributed, or transmitted in any form or by any means, or stored in a database or retrieval system, without the prior written permission of the publisher.

Edited by Darrin Griffiths, EdD, & James Ryan PhD
Copy-Edited by Steve Viau, Pointed View Editing
Book design by Jim Bisakowski – www.bookdesign.ca

ISBN 978-0-9918626-3-4

Word & Deed Publishing Incorporated
1860 Appleby Line, Suite #778
Burlington, Ontario, Canada, L7L 7H7
(Toll Free) 1-866-601-1213

Visit our website at
www.wordanddeedpublishing.com

Praise for Case Studies for Inclusive Educators and Leaders

We are living through a global period of xenophobia, divisiveness, and new and old exclusions that is trickling down to our schools. There is no better way to teach inclusion than through the use of complex cases that make us think about how we normalize and/or disrupt exclusion in and out of schools. The cases in this book are excellent tools for stimulating in-class discussion and professional development, and it is in these educational spaces that we can begin to learn how to challenge the bullies who want to divide us.
— *Gary Anderson, Dept. of Educational Leadership, NYU*

This is a compelling text with useful practical guides for educators and field practitioners broadly defined. The international scope of the book makes it highly significant and relevant, pointing out the nuances, challenges and possibilities of inclusivity, social justice and equity education in contemporary times. This work clearly offers intellectual openings for critical dialogues, social criticisms and speculative imaginaries of new educational futurity.
— *George J. Sefa Dei, Professor of Social Justice Education & Director, Centre for Integrative Anti-Racism Studies, OISE, University of Toronto*

"We are living in a context fraught with tensions, conflicts and injustices of every kind. Griffiths and Ryan offer us hope not by providing easy answers, on the contrary by presenting us with an opportunity to reflect, to look into our inner self, our own value system, our own biases, our own prejudices and encouraging us to engage in responsive leadership - a leadership that is spurred by strong ethical behaviour. Each case provides the reader with an opportunity for growth. It is indeed a timely work, to be recommended."
— *Christopher Bezzina, University of Malta and Uppsala University, Sweden*

This book provides great case studies of inclusion that will spark reflection and discussion for educational leaders to act. "None of us enter the field of educational leadership not to take actions." This is a quote within this book that resonates with me because it highlights a dichotomy, one that is reassuring and problematic at the same time. As educational leaders we bring our lived experiences to our practices and decision making each day and we need to have mechanisms in place, whether that be a critical mentor, an advisory committee, or a intentional new learning experiences, that will challenge our biases to ensure that the "actions" we are taking provide equitable access and opportunity for all students and staff to feel valued, safe, accepted, and supported if we are committed to improving outcomes for all students.

—*Manny Figueiredo, Director of Education, Hamilton-Wentworth District School Board, Ontario, Canada*

I appreciate the pedagogical aspiration of this book: highlighting the dilemmas of inclusive practice, avoiding neat answers and provoking us to form our own conclusions. It brings inclusion out into the open for discussion. It challenges us to enter into debates about what inclusion really means, in practice not just in ambition. It is an unsettling book, without resolutions, reflecting the realities of lived experience but with a desire to move beyond the experiential to forge principles for inclusive practice.

—*Professor Trevor Gale, Head, School of Education, The University of Glasgow*

This assemblage of essays could not come at a more important historical moment, not only because reactionary populism and the mimetic scapegoating of immigrants is afoot worldwide, and despotic leaders of nation states are encouraging their constituencies to become a safe refuge for acrimony, but also because the contributors speak so presciently to the urgent and everyday issues facing students, teachers, parents and the communities in which they live and labor. What is left today of the public sphere is peeling away like rancid fruit, while citizens are being persuaded by swaggering demagogues and their extortionist cronies that they are better off compliantly giving up their freedom in return for maximum security against outsiders--the images of which have been conjured up by pathological liars such as Donald Trump, who enjoys playing puppeteer behind the smoke and mirrors of celebrity. In such times many teachers, overburdened by despair and overworked by the demands of capital, remain bereft of inclusive leadership and teaching strategies so urgently needed in order to reclaim lost territory, to regain new spaces of hope and possibility, and to introduce variations and invent new forms of inclusive communities of learners as warranted by today's pedagogical necessity. Editors Darrin Griffiths and James Ryan and their stellar international cast of authors have together created a fundamental, expansive and indispensable book that probes deeply into the issues surrounding case studies, stressing the importance of contextual specificity. This is a fiercely urgent book that I would urge all educators to engage. This is a fiercely urgent book that I would encourage all educators to engage. Every educational researcher, teacher, administrator and policymaker--from Toronto's Kensington Market, to Silicon Valley, to the hinterlands of the Italian Alps--would do well to make this reading a priority. It is heartening to read so many voices--39 in fact--united in the struggle for justice.

—*Peter McLaren, Distinguished Professor in Critical Studies, the Donna Ford Attallah College of Educational Studies, Chapman University and author of Pedagogy of Insurrection*

Darrin Griffiths and James Ryan, who are well-respected scholars and long-standing educators, have assembled a brilliant collage of international authors to provide their readers with 39 concise, engaging, morally problematic and provocative case studies, around the theme of inclusion. Based on current learning community realities, these cases introduce an array of well-formed issues, dilemmas, quandaries and imperatives. To work through the accompanying case questions is to be sensitized, educated, equipped and ethically transformed.

—*Keith D. Walker, Professor, Educational Administration, University of Saskatchewan*

Case Studies for Inclusive Educators & Leaders is an thought-provoking collection that collectively illustrates the diversity of what inclusive education means in various contexts. Each case goes beyond telling a story—indeed, authors question and critique seldom-interrogated concepts such as leadership, education and context as they seek to understand and explain what inclusion looks like in 21st century schools. Chapters offer a sophisticated mix of theoretical exploration and practical applications. Recommended for educational leaders, faculty in leadership preparation programs and professional development providers.

—*Professor Jeffrey S. Brooks, Associate Dean, Research and Innovation, RMIT University School of Education*

"Exclusion in schools and societies--exceedingly various in its forms and targets--can be particularly difficult to interrupt when routinized and normalized, or as we see increasingly today, when masked by false claims to democracy. As educators and leaders strive toward inclusion in the most robust and complex sense, we need look no further than this collection by Griffiths, Ryan, and colleagues that magnifies the complexities, contingencies, and contradictions of doing so. The refusal to oversimplify that defines the vast array of richly detailed cases only pushes readers further to grapple, question, dialogue, and imagine.
—*Kevin Kumashiro, author of "Against Common Sense:
Teaching and Learning Toward Social Justice"*

Inclusivity, equity, diversity and difference are all flushed out in Case Studies for Inclusive Educators and Leaders, where it is shown that to treat everybody equally does not mean treating them the same. In Case Studies, inclusivity and equity are poetically dealt with where the authors show – with elegance – the vision and the courage required to bring into existence a better and more hopeful, inclusive and equitable future. Case Studies is a required reading for those who dare to educate and lead with their eyes wide-open and their consciousness wide-awake.
—*Awad Ibrahim, Professor, Faculty of Education, University of Ottawa*

This book presents a fascinating selection of the many multifaceted challenges and dilemmas involved in navigating the complex world of schooling. It integrates the perspectives of teachers, school leaders, families and other professionals in ways that sensitise the reader to the experiences of children at risk of marginalisation or exclusion. Questions at the end of each chapter encourage a flexible, solution focused approach to managing difficult situations without prejudice. As a casebook for inclusive education, it makes an invaluable contribution to the literature.
—*Lani Florian, Bell Chair of Education, Moray House School of Education,
The University of Edinburgh.*

These are short, well-written, thought-provoking, excellently-resourced cases that probe the teacher's dilemma in relation to the excluded student, accompanied by key questions and relevant teaching strategies. Each chapter is exceptionally well-organized, but in its totality, this book is not an easy read...I was personally troubled as I was drawn into cases of exclusion, confusion, and delusion that expose a wide range of traditional, exclusion-oriented norms.

I strongly recommend Case Studies for Inclusive Educators and Leaders. This collection is a profound, fresh, and disturbing journey into the world of exclusionary practices. It will tear off the veneer of complacency that hides school-based exclusionary practices and help prepare readers in the ongoing struggle towards inclusion.

—*Glenn Rideout, PhD, Associate Dean, Graduate Studies and Research, Faculty of Education, University of Windsor*

Griffiths and Ryan's diligent efforts to retrieve narratives from the field of education detailing inclusive practices has definitely paid off! This compilation of stories from educators, leaders, and scholars in the field is a must-read for anyone invested in public education and the success of students. This edited book captures everyday scenarios in teaching-case study format that demonstrates efforts to create more inclusive schools. Readers are given the opportunity to handle the often-complicated dilemmas that educators experience first-hand every day. These exercises will help educators understand inclusion in deeper ways, and ultimately assist them to do something about the pernicious exclusive practices that plague our schools and communities.

—*Katina Pollock, Associate Professor, Western University*

This book is an invaluable resource for those who want to test their assumptions about exclusionary practices and policies in schools and to reflect imaginatively and critically on the difficult choices involved in making education a flourishing and successful experience for everyone. No simple answers are offered. Instead, educators and leaders are able to work with a range of carefully selected and accessibly presented cases rooted in the complexities and dilemmas of real-life school situations and contexts. The book practices what it preaches, by treating educators and school leaders inclusively. They are invited to engage with the cases as active, professional learners capable of enhancing their own understanding and grappling with the challenging issues raised.

—*Philip A. Woods, PhD FRSA, Professor of Educational Policy, Democracy and Leadership, University of Hertfordshire, UK*

Darrin Griffiths & James Ryan have assembled an outstanding set of cases for educators and education leaders who strive to foster socially just schools. The cases, written by scholars from around the world, offer intensely real scenarios that occur in today's schools. This is a wonderful teaching tool that will empower educators and leaders to take head on complex cases of exclusion and injustice and turn them into opportunities to foster acceptance, understanding, and fair outcomes for all students.

—Casey D. Cobb, Ph.D. Neag Professor of Educational Policy,
Neag School of Education, University of Connecticut

Dedication

This book is dedicated to all educators who strive for inclusion.

Contents

Praise for Case Studies for Inclusive Educators and Leaders . .i

Dedication ix

Foreword xv
Ira Bogotch, Florida Atlantic University, Florida, U.S.A. and Sara Bogotch, EBS Healthcare, U.S.A.

Introduction: Cases for Inclusion 1
James Ryan, OISE/University of Toronto, Ontario, Canada

Case #1. Enhancing Diversity and Equity at Tradition University 11
William B. Harvey, American Association for Access, Equity and Diversity, in Washington, D.C., U.S.A.

Case #2. The Husky or the March?: Which Way to Student Solidarity 17
Karleen Pendleton Jiménez, Trent University, Canada

Case #3. The Consequence of Islamaphobia in K-12 Schools: A Case to Remedy Bullying 23
Bobbie Plough, California State University, East Bay, U.S.A., and Brad J. Porfilio, Seattle University, U.S.A.

Case #4. How Can We Support Teachers To Become More Inclusive in Secondary School? 31
Suzanne Carrington, Queensland University of Technology, Australia, and Jane Vanelli, Ferny Grove State High School, Australia

Case #5. Inclusive Communities? Supporting Sexual Minority and Gender Non-conforming Youth in Catholic Public Schools. 39
Barbara Hamilton, Calgary Catholic School District, Canada, and Carmen Mombourquette, University of Lethbridge, Canada

Case #6. Including Homeless Children in an Elite School: Arzoo's Story. 49
Divya Murali, Sveta Davé Chakravarty, and Shashi Mendiratta, The Ferdinand Centre for Education for Social Justice, New Delhi, India

Case #7. "He's here everyday but, take him away!" 57
Chris Gilham, St. Francis Xavier University, Canada

Case #8. Negotiating and Navigating Disability in Inclusive
Settings 61
Melissa K. Driver, Kennesaw State University, U.S.A.

Case #9. Inclusion to Prevent Exclusion: A Tale of Two Schools 67
Louise Gazeley, University of Sussex, UK

Case #10. Brentwood High School 73
Lynn Butler-Kisber, McGill University, Canada

Case #11. RACE: A Polarizing Force. 79
Philip McAdoo, The University of Pennsylvania, U.S.A.

Case #12. Including Sophie: Autism, Dyslexia, and Mental Health 85
Jenn de Lugt, University of Regina, Canada

Case #13. Wendy or Chad? Supporting Transgender Youth in
Elementary Schools. 91
Bud Harrelson, University of North Carolina at Chapel Hill, U.S.A,
and Kathleen Brown, University of North Carolina at Chapel Hill,
U.S.A.

Case #14. Including Older Pupils With Challenging Behaviour:
A Case Study Within a Secondary School in England . 99
Carl Parsons, University of Greenwich, London, UK

Case #15. The Complexity of Curriculum Decision-Making:
Defining a Strategic Course for Student Achievement
in light of School And District Policy 105
Lindsay Kwock Hu, University of Southern California, U.S.A.

Case #16. Unexpected Bus Duty: Lessons on Inclusion from a
Field Trip 109
Steve Sider, Wilfrid Laurier University, Canada

Case #17. Facing High School: A Mother Reflects on Her Son's
Journey Through Inclusive Classrooms 115
Diane Linder Berman Hunter College & Stafford Technical Center,
and David J. Connor, Hunter College, City University of New York,
U.S.A.

Case #18. The Dilemma of Christmas in the Secular Public
School 123
C. Darius Stonebanks, Bishop's University, Canada

Case #19. I Didn't See This Coming 129
          Cindy Diehl-Yang, VGM Group, U.S.A., and Nicholas J. Pace,
          University of Nebraska-Lincoln, U.S.A.

Case #20. Is This Inclusion? 137
          Linda Chmiliar, Athabaska University, Canada

Case #21. Linguistic Exclusion From Above 143
          Eleni Oikonomidoy, University of Nevada, Reno, U.S.A.

Case #22. Donna Becomes Don: A Call for School Districts to
          Better Serve Transgender Youth 149
          Nan Stevens, Thompson Rivers University, Canada

Case #23. Punthea's Father: A Study in PTSD 157
          Robert E. White, St. Francis Xavier University, Canada

Case #24. Looking at the "Big Picture" and Long-term
          Outcomes: Partnering with Parents and Self-
          Advocates to Ensure Quality Outcomes for Students
          with Intellectual Disabilities. 163
          Lynne Sommerstein, S.U.N.Y. Buffalo State, U.S.A., and Diane Lea
          Ryndak, The University of North Carolina at Greensboro, U.S.A.

Case #25. Katie's Dilemma 171
          Cam Cobb, University of Windsor, Canada

Case #26. Disrupting Expectations: Challenges to Academic
          Inclusion in a "College For All" Culture 177
          Michelle J. Bellino, University of Michigan, U.S.A., and Nathan
          Phipps, University of Michigan, U.S.A.

Case #27. Hum ... Social Justice? But the school is doing well! . .187
          Jhonel Morvan, Brock University & Ontario Ministry of Education,
          Canada

Case #28. Nang Tat's New Life. 195
          Troy Boddy, Montgomery County Public Schools in Rockville,
          Maryland, U.S.A.

Case #29. A Question of Gender Dysphoria in a Preschool Age
          Child 201
          Camille Quinton, Prairie Rose School Division, Alberta, Canada

Case #30. The Challenges of the Lavendale Juvenile Center 207
          Ray Tonchen Jr., Wayne State University, U.S.A.

Case #31. The Case of the Service Dog................213
    Adelee J. Penner, Alberta Education, Canada
    & Carmen Mombourquette, University of Lethbridge, Canada

Case #32. Indigenous Peoples and Inclusivity in Education 219
    John Roberts, Mohawk College, Hamilton, Ontario, Canada

Case #33. Including Tony.......................225
    Vernita Mayfield, Leadervation Learning, Denver, Colorado, USA

Case #34. Gay Boys Do Cry: Homophobia and Victimization in Canadian School Culture 231
    André P. Grace, University of Alberta, Canada

Case #35. Doing Things Right or Doing the Right Things: The Case of Inclusion in the Republic of Ireland 239
    Carol-Ann O'Stórain, Miriam Twomey, Michael Shevlin, & Conor Mc Guckin, School of Education, Trinity College Dublin, Ireland

Case #36. Educator Bias and Judgement and Student Discipline. .255
    Bill de la Cruz, Denver Public Schools, Colorado, U.S.A.

Case #37. Stacey Is Not Attending School...............263
    Debbie Donsky, Ontario Ministry of Education, Canada, and Darrin Griffiths, Niagara University, Ontario, Canada

Case #38. Including Samir: Resistance to Inclusion - how to help school communities embrace integration, and moderate/severe disabilities..................269
    DeLacy Ganley, Claremount Graduate University, U.S.A., and Samara Suafo'a, Claremount Graduate University, U.S.A.

Case #39. Navigating Religion, Creed, and Accommodation . . .279
    Hiren Mistry, OISE/University of Toronto, Canada

Afterword 289
    Denise Armstrong, Brock University, Ontario, Canada

Contributors 297

About the Editors 313

Foreword

Inclusive Education

Ira Bogotch & Sara Bogotch

In this Foreword, we will try to give you a taste of the many rabbit holes that you are about to jump into as you read this book of cases, compiled by Darrin Griffiths and James Ryan. Each case presents a difficult—and often moral—dilemma. The case authors provide specific contexts, settings, and guiding policies all leading to a conflict or a problem statement. But as you read the cases, you will need to be prepared for there *not* to be a beginning, a middle, and, especially, an end. The cases here are unique, in that they stop before there are any resolutions, moral or pragmatic. The cases invite you into the complex world of educational leadership made explicitly real. Hopefully, that invitation leads you to read widely and think deeply; the answers to the cases will not emerge from your mind fully formed. You land inside the rabbit holes searching for meanings so that you can offer intelligent suggestions and make tentative hypotheses, but never to give definitive answers. Why? Because as an educational leader you will never be in an ideal situation where certainty is your guide. Your quest, your mission, is to put the good of the child(ren) ahead of constraints, restraints, and the realities of working in imperfect settings. Should you choose deliberately to act as a leader for social justice, then that good will extend out to families, communities, and even societies themselves.

Whether you are using this text as an instructor for aspiring leaders, in professional development sessions, or if you yourself are engaged in leadership development, the learning curve will be steep; however, it will be well worth your time.

The two signs below can be said to reflect two sides of the inclusive education coin. In the sign entitled WE WELCOME, you see a version of the universal declaration of rights for everyone. It is an all-inclusive ideal – a world to which many of us aspire. Right below it is a sign hanging in the Special Education wing of a local elementary school. The message here recognizes specific needs of individual students or groups of students. Do we treat all children the same or do we educate each student according to what s/he needs? Can we do both? How?

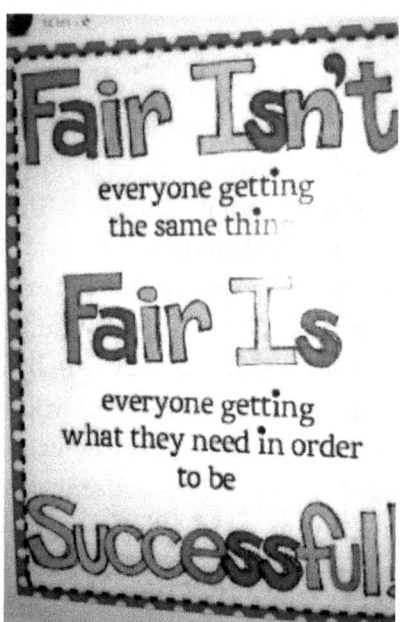

Professional Judgments Inside Seven Rabbit Holes

Rabbit Hole #1: In your professional judgment as an educational leader, which of the two signs reflects *your philosophy* or, in other words, the values guiding your educational decisions?

Rabbit Hole #2: How do you handle dilemmas (e.g., when both parties to a dispute have right – ethical or legal - on their side] in your everyday practices?

Rabbit Hole #3: Physically and mentally (with respect to your own health], are you able to live with unresolved contradictions, tensions, and on-going conflicts as part of your daily routines?

Rabbit Hole #4: Do you think that compromise is the best way out from difficult situations?

Rabbit Hole #5: Do you consider yourself a pragmatist, a realist, and a decision-maker; or, do you think that too often talk devolves into a waste of your time?

Rabbit Hole #6: Is your chosen *modus operandi* to handle problems one at a time as they emerge, child by child, incident by incident?

Rabbit Hole #7: Do you prefer neat and tidy answers to a seemingly endless series of questions?

None of us enter the field of educational leadership *not* to take actions. Once we are made aware of a problem, big or small, our collective disposition is to act. A critical pragmatic question is, how much time do any of us have on-the-job for deliberation and professional judgments? Even if you think that the best way to learn the intricacies of school or university leadership is through experiences on-the-job, what is always missing are continuous study and deliberation. Nowhere does discussion and debate happen better than in an academic setting on a university campus. Yes, as a university professor, the first author is biased. Yet, we know too well what life is like for school/university leaders once on-the-job. True, you may love your job, but there is rarely enough time, resources, or training to make inclusive education work as an ideal. All of this has led us to list a few warning signs.

Warning Labels on Inclusive Education

Whatever you decide inclusive education should be, it ought to come with warning labels that might read:

> If a child is silent for prolonged periods of time in class, stares out into space, sits apart from the other children, cries periodically (or continuously), works alone on an iPad, or is disruptive, then your professional judgment must involve the student. Many of these students may communicate what they want/need to become self-confident, and it is our job to actively listen. That's educational leadership!

> If a child has been diagnosed with, for example, autism, an intellectual disability, or has physical limitations, then your professional judgment is to involve an interdisciplinary team to design (or redesign) a plan of individualized education and ensure that *everyone* involved knows the plan inside and out. That's team leadership!

> If your school and/or district do not provide adequate training for all staff, or if the trained staff are overwhelmed and without sufficient support and resources to do a quality job, or if the team members do not have collegial relations, then your professional judgment must include strategies to address systems and personnel issues. That's strategic leadership!

Whither Social Justice?

To what end(s) are we to fulfill the hopes and dreams of education? Inclusive education is one more step in the direction of promoting leadership for social justice. As policy, it aims towards making educational institutions a welcoming refuge for all, regardless of race, religion, nationality, class, sexual orientation, intellectual disability, or physical limitation. By policy, when a school or district is named as an inclusive community, then it does not single out specific groups of students. Yet as educators who diagnose problems and issues, we know that each child has specific needs that ought to be met educationally, socially, and emotionally. Figuring out the right setting, the right curriculum, the right pedagogy, the right levels of instruction, the right individuals to relate to the child, and the right team needed to make the above decisions, are all part of the inclusion process. It involves planning, implementation, and monitoring, not simply for compliance, but for quality and the good of the child. We know that something can go wrong at any point inside educational institutions, so let's be as prepared as possible. This is where these case study discussions can be so valuable.

Your job is to align instruction, curricula, and extracurricular programs with equity, based on the needs of children and adults. In so doing, you fulfill your moral purposes as an educational leader. This is a necessary function; however, it is not sufficient in terms of leadership for social justice. What we mean here is that you still are obligated to ensure that the opportunities you are able to create within schools and universities are translated out into communities and societies. Social justice expands the boundaries of your formal job description. It obligates you to act beyond school and engage in social, political, and economic struggles for equal opportunities for all. Unfortunately, not all educators embrace this external political and moral dimension to their jobs.

The relationship between inclusive education and social justice is always contingent on contexts and cultures—and never comes with any guarantees. Thus, all of us should seek to make our lessons relevant to social, political, and economic opportunities outside school. To do so, we need to exercise our rights as citizens. As we write this foreword, we see the high school students in Parkland, Florida—along with their upper-middle-class families—pushing for changes, not just inside schools, that is, school safety, but for society (US) as a whole, that is, gun control and greater mental illness resources. The alleged shooter was excluded, not only from this particular high school, but also from other social and mental health institutions affiliated with the school system. Everyone acknowledges how the school system, the mental health system, the police, and even the FBI, could not connect the dots prior to this horrible tragedy. The responsibilities of inclusive education and leadership for social justice are to connect the dots, close the gaps, and engage in both educational and political processes. For too long, adult educators have constructed an exclusionary model of education, delimiting issues of equity/opportunities to within-school teaching and learning. This arrangement has prevented educators (and their students) from engaging in broader social, political, and economic activities. For inclusion to work, even imperfectly, educators need to extend their own mindsets beyond their classrooms and educational institutions and engage with societal debates. Like the cases in this volume, we will see the many possibilities that can emerge from educators jumping into this social-justice rabbit hole.

Introduction: Cases for Inclusion

James Ryan

This book is for those who wish to make schools more inclusive places. It presents case studies of everyday problem scenarios with which teachers, administrators and parents must deal. In one way or another, all these cases involve issues of exclusion/inclusion. They offer readers the opportunity to think about particular problem situations that they may encounter, and to devise solutions to them. Our hope is that the cases—and the related questions and activities—will assist educators to understand, reflect upon, and deal with, the many exclusive issues that they come across each and every day, so that they will be better prepared to make our schools and communities more inclusive places to work, learn, and live.

As the cases will reveal, exclusion is neither easy to recognize nor to deal with. Unbidden, it routinely intrudes on our lives. Exclusion occurs in many ways – as we are left out of conversations that are important to us, decisions that affect us, and valued activities in which others engage. It inserts itself into our personal lives, our places of work, and our institutions of learning. Exclusion may be obvious. We may know, for example, that we have not had a say in the new guidelines just passed down from central office. But exclusion may also be difficult to see – we may not be aware that deliberations about the new guidelines are taking place. Exclusion may materialize spontaneously. But it also may be predictable, the product of longstanding patterns that we have come to anticipate. We may know ahead of time, for example, that we are going to be left out of conversations and decisions about new guidelines.

Exclusion may be intentionally engineered for particular purposes.

Central office officials may, for example, purposely leave particular people out of deliberations over new guidelines. Just as likely, though, exclusion is the result of practices that we take for granted, part of institutional norms that appear on the surface to be benign, necessary, and ethical. All parties associated with new guidelines, for example, may assume that decisions ought to be left to the few people they believe are best able to design them. They may feel comfortable with their exclusion because it has always been done in this way. Most of us have experienced these kinds of exclusion. Despite our social or organizational positions, our professional or personal acuities, or our moral or political orientations, every one of us, in one way or another, will experience some form of exclusion over the course of our lifetimes.

Exclusion can be painful; it hurts. We all have felt the sting of not measuring up – of being labelled as too large or small, too clever or inept, or too conforming or rebellious. We all know what exclusion feels like (Ryan, 2006). For some, however, exclusion can be just a temporary condition, occurring sporadically in context-specific events. Others may have the resources to counter exclusion. Making use of their positions, acuities and/or affiliations, they are able to be part of conversations, decisions, and activities that are meaningful to them, sidestepping the obstacles that could have prevented their inclusion. Those who can do this are privileged. The privileges that accompany their positions, acuities, and affiliations ensure their inclusion.

But not everyone is so easily included. Indeed, many who do not possess the privileges required for inclusion are routinely excluded from what life has to offer. Those with skin colour that is not white, ethnicities, cultures, and languages that are not of European origin, body shapes that are not ideal, women, LBTGQ individuals, the poor, and the physically, emotionally, and psychologically challenged are systemically excluded over and over again. For them, exclusion is not temporary, spontaneous, or surmountable. Instead, it is persistent, pervasive, and seemingly unresolvable. It affects every aspect of their lives; it shapes their personal interactions, their professional relationships, and, more profoundly, their life prospects. They routinely endure hurt, shame, embarrassment, and pain in the contexts in which they live, work, and learn.

This is not to say that those concerned with exclusion have not in recent years attempted to do something about it. Indeed, both individuals and institutions have designed practices and policies that promote inclusion. One of the areas in which this has happened is education. Acknowledging that exclusion extends beyond ability, to issues of race, ethnicity, culture, language, religion, sexual orientation, and gender, among others, some educators have actively sought to identify exclusive practices and do something about them. The contributors to this volume are one example. Scholars have also shown concern over exclusion. The numbers of studies, scholarly articles, and books in this area have increased over the past few years. Education organizations have also entered the fray. The Ontario government (2009), for example, has implemented guidelines directed specifically at equity and inclusion in education. They are designed to ensure, in increasingly diverse contexts, that "students are engaged, included, and respected, and that they see themselves reflected in their learning environment" (p. 5). Governments have also been active in devising or adjusting leadership frameworks to provide equitable and inclusive guidelines for administrators (e.g., European Policy Network on School Leadership, 2010).

While the above initiatives are encouraging, they nevertheless represent islands in a rapidly encroaching sea of exclusion. Nationalist sentiments appear to be on the rise, and central to these efforts are campaigns to exclude groups of people. Emblematic of this nationalist fever are the words and deeds of the president of the United States, Donald Trump. Derogatory and demeaning comments about other countries and cultures, promises to build a wall to keep Mexican people out, threats to deport the children of undocumented immigrants, unflattering remarks about women, and executive orders to prevent citizens of Muslim countries from entering the United States represent just a few of the exclusive sentiments of one of the most powerful people in the world.

While presidential orders may seek to keep so-called undesirables out of the United States, they also are having a significant impact on marginalized communities within. Presidential tweets, orders, and pronouncements have emboldened progenitors of exclusion. Castrellon, Rivarola, and Lopez (2017) indicate that hate crimes and hateful harassment have increased in the United States since the election of President Trump. They observe that "the haters came out of the woodwork and violence suddenly became mainstream" (p. 941). More than this, though, recent pronouncements have given licence for organizations to treat their members poorly. In California, for example, immigration officials are more actively trying to deport illegal immigrants, prompting employers to feel that it is okay to mistreat employees who are in the country illegally (Brunhuber, 2018). The consequence of all this is that marginalized communities in the United States feel angry, anxious, and threatened; they are constantly reminded that they are second-class citizens, neither wanted nor accepted (Castrellon, Rivarola & Lopez, 2017).

The effects of the Trump administration's actions are not restricted to the United States, or, for that matter, the countries and people Trump has targeted. They also have had an impact on other countries. In Canada, for example, as in the United States, reports of racism and violence have increased since the American election (Carter, 2016). Some of these incidents are directly related to Trump's election. Examples abound. In a Hamilton, Ontario store, for example, a black woman was confronted by a white man in a checkout line, who pointed to a picture of Trump, saying that he was glad that he was elected and hoped that "he cleans up the whole of North America" (Carter, 2016, p. 2). Asked to explain what he meant, he replied that "You all (non-white people) shouldn't even be here, you're murderers and killers ... I hope he gets rid of all of you." Commenting on incidents such as this, Bernie Farber, Executive Director of the Mosaic Institute, surmised that "Trump has given permission for the racists ... to pop their heads up ... and get busy." He also notes, though, that while that this is not something new to them, "it's just a shot of adrenalin" (CBC, 2016).

These exclusive sentiments and practices inevitably seep into all of our institutions, including education, excluding men, women, and children in the process. But while the American presidential administration is a problem for inclusive-minded educators around the world, it is not the only one. Other serious—and longer-term—challenges can be traced to encroaching neoliberal reforms. Anderson (2017) notes that recent Trump-inspired education reforms in the United States, while concerning, have merely deepened and expanded the neoliberal policies of the previous administrations. Based on valued market principles, these reforms have favored private schools, enabled the infiltration of private business interests, instituted comprehensive testing regimes, and fostered competition among schools and families. Unfortunately, these programs have not worked well for marginalized groups. Most obviously, they have increased the scope of exclusion in education, both in the United States and elsewhere. In doing so, these reforms have amplified already extreme levels of inequalities (Anderson, 2017; Ryan, 2012).

Trump-inspired and neoliberal reforms are not the only threats to inclusion. Indeed, the very ways in which schools are organized make it difficult to include different others. Western educational institutions are at least partly responsible for exacerbating, if not generating, exclusion. This inability to accommodate diversity can be traced, in part, to the way in which educational institutions were originally organized. Emulating an industrial model, Western educational institutions were designed to process large numbers of students in the most efficient way possible (See for example, Callahan, 1962). They worked on the assumption that a relatively few number of teachers can effectively teach a much larger number of students. Successful operation, however, demanded a considerable degree of uniformity; students had to conform to certain prototypes, that is, they had to be docile, intellectually, emotionally, and physically able, speak the language of the classroom, and possess knowledge, skills, and values compatible with certain cultural, class, gender, sexual orientation, geographical, racial, religious, and many other unique types of, backgrounds. Buildings were, and, for the most part, still are, designed, teachers trained, resources allocated, schedules arranged, and curricula created specifically to serve these prototypes. Schools organized in this way, however, do not easily accommodate those who fail to conform to these prototypes, and as a result they routinely exclude students.

For the most part, the basic DNA of this industrial model persists today; most Western contemporary schools are organized to efficiently process large numbers of particular kinds of students. Unfortunately, these organizations cannot easily accommodate the increasingly diverse student populations that attend present-day schools. Most education systems are not well prepared to cope with diversity or to promote inclusion. More often than not, individual educators, rather than institutions or systems, are the ones who have to devise strategies to include students who display differences.

Contemporary inclusive-minded educators have their work cut out for them. They have to contend with increasing numbers of policies, practices, and organizational patterns that routinely exclude students, parents, and communities. While some exclusive measures are blatantly obvious, others are not. Indeed, the best-intentioned policies can themselves be exclusive. For example, policies that focus on school improvement or raising achievement levels, without acknowledging the diversity in school communities, can exclude many. But these practices may not always be easy to see or understand, buried as they may be in benign-looking policies, practices, or reforms. School life is complex, and exclusion—whether it be slight and fleeting or significant and enduring—is not always apparent, particularly to those who are not routinely subject to it.

Another reason that exclusion may be difficult to detect is that inclusive-minded educators may themselves be unwittingly engaged in exclusive actions. Educators may simply not be aware that what they are doing is exclusive. Responding more often to aggressive male students than more docile female students, favoring so-called classic literature over less well-known but culturally relevant sources, pining for the good old days when teaching more uniform groups of students was supposedly easier, or favoring certain parent groups over others, constitute just a few ways in which well-meaning educators can foster exclusive sentiment and practice. But inclusive-minded educators can also prop up exclusion in more conscious ways. In some circumstances, educators may feel that they will have to sacrifice inclusion for other, more valued, ends. Teachers may want to exclude certain students from their classrooms because they believe that their lessons will work better without these students, or leaders may not want to include teachers in decision-making because they fear that including them may make it more difficult to promote their agendas. The final—and perhaps most difficult to admit—reason for unwittingly promoting exclusion is that inclusive-minded educators may harbour deep-seated but unacknowledged exclusive sentiments (Ryan,

2003). They may unknowingly hold racist, sexist, homophobic, or classist views, and routinely put them into practice without understanding their motivation for doing so nor the consequence of their actions.

Noticing exclusion is challenging enough. But doing something about it, once detected, can be even more challenging for educators. To begin with, inclusive-minded educators work in environments, cultures, and organizations that are not always conducive to inclusive initiatives. Market-friendly policies, aggressive testing regimes, and corporate generated curricula make it difficult for educators to exercise inclusive teaching and leadership practices. More directly though, the people with whom educators work may oppose their inclusive efforts (Ryan, 2012). Powerful administrators, fellow teachers, and community members may actively oppose inclusive initiatives. Among other things, they may have agendas that do not coincide with inclusive priorities. So inclusive-minded educators will have to find ways to promote their inclusive initiatives in environments that resist their efforts (Ryan & Armstrong, 2016). This may involve both understanding these environments and choosing the right strategies to move forward.

Choosing the appropriate inclusive strategies is rarely a straightforward matter, even after educators have correctly identified exclusive practices. Besides accounting for potential resistance to their actions, inclusive-minded educators will often have to choose between two or more competing inclusive options. Selecting one may mean ignoring or negating the other. Allowing a guide dog in the school may assist a visually impaired student, but it may also exclude allergic-sensitive students from certain activities and spaces. Including a student with behavioral issues in regular classroom activities may make it difficult for other students to be involved in the same activities. Initiating inclusive measures not supported by central office may bring on greater surveillance and make it more difficult to promote such initiatives in the future. Siding with one community group over another may damage future relationships with one of the groups. Despite such challenges, educators will at some point have to make a choice.

The complexities of the situations with which educators are typically confronted present them with a number of plausible responses. In the Forward to this book, Bogotch and Bogotch, making a reference to *Alice in Wonderland*, observe that educators have a number of rabbit holes from which to choose when they encounter exclusive practices. In many of these cases, there will be no right or definitive action, and more than one path can achieve the desired end. No universal or sure-fire solutions to these problems exist. Their complexities, context-specific natures, and the rapidly shifting terrains in which they occur, resist ready-made, already-prescribed, or neatly tailored solutions. But whatever choice they eventually make, educators should be able to justify them, understand the consequences of their actions, and be prepared to live with them. The cases in this book provide educators with the opportunities to do this.

The cases presented in the book are intended to provide educators with simulations of complex situations in which educators routinely find themselves. These situations have no easy solution. The cases themselves do not provide resolutions; they stop short of that. Readers are expected to assess the situations and devise their own solutions to them. In doing so, they will have the opportunity to reflect on their own views of inclusion, understand how exclusion manifests in real-life situations, consider potential alternative solutions, and assess the consequences of their eventual choices, just as they would do in actual situations.

The cases span a range of contexts and countries, including the United States, Canada, the United Kingdom, India and Australia. They feature issues associated with what many see as inclusion – physical and intellectual ability. But they also probe many other inclusive issues, including gender, transgender, sexuality, race, immigration, language, religion, age, behaviour, and social class, among others. These issues surface in pedagogy, curriculum, extra-curricular activities, leadership, management, and community and family relationships issues. Readers will have the opportunity to consider the problems described in the cases, to clarify them, and to make an attempt to devise solutions to them. Readers can use the questions and teaching suggestions at the end of each case for their deliberations if they choose, or they can simply approach the described scenarios as they see fit.

The scenarios in this book depict situations with which inclusive-minded educators must deal on a daily basis. These problem-related episodes routinely emerge in the work lives of most educators, and educators' ability to promote inclusion will hinge on the way in which they are able to deal with these immediate and context-specific issues. Recognizing, understanding, and doing something about these exclusive situations is a vital step in promoting inclusion. Failure to address these workplace issues, on the other hand, enables exclusion. It is crucially important, then, that educators take action when they encounter exclusive practices. But while educators may figure how to deal with particular situations within their own workplaces, their actions may not necessarily result in widespread or long-term solutions. And so it is also important that educators understand why exclusion continues to rear its head in their schools, and what they can do beyond resolving their immediate exclusive issues to ensure that these episodes are neither repeated in their schools nor in other educational institutions near and far.

Sustained and widespread solutions to destructive, exclusive practices will require substantive changes to the larger systems that serve students and their communities. In order to achieve such ends, those who wish to promote inclusion will have to supplement their efforts to solve their immediate problems with actions that target larger institutions. Meaningful change will only come about when the entire educational apparatus is challenged and changed. If inclusive-minded educators are to someday work in diversity-friendly organizations then they and their allies will have to change the ways in which we think about and operationalize contemporary education. Doing so would mean promoting more inclusive alternatives to current professional discourses, teacher training, building designs, curricula, pedagogy, scheduling, and leadership, among many other elements of contemporary schooling. Those who engage in these efforts must keep in mind, though, these actions will be just a first step in a long and challenging journey. This journey, however, will be well worth the effort.

References

Anderson, G. (2017). How education researchers have colluded in the rise of neoliberalism: what should the role of academics be in these Trumpian times? *International Journal of Qualitative Studies in Education* 30 (10), 1006-1012.

Brunhuber, K. (2018). Immigrants and cops caught in sanctuary 'war' between Trump and California. CBC News. Accessed Mar 13, 2018 11:50 AM ET (http://www.cbc.ca/news/world/california-sanctuary-laws-trump-1.4573683)

Callahan, R. (1962). *Education and the cult of efficiency.* Chicago: University of Chicago Press.

CBC News. (2016). Trump accused of giving 'a shot of adrenalin' to Canadian racists. November 17, 2016 (http://www.cbc.ca/news/canada/donald-trump-racist-incidents-canada-1.3853681).

Carter, A. (2016) Hamilton woman faces checkout line racism fueled by Trump win. *CBC News.* Accessed November 14, 2016 (http://www.cbc.ca/news/canada/hamilton/trump-1.3849738)

Castrellon, L., Rivarola, A. & Lopez, G. (2017). We are not alternative facts: Feeling, existing and resisting in the era of Trump. *International Journal of Qualitative Studies inEducation* 30 (10), 936-945.

European Policy Network on School Leadership. (2010). *Promoting the policy agenda on school leadership from the perspective of equity and learning.* EPNoSL.

Government of Ontario (2009). *Realizing the promise of diversity: Ontario's equity and inclusive education strategy.* Toronto: Ontario Ministry of Education.

Ryan, J. (2012). *Struggling for Inclusion: Educational Leadership in Neoliberal Times.* Greenwich, CT: Information Age Publishing.

Ryan, J.(2006). *Inclusive Leadership.* San Francisco: Jossey-Bass.

Ryan, J. (2003). *Leading diverse schools.* Dordrecht, NL: Kluwer.

Ryan, J. & Armstrong, D. (Eds.) (2016). *Working (With/out) the System: Educational Leadership, Micropolitics and Social Justice.* Charlotte, NC: Information Age Publishing.

Case #1

Enhancing Diversity and Equity at Tradition University

William B. Harvey

Introduction

To help move Tradition University forward on its stated commitment to diversity and equity, the institution hired a chief diversity officer who, upon his appointment, cautioned the members of the community that no one person alone would be able to change the institutional culture. This case examines various circumstances that, policy statements notwithstanding, hindered the university from moving towards its stated goals and it calls attention to a measure of covert resistance that is embedded in the customs, traditions, and practices of the institution. Efforts to include administrators, students, and faculty in moving the diversity agenda forward are considered, and lead to the realization that institutional self-examination, an openness to change, and appropriate resources are critical to realizing success in this endeavor.

Overview/Analysis

At Tradition University, a highly regarded, very selective, postsecondary institution, the decision to hire a chief diversity officer at the vice-presidential level was not made lightly. TRU, as the University is known, affectionately to its supporters, and sarcastically to its detractors, dates its history back to the colonial era, and changes its social practices and culture slowly and with lengthy deliberation. Charging discrimination and racism, African American students had become loudly critical of the campus atmosphere and of their treatment by some of their peers and professors. When the physical assault of an undergraduate African American female did not lead to the identification of a suspect and consequently no charges were filed by the university police against anyone, the resultant national publicity tarnished the image of the institution, raised concern among both the administration and alumni, and moved a sluggish search process for the cabinet level position to its conclusion.

Upon his introduction to the Board of Trustees in a public ceremony, the new Chief Officer for Diversity and Equity (CODE) shared his perspective that a more tolerant and inclusive culture, that he believed TRU both wanted and needed, could only be realized with the support and participation of all sectors of the community. At an institution where custom and legacy so strongly impacted attitudes and behavior, he said, change could not be achieved by one person alone, regardless of his title or portfolio. Initiatives that could implement the university's stated values would need the endorsement and embrace of senior administrators, faculty, trustees, student leaders, and even concerned alumni in order for TRU to become a move diverse and equitable institution.

The creation of the CODE position presented an interesting situation for the university because it could be viewed as an implicit acknowledgement that the institution had been less than judicious in its past efforts to incorporate diversity across the operational spectrum. TRU recognized that more thoughtful planning and coordinated action must be taken to meet both the challenges and opportunities that will be presented by the phalanx of demographic, economic, political, and social changes that are taking place as the twenty-first century unfolds. At the same time, the interjection of the CODE as a change agent into a change-averse environment indicated that he would face challenges from various constituent groups as well as a measure of passive resistance to suggested modifications in existing practice and policy.

For example, his suggestions for increasing the outreach to potential students of color through visitations to urban high schools were met with questions about the quality of the applicants and about the safety of the admissions staff. Recommendations for diversifying the faculty by connecting to graduate students of color in various fields and establishing a recruitment pipeline caused concerns about affecting the integrity of future searches. Expressions of concern raised by the CODE about the near total exclusion of the contributions of people of color in the curricular offerings evoked sharp reminders about faculty prerogatives and the primacy of the canon.

Problem Statement

Although one of the justifications of the American academy has been its presentation as an ethically-rooted laboratory of inquiry, dedicated to the pursuit of truth and enlightenment without regard to ideology and with unadulterated objectivity, the reality has been quite different. Colleges and universities serve the crucial function of identifying and preparing the individuals who will maintain and extend the continuity and direction of the social order – they separate those who will be leaders from those who will be led, and TRU has served this purpose demonstrably. From its inception the university, like the larger society in which it is embedded, has subscribed to and supported the doctrine of white supremacy, though this is a difficult and painful acknowledgement for the institution to make.

The founder of TRU, his well-known celebration of the principles of equality and justice for all notwithstanding, also articulated the concept of a "natural aristocracy" of talent and virtue, which was the result of his own scientifically researched comparative studies. By establishing a foundation of supposedly unassailable biological and historical "facts" that placed individuals of European descent on an intellectual and cultural level above all other races and societies, the university elevated the doctrine of white supremacy to a position that placed its validity and appropriateness beyond question. Thus, the legitimization of white supremacy via the university occurred partly through the manipulation of "objective scholarship", which was then manifested through discriminatory actions. The validation of the ideology then served as the basis for the construction of an interlocking complex of political, economic, social, artistic, and religious structures which reinforced the central concept and discouraged changes or challenges to the system.

It was not until the launch of the Civil Rights movement in the 1960's that TRU, like other institutions of higher learning, even attempted to disengaged from practices that clearly contradicted the national ideals of fairness and equality. When that grass-roots uprising of African Americans occurred, it brought into public display the overt racism and discrimination that prevailed throughout the nation and forced the realization that TRU had at best overlooked, and at worst actively supported racist practices. The assertion that people of color were inferior to whites validated their mistreatment and persecution, even within the pristine halls of this institution.

Until the latter part of the twentieth century, colleges and universities positioned themselves as "ivory towers", which dictated a policy of non-engagement on such social problems as racial segregation. While TRU does not acknowledge a covert, participatory role in the creation and maintenance of a deliberately unequal society, the intention to become more diverse reconciles a disjunction between praising America's unrealized national ideals while manifesting a contrary pattern of actions and behaviors. TRU must be prepared to accept responsibility for its duplicitous history and use all of the intellectual and technical tools at its disposal in order to lead by example and move the larger society towards the elimination of prejudice and discrimination. It is especially important for senior white male faculty and administrators to assume some measure of ownership of the necessity to increase institutional diversity and accept responsibility to expand this perspective throughout the academy. There are many areas where change must occur, including the following:

- TRU must identify, cultivate, enroll, support, and graduate substantially larger numbers of students from underserved communities and prepare them to go forward to exercise leadership within their respective groups and the larger society. African American students have been faced with numerous racist encounters since the university desegregated in the 1970's—even up until the present day—and the TRU culture continues to create problematic encounters for these students. In order to reduce the sense of marginalization that is experienced by students of color, they must be admitted to the institution in numbers that comprise a critical mass.

- Meaningful academic and social opportunities for white students to engage and interact with their peers of color must be created at TRU because the successful deracialization of American society is contingent on an informed acceptance by these students that in the evolving social order, their race offers them an equal, ***rather than a favored***, role for participation and advancement in their endeavors.

- TRU must insure that faculty members from underrepresented groups are present in numbers that extend beyond mere tokenism so that a clear message is conveyed to all students that members of all races have the intellectual capability to hold such positions. The paucity of faculty of color in the academy is frequently attributed to the small pool of qualified individuals who hold the appropriate credentials and accomplishment to be considered for these positions at predominantly white college and universities, though these academicians are prevalent at historically black colleges and universities. The increased representation of faculty of color on predominantly white college and university campuses, especially those who have earned tenure, sends a message to white students regarding the intellectual capacity of the various groups they represent, while also providing tangible role models for students from the underrepresented communities.

Curricula must be broadened to debunk the myth that only people of European ancestry have been architects of and contributors to the development of American society, and acknowledge that there are antecedents to this civilization in various locations around the globe, including Africa and South America, and not exclusively in Western Europe. Providing a complete and critical education for all college students about the nation's racial history, including the historical and contemporary realities of racial prejudice, stereotyping, and discrimination is a responsibility that TRU has abdicated. Only recently has the institution begun to move away from the broadly held orientation that centered "authentic" knowledge almost exclusively within the realm of Western European males, while ignoring the perspectives, points-of-view, and even the substantive contributions of people of color to the development of the society.

Case Questions

1. What methods, strategies, or approaches can be used to help the various TRU constituencies understand that the institution has been complicit in supporting racism in American society?
2. What methods, strategies, or approaches can be used to help TRU officials develop creative, effective ways to identify, recruit, and enroll, and graduate more students of color?
3. What methods, strategies, or approaches can be used to help TRU officials develop creative, effective ways to identify, recruit, and retain more faculty of color?
4. What methods, strategies, or approaches can be used to help TRU officials identify ways to enhance the representation of the achievements and contributions of people of color and incorporate them into the existing curricula?
5. How can TRU use the array of new-era tools and devices to reconfigure the collegiate experience to celebrate diversity in order to impact the values development of students and to develop examples that can be duplicated by other higher education institutions?

Case #2

The Husky or the March?:
Which Way to Student Solidarity

Karleen Pendleton Jiménez

Introduction

Several grade 6 students want to perform a skit about accepting diversity, but their teacher refuses. The teacher wishes to present a traditional play, fearing that the students' skit might be too political and increase racial tensions. The principal must decide whose performances will be included in the school assembly, and how to best address conflicting claims of marginalization.

Overview

"They want to make a skit," Rosa Martínez explains to Principal McCann. "They should be allowed to make their skit."

Rosa Martínez is a Latina-Canadian in her mid-forties, with a daughter, Leila, in Grade 6. She is a professor of sociology at the local university and is highly articulate and knowledgeable; on at least one prior occasion she has referenced the Provincial Human Rights Code with regard to her daughter's education. In that instance, some of the boys on the playground were teasing some of the girls who had begun wearing bras. Out of earshot from teachers, their comments became lewd, and the girls stormed Principal McCann's office in tears.

Principal McCann had not even had the opportunity to meet with all of the students involved, let alone their parents, before Ms. Martínez had telephoned to report her concern and citations from the Code. While it was part of her job, Principal McCann still became irritated when parents did not give her adequate time to complete proper procedures. In that case, she doled out numerous lectures and punishments, but still managed to disappoint Ms. Martínez by not offering school-wide sexual harassment training. She believed that the school community was not sexist as a whole, rather it was a problem particular to those students.

Principal McCann had started off on the wrong foot with Ms. Martínez. Ms. Martínez had come to the school's annual information day when she first moved into the area. Believing she was a new immigrant to Canada, Principal McCann advised her in slow, clear words that Ms. Martínez could learn about Canada from the New Canadian Centre. Principal McCann was just trying to be welcoming, but was met with a cool, curt response from Ms. Martínez, "Thank you very much, but I was born in Canada." Principal McCann felt embarrassed and apologized, but the event left an awkward feeling between them.

Principal McCann is in her mid-fifties, and has lived in Percy her entire life, save for the five years it took to complete her undergraduate and education degrees. Many people in the community know Principal McCann personally, or, if not her, other members of her family. The McCann family arrived from Ireland in the 1800s, helping to found a nearby mill. Percy is a city of 80,000 people, surrounded by farming towns. It is a place where urban and rural people come together for family get-togethers, cultural events, shopping, sports, work, and schools. Rural students sometimes sit on buses for over an hour before they are dropped at Percy Schools. However, the biggest outsiders on Percy streets are the university students and faculty, because they often come from far away, have more money, and embrace progressive agendas.

The weekend before the skit request, Ms. Martínez had taken her daughter to a large march in a metropolitan centre, protesting the election of a divisive political leader. In response to the leader's explicit racist and sexist campaign, protesters created beautiful signs and chants that embraced diversity, supporting groups such as women, immigrants,

Muslims, LGBTTQI2S (lesbian, gay, bisexual, transgender, transsexual, queer, intersex, and two spirited people) and Jewish people. Leila was so excited by the big crowd and the loving messages that when she returned she told her friends all about it. Her two best friends are Marc, the son of a lesbian couple, and Miriam, who is the youngest daughter of one of the few Jewish families in town. The three brainstormed the idea to create a skit as their grade 6 performance at the Spring school assembly – it would be about welcoming and accepting students' differences, and be set at a skateboarding tournament.

The assembly is a favourite of students and staff each year, and each class showcases their talents. Leila, Marc, and Miriam are in Mrs. Evergreen's grade 6 class, known for its annual play about a group of different animals (bear, fox, turtle, otter, bat, bugs, and a husky) that head off down the river for a sometimes scary, but mostly wholesome adventure. "It has become a school tradition to perform this play," Mrs. Evergreen had explained to Leila, Marc, and Miriam, when she apologized that they would not be able to perform their diversity skit.

Prior to the meeting between Ms. Martinez and Principal McCann, Principal McCann had chatted with Mrs. Evergreen to understand what had transpired. Through that conversation, Mrs. Evergreen explained that, "Husky and His Friends on the Roaring Rapids," was an important tradition for her classroom and the school. She also commented that she was worried that the skit Leila, Marc, and Miriam had proposed would make the white students, and especially the rural kids, feel guilty or left out. The majority of the students in her class come from white, Christian, heterosexual, working-class and middle-class backgrounds, some rural and some urban. However, in addition to the diversity of Leila, Marc and Miriam, there is also one First Nations girl, and twin brothers newly arrived from Syria. Mrs. Evergreen felt the assembly was supposed to be about celebration, not about politics, and she didn't feel comfortable leading a political presentation.

Problem Statement

Principal McCann has a policy of not interfering with her teachers' decisions about their assembly performances, but is increasingly aware (especially with the arrival of several refugee families) that the school has done little to educate students and staff on incorporating multiculturalism into their classrooms. She is upset that Mrs. Evergreen is refusing to do the presentation in the name of protecting the rural students. In the past she has observed rural students as sometimes being more understanding of other marginalized children in the school than their urban counterparts. Still, if she found a way to give the students a chance to present their skit, it would need to be carefully facilitated so that it did not polarize the school community. Last fall, racial tensions blew up at a neighbouring school when an immigrant student was falsely accused of stealing another student's phone. Principal McCann does not feel confident about her own capacity to provide multicultural instruction or resources for her school community.

Case Discussion Questions

1. Should Principal McCann allow Leila, Marc, and Miriam to perform their skit? If so, should anyone else be involved in creating and performing it? If the teacher, Mrs. Evergreen, is correct and other students might feel offended by the student skit, what other actions could Principal McCann take to encourage school-wide community-building, and to protect Leila, Marc, and Miriam from being singled out?
2. Should Principal McCann ask Mrs. Evergreen to put aside her animal adventure play for one year and support her students in creating the diversity skateboarding skit? What role do traditions play in an organization's culture? Which traditions should be kept or discarded and why?
3. Race and ethnicity were pushed to the forefront as the key issues involved in the decision on whether to allow the students' skit to be presented. However, the student Leila had been inspired by a march that brought many issues together: race, immigration,

gender, sexuality, and religion. What guidance could be offered to the students that honours their interest in accepting and celebrating many types of differences?
4. What resources might Principal McCann access to help educate herself on how to tactfully incorporate social justice education in her school? Who could she speak to for advice on how to move forward?
5. What policies and laws could Principal McCann examine to help guide her decision about whether to allow the presentation of the student skit?
6. Where might Principal McCann find qualified guest speakers or facilitators on issues of diversity and social justice?
7. What is needed to encourage schools to incorporate social justice and diversity education before a parent feels compelled to threaten legal action?

Teaching Strategies

A school level initiative, with invitations to the community, is required to intervene in the numerous types of exclusion and marginalization described by participants. There are multiple—and creative—opportunities for teaching about diversity and social justice.
1. At the next staff meeting, give teachers time to write and submit anonymously: i) Any questions they have about social justice and diversity; ii) Any problems they might have witnessed or overheard at their school; iii) Any ways in which they might feel personally marginalized or excluded; and, iv) Any words or actions they have witnessed that have promoted acceptance of diversity at their school. Compile the answers, synthesize, and present them at the next staff meeting. Be sure that anonymity is still maintained (i.e., you may need to generalize some statements). Offer staff the opportunity to discuss the findings together, and to brainstorm ideas for creating a more inclusive school climate.
2. Provide a social justice and diversity film series for staff. You may need to pick short films or excerpts from films, given time

limitations. You could begin or conclude staff meetings with the film and a short discussion. Allow teachers to discuss in pairs or groups as well.
3. Ask teachers of all grade levels to create an arts-based lesson plan that incorporates social justice and diversity. Using words and images, ask students to respond to the same questions that teachers were asked above: 1) Any questions they have about social justice and diversity; 2) Any problems they might have witnessed or overheard at their school; 3) Any ways in which they might feel personally marginalized or excluded; and, 4) Any words or actions they have witnessed that have promoted acceptance of diversity at their school. Depending on grade level and interest, the creations could be simple drawings, brief text observations, photo journals, videos, paintings, audio recordings, music, drama, etc. Connect the assignment to curricular expectations. Hold an art exhibition for students, parents, and staff, to walk through the school and learn from the many student perspectives as expressed through their artwork. Students have the option of their art being anonymous or named.
4. Finally, provide the students Marc, Leila, and Miriam with an instructor who can use writing prompts and improvisational exercises to build a script together, and to help guide the performance. Perhaps this can be accomplished through the creation of a social justice club with a supportive advisor.

References

Bornstein, K. (1998). *My gender workbook*. New York: Routledge.

Chasnoff, D. (Co-Director), & Cohen H. S. (Co-director). (1996). *It's elementary: Talking about gay issues in schools* [documentary film]. USA: New Day Films.

Pollock, M. (Ed.). (2008). *Everyday antiracism: Getting real about race in school*. NY: The New Press.

Terrell, R.D., & Lindsey, R. B. (2008). *Culturally proficient leadership: A personal journey begins within*. Thousand Oaks, CA: Corwin Press.

Case #3

The Consequence of Islamaphobia in K-12 Schools:
A Case to Remedy Bullying

Bobbie Plough & Brad J. Porfilio

Introduction

This case represents the San Diego Unified School District board members' and superintendent's initial attempt to address the concern regarding Islamaphobia, which manifested in bullying of numerous Islamic, or those who are perceived to be Arab, children in their schools in 2016.

Overview/Analysis

According to the Islamophobia Research and Documentation Project (IRDP), Islamophia was first coined in the Runnymede Trust Report in 1991 and defined as "unfounded hostility towards Muslims, and therefore fear or dislike of all or most Muslims".[1] Some Muslim groups felt compelled to use this term because Muslims in numerous Western countries encountered discrimination, exclusion, and hostility for holding cultural and religious beliefs and practices that differ from

---

1   Islamophobia Research & Documentation Project (n.d.) Retrieved from http://crg.berkeley.edu/content/islamophobia

Judeo-Christian practices, which are the foundation for developing political, social and economic relationships in Western contexts for more than 600 years. The fear or dislike of Muslims, and for those who are perceived to be Arab, was exacerbated on September 11, 2001, when it was learned Osama bin Laden, leader of the Islamic militant network al Qaeda, was responsible for engaging 19 men to launch terrorist attacks across the U.S. The attacks resulted in the of killing 2,996 people and wounded more than 6,000 others, as well as the loss of 10-13 billion dollars of property and infrastructure.[2]

Sadly, since the devastating terrorist attacks launched by al Qaeda on U.S. soil, social, political, and economic leaders in the U.S. have engaged in a propaganda campaign in order to dehumanize Muslim people and vilify Islam. U.S. powerbrokers have continually characterized Muslims as "uncivilized," as well as stated that Islam is "evil" and the seed solely responsible for several terrorists attacks committed by Muslims which have occurred in Europe and the U.S. since 9/11. The characterizations of Islam and Muslims are clearly false. President Obama argued that "radical Islam terror" in political discourse would come to "conflate 'murderers' with "the billion Muslims that exist around the world, including in this country, who are peaceful.""[3] The process of dehumanizing and vilifying Muslims and Islam has resulted in numerous Muslims, or those perceived as Arab, enduring hate crimes across the U.S.

The Anti-Islamic and Muslim sentiment that undergirds political discourse and shapes life in communities across the U.S. had filtered into numerous educational communities in 2015, resulting in toxic environments for children who are Muslims, or are perceived as Arabic. For example, bullying incidents aimed at Muslim children in California escalated after the 2015 terrorist shooting and attempted bombing in

---

2   Aurelie Corinthios (29, January, 2017). How many terrorist Attacks in the U.S. have been carried out by immigrants from the 7 banned Muslim countries? People Online, Retrieved from http://people.com/politics/donald-trump-refugee-muslim-ban-terrterrorist-attack-us-statistics/terrorist-attack-us-statistics/

3   Donald Trump: US will wipe out 'Islamic terror groups' (20, January, 2017). Al Jazeera. Retrieved from http://www.aljazeera.com/news/2017/01/donald-trump-wipe-islamic-terror-groups-170121044142466.html

San Bernardino. Six months later San Diego Unified School District (SDUSD) board members listened to young victims of bullying as they shared their stories and asked leaders to address the growing problem of bullying of Muslim students in their schools. Hundreds of members of the Muslim community attended the meeting, with parents holding up signs that read "Protect Our Kids."

The local NBC affiliate in San Diego reported the story and shared the words of the children who spoke at the board meeting.[4] A 6th grade girl described how she was bullied and called names by a group of three boys. When she told her teacher, the girl said nothing was done about her concerns. "I didn't feel safe. I told my teacher I didn't feel safe. I told her I want to be safe, but she didn't react to that," the girl explained. The girl told the school board that the boys hit, punched, and kicked her. One day, they pushed her, causing her to bleed after suffering an injury to her teeth. The girl said she and one other student felt they were being targeted and bullied because of their religion. "We were the only two Muslims and we were the only two to get bullied," she said. "Several times I felt depressed and thought of leaving everything behind – to a place where no one is there."

A 5th grade Muslim student told the board about how a classmate would often stare at her and her mother in a "nasty way" and ask her why her mother wore a head scarf. After months of these types of questions, the girl said her classmate purposely stepped on her hand one day, sending her to the emergency room. "On my way to the hospital, I was thinking, 'Why would that happen just because my mom looks different than my classmate's mom?' the student told the SDUSD board.

After approaching the podium, a 4th grade boy said that one day in class he and fellow students were talking about different cultures. He shared that he was Muslim. "A kid in my class told me that, '[Donald] Trump was going to beat Muslims up – including you. He also said that Muslims were the worst people,'" the boy recalled. "After hearing his

---

4   Monica Garske (27, July 2016). San Diego Unified school board will address Islamaphobia and bullying of students. *NBC7 San Diego.* Retrieved from http://www.nbcsandiego.com/news/local/San-Diego-Unified-School-District-Islamophobia-Muslim-Students-CAIR-Plan-388390272.html

words, I was scared and started crying. I started crying because Muslims are my family and I don't want anyone to hurt my family," he added. The boy also said he told his teacher about the bullying, but nothing was done by the teacher.

A 16-year-old senior with many leadership roles at his high school also talked about how his religion has played a role in the way fellow students and teachers look at him. "I can't even begin to tell you how many times I've felt inferior because I look foreign. I've had people exclude me, spread rumors about me because of my faith or had my ideas trampled upon," he said.

Six months after the board meeting, Governor Jerry Brown signed the Safe Place to Learn Act (CA Assembly Bill 2845).[5] The law prevents discrimination, harassment, and bullying against Muslim and Sikh students in the classrooms of CA, and provides teachers, staff, and administrators with resources that will help them to identify, prevent, and find a solution to bullying and discrimination happening in their schools.

While previous law requires school districts to provide certificated employees with existing school-site and community resources and information in support of lesbian, gay, bisexual, transgender, and questioning pupils, this law adds the support of pupils who face bias or bullying on the basis of religious affiliation or perceived religious affiliation. Additionally, this law mandates the creation of a list including statewide resources and community-based organizations to provide support to youth, and their families, who have been subjected to school-based discrimination, harassment, intimidation, or bullying on the basis of religious affiliation, nationality, race, or ethnicity, or perceived religious affiliation, nationality, race, or ethnicity.

Unfortunately, the Safe Place to Learn Act was not embraced by some segments of the community. In fact, State Senator Joel Anderson, representing a neighboring area in San Diego County was one of only

---

5   Safe Places to Learn Act of 2016, A.B. 2845, California State Assembly (2016). Retrieved from https://leginfo.legislature.ca.gov/faces/billNavClient.xhtml?bill_id=201520160AB2845.

three State senators who opposed the bill.[6] He told the *San Diego Union-Tribune*, "Religious bullying of any faith is wrong, and I would have supported a bill that was inclusive of all faiths." Social media raised comments such as "What about the laws protecting Christian students from traditional Islam supremacy and the ensuing suppression that comes with that?" Other comments called for closing mosques and banning the Koran as a holy book, describing it as a manual of torture and mayhem. One post encouraged readers to stockpile weapons and ammunition to fight a revolution against Islam.

Problem Statement

The school board members and Superintendent listened intently as students shared their narratives of being bullied in their schools. Clearly, the Board of Education and Superintendent did not have the information, or did not act upon it, regarding the bullying of Muslim students in San Diego Unified School District. After the board's vote, the SDUSD superintendent ensured that she would partner with the Muslim community, including the Council on American-Islamic Relations, and visit with parents and students to help develop a comprehensive strategy to battle bullying. This included providing data on Muslim student reports of bullying on a monthly basis. Those monthly reports would be posted online.

Case Problems

Exercise 1: What should have been done?

- What methods would ensure that information is communicated to the Superintendent, School Board, principals, or other pertinent leaders?

---

6 Pollak, Joel B. (2016, October 5). Jerry Brown signs law to stop (only) anti-Muslim bullying. Retrieved from http://www.breitbart.com/california/2016/10/05/jerry-brown-signs-law-protect-muslim-kids-bullying/

- What were the actions the Superintendent and School Board might have taken or policies enacted to prevent bullying of Muslim students?

Exercise 2: Engaging the community.

After the narratives were shared at the Board meeting, the Superintendent promised to engage the Muslim community and the Board of Education directed the Superintendent to deliver a report in the following months.

- In addition to partnering with the Muslim community, what specific actions might principals, teachers, staff, and students take to engage the broader community to promote understanding of what political, social, and economic forces give rise Islamaphobia, and how they have led to the bullying of Muslim children, and those who appear to be Arab, in K-12 schools in the U.S.?
- Describe a step-by-step process for school personnel to engage the community in addressing this issue.
- What resources outside of the school could the principal access to build a culture free from hate and hostility in K-12 schools?
- Describe some policies, practices, and pedagogies designed to ensure a school environment is conducive to learning for all students.
- Are there national, state, and local resources that can be leveraged to provide information and support the process?
- What are some strategies for guiding schoolteachers, school administrators, and children to understand how political leaders have used mass media outlets to demonize and vilify Islam and Muslim people?
- How does the school harness social media to challenge pernicious stereotypes associated with Islam and Muslim people, as well as bring an understanding and appreciation of Islam and Muslim people?

Reading Resources

Gardner, Rod, Yasemin Karakaşoğlus, and Sigrid Luchtenberg. "Islamophobia in the media: a response from multicultural education 1." Intercultural Education 19.2 (2008): 119-136.

Ramarajan, Dhaya, and Marcella Runell. "Confronting Islamophobia in education 1." *Intercultural Education* 18.2 (2007): 87-97.

Walton, Gerald, and Blair Niblett. "Investigating the problem of bullying through photo elicitation." *Journal of Youth Studies* 16.5 (2013): 646-662.

Zine, Jasmin. Staying on the straight path: A critical ethnography of Islamic schooling in Ontario. National Library of Canada= Bibliothèque nationale du Canada, 2005.

References

'CALIPHORNIA' far left Governor Jerry Brown signs 'anti-Islamaphobia' bill just for Muslim students (2016, September 28). Retrieved from http://www.barenakedislam.com/2016/09/28/caliphornia-far-left-governor-jerry-brown-signs-anti-islamophobia-bill-just-for-muslim-students/

Corinthios, A. (29, January, 2017). How many terrorist Attacks in the U.S. have been carried out by immigrants from the 7 banned Muslim countries? *People Online,* Retrieved from http://people.com/politics/donald-trump-refugee-muslim-ban-terrorist-attack-us-statistics/

Council on American-Islamic Relations. Retrieved from https://www.cair.com/about-us.html Islamaphobia Research and Documentation Project (n.d.). Retrieved from http://crg.berkeley.edu/content/islamaphobia

Pollak, J. B. (2016, October 5). Jerry Brown signs law to stop (only) anti-Muslim bullying. Retrieved from http://www.breitbart.com/california/2016/10/05/jerry-brown-signs-law-protect-muslim-kids-bullying/

Safe Places to Learn Act of 2016, A.B. 2845, California State Assembly (2016). Retrieved from https://leginfo.legislature.ca.gov/faces/billNavClient.xhtml?bill_id=201520160AB2845.

Trump, D. (20, January, 2017). US will wipe out 'Islamic terror groups' *Al Jazeera.* Retrieved from http://www.aljazeera.com/news/2017/01/donald-trump-wipe-islamic-terror-groups-170121044142466.html

Case #4

How Can We Support Teachers To Become More Inclusive in Secondary School?

Suzanne Carrington & Jane Vanelli

Introduction

This case study is situated in a secondary school in Australia, where all students have the right to attend their local school. We describe how Janet, the leader of the inclusion program, facilitated a whole school approach to differentiated teaching to support learners with disabilities. Challenging issues are explored, such as leadership for a whole school approach to inclusion, professional development for teachers, and support for culture change. The case explores the barriers, negotiations, and changes to thinking that are required to support an inclusive approach to planning and practice in the classroom. This case engages readers in theorising about equality in education through consideration of what is required for a whole school approach to inclusion. The case will be of interest to school leaders and classroom teachers.

Overview

The population in Australia is diverse, and it is a challenge for schools to respond to the broad range of student cultural, socioeconomic, and ability backgrounds. Considerable efforts have been made in recent years to address issues of equity within the education system, and teachers are expected to teach the diverse range of learners in their school. This case study is situated in a government-funded secondary school in Australia. The school has a population of 1800 students, spanning Years 7 to 12 (ages approximately 12-17 years). The school enrolment includes approximately 75 students with disabilities and an additional 150+ students identified as having learning difficulties. The school is viewed as providing leadership in inclusive education. There are a number of specialist teaching staff and teacher assistants in the school who provide support to the students with disabilities in mainstream classrooms.

As the number of students with disability enrolled at the school increased, more specialist teachers with similar philosophical ideas were employed to support differentiation of teaching for students with disability in an inclusive program. Resources were developed by the specialist teachers to support curriculum planning. Initially, progress was slow and there were some barriers for students with disabilities to access all areas of the curriculum. Many mainstream classroom teachers were feeling inadequately prepared to support students with disabilities, and some teachers were unwilling to engage in an inclusive approach due to their own prejudices.

In 2013, the education department launched a new initiative to support the implementation of an inclusive approach to education. Janet, the leader of the program, was tasked with undertaking an action research project, which would result in implementation of a specific change in the practices at the case study secondary school. This project involved data collection that included conversations with staff. The project identified that teachers were insular in their approach to recognising and understanding students' abilities and limitations, both academically and socially. This meant that information about how students were successfully supported in a class was often retained by the teacher and not passed on as students moved through the school. As a result Janet developed and implemented a classroom differentiation and tracking tool, called the *Differentiation Class Profile*, as a means of communication about student progress between staff in the case study secondary school (See Appendix 1). This tool provided a centralised record of data, such as attendance, standardised test scores, and academic achievements, as well as a record of what type of teaching adjustments were utilised in different years and subject areas.

Despite ongoing professional development and working collaboratively on embedding inclusivity into classrooms, Janet was not prepared for the staff dissatisfaction about the new initiatives. There was a need to consider whether there were other barriers that were preventing the acceptance of an inclusive approach that required teachers to use the *Differentiation Class Profile* to support teachers working with students with disabilities.

Consequently, a range of consultations occurred, with teaching representatives from all faculties, school-based union representatives and the executive leadership team, to discover the underlying reasons for the lack of engagement and support. Teachers were under considerable pressure to implement a new Australian Curriculum in their classrooms, and to develop and trial curriculum plans and new resources. Teachers stated that they felt overworked and overwhelmed at the amount of changes they were required to implement at the same time. They perceived that the 'added' work required in the inclusive approach would be onerous and time consuming, that people would make judgements on or about their work, and that it was another system compliance. Partly the teachers' reluctance was due to their lack of understanding about how useful the *Differentiation Class Profile* could be. The teachers did not understand how the tool could be used to collect data about students' performance and participation at school, along with data about successful adjustments and support strategies. They did not understand that this tool, and the whole school process, could inform their future planning and practice and save time in the future. It was also recognised that the workforce comprised an older teaching staff; one whose notions of classroom inclusion were being challenged, and where they did not fully understand that supporting the diverse needs of students in their school community was their responsibility.

Problem Statement

The school executive leadership team identified that a whole-school approach to inclusive education was required. The leadership team needed to promote the procedure and management of recording and tracking data, establish the importance of data collection using the *Differentiation Class Profile* (e.g., academic data, behavior data, teaching adjustments, student profile data), and promote how to use the data to inform classroom practice. The whole-school approach to inclusion consequently involved ongoing professional development and coaching of faculty staff who were resistant to embracing change, along with enabling them to meet their teaching responsibilities for an inclusive approach. These approaches required leadership and teacher commitment to working cooperatively in teaching teams across the faculties and year levels of the secondary school. Janet was overwhelmed and frustrated with the slow progress of adopting a whole school approach. She was not sure how to address the barriers, negotiations, and changes to thinking that were needed to support an inclusive approach to planning and practice in the classroom.

Discussion Questions

In the following section, we identify a range of issues and questions to support a discussion about the case study:

1. How could a consideration of teacher beliefs and values be included as a component of the action research to enhance the leadership of a whole school approach?
2. How can school leadership influence the implementation of a whole school approach to differentiation in the secondary school?
3. This case study raises questions about how to prepare the staff for a change agenda. Should consideration and support for staff be considered for engagement in a whole school change *prior* to the action-research project *or* as a component of it? How could this be supported in a school?

4. The *Differentiation Class Profile* was developed without mainstream staff consultation. Consider how the leader of the inclusion program could have worked in a more consultative manner to facilitate ownership and commitment.
5. How can school leaders facilitate the change in beliefs and values to support a more inclusive culture at a school?
6. Was the leader of the inclusion program the best person to lead this change within the school? Was she stereotyped as fulfilling a specific role in the school leadership team? What implications are there from this case study that can inform ethical school leadership in secondary schools?
7. What type of professional development is required to develop teachers' understanding about how data can be utilised to drive the inclusion agenda in schools?

Teaching Strategies

State High School – Differentiation Class Profile

Department:	xxxxxxx		Class:	xxxxx		Individual Class Data Goals:			
Teacher:	xxxxxx		Year/Semester:	XXXX/X		%A xx	%B xx	%C xx	

Mark check box to indicate data used	Data Check – where is the student at?		Pre-knowledge Check – ways of gathering information on student's current knowledge and skills	
	☐ Attendance data ☐ Standard tests – NAPLAN ☐ One School Student Summary	☐ Reporting results ☐ G & T data ☐ SEP/LD data	☐ Diagnostic test in class ☐ Results from previous unit ☐ Student interest	☐ In class test of content understanding ☐ G & T documentation/reports ☐ Resources available	☐ In class test of skills and processes ☐ SEP/LD – IEP's and strategies ☐ Other (please specify)

Student name	ATSI	ESL INT	Spec Provs	D/E	A/B	G&T	SEP	LD	Other	Adjustment Codes	Comments (optional)

State High School – Differentiation Class Profile

Teaching Adjustments

#	Adjustment	#	Adjustment
1	Provide visual cues	19	Negotiate contract of work completion
2	Use concrete materials	20	Use ICT's to support learning
3	Provide scaffolding	21	Use adaptive technology
4	Divide process into small steps	22	Monitor comprehension
5	Adjust layout of resources	23	Allow regular breaks
6	Provide graphic organisers	24	Establish a set routine
7	Use adjusted handouts	25	Allow oral responses instead of written
8	Use teacher aide to read/scribe notes	26	Cater to learning style
9	Give power points as handouts	27	Slow pace of instruction
10	Place handouts on intranet	28	Allow opportunities for revision
11	Enlarge handouts	29	Check student notebooks
12	Use peer support/reciprocal teaching	30	Give personal cues to begin work
13	Allow additional time to complete task	31	Structure mixed ability learning groups
14	Pre-teach new vocabulary & concepts	32	Adjust seating plan
15	Present information in a multi-sensory manner	33	Structure extra challenges (class & homework)
16	Adjust homework task/requirements	34	Provide more complex/challenging stimulus
17	Provide exemplars/model responses	35	Provide choice of homework tasks & response types
18	Provide additional readings	36	Use digital media as reflection/improvement tool

Assessment Adjustments

Bookwork
- a Use adjusted notes/theory book
- b Adjust criteria for bookwork assessment
- c Offer alternative responses

Exams
- d Adjust language
- e Adjust layout
- f Adjust criteria
- g Provide reader/scribe
- h Add visual clues/prompts
- i Allow additional time
- j Provide quiet work environment
- k Computer allowed

Assignment
- l Adjust language
- m Adjust layout
- n Adjust criteria
- o Adjust length of task
- p Provide scaffolding
- q Allow extra time to complete

Practicals
- r Provide peer tutor/buddy
- s Use teacher aide assistance for safety
- t able to work in a smaller group
- u Able to work individually
- v Provide step by step instructions
- w Model expectations
- x Provide visual clues
- y Record practical performances
- z Adjust length of assessment

Data Locations

OneSchool → School Management → Class Dashboard
OneSchool → Student Profile

ATSI:	OneSchool → School Management → Class Dashboard
ESL:	OneSchool → School Management → Class Dashboard
International:	OneSchool → School Management → Class Dashboard
Special provision:	Intranet → Senior School → Special Provision folder
D/E Students:	Intranet → School Data → Student Academic Reports
A/B Students:	Intranet → School Data → Student Academic Reports
G&T:	Intranet → T&L tab → G&T folder
NAPLAN:	Intranet → Junior Schooling → NAPLAN Data (year)
SEP:	Intranet → SEP/LD → Student List → Individual Profiles (year level) → IEP
LD:	Intranet → SEP/LD → Student List → Individual Profiles (year level)
Behaviour:	OneSchool Student Profile → Behaviour Profile
Attendance:	OneSchool Student Profile → Absences or previous Report Cards or IDAttend

Instructions

When: To be completed by the end of the third week of each semester/term
Who: All teachers
Where: G Drive*File name*
File name:

How:

Individual Class Goals are drawn from previous achievement data of the class, ie; an impact class might set a goal of 50% A-C, whereas and extension class might set a goal of 95% A-B. Aim for 3-5% improvement each semester.

Student Information table
- Use the data sources to fill in the categories for your class
- Name specific students - write letter or numbers to indicate appropriate strategies
- Strategies are in two sections – Teaching Strategies and Assessment Strategies - choose from both to accommodate the learning needs of your individual students
- Comments are optional

Case #5

Inclusive Communities?
Supporting Sexual Minority And Gender Non-conforming Youth in Catholic Public Schools.

Barbara Hamilton & Carmen Mombourquette

Recently in Alberta, Canada, the provincial framework *Inspiring Education* has called for a shift of the entire education system to become student-centered (Alberta Education, 2010). This shift in practice, leadership, and governance, away from a system-centered approach towards a student-centered focus, is a process that will occur by implementing a variety of initiatives over the next 15 years; despite many opportunities, there will certainly be challenges along the way. Specifically, this case will examine how Catholic school boards will meet their mandate to "establish, implement and maintain a policy respecting the board's obligation under subsection (1)(d) to provide a welcoming, caring, respectful and safe learning environment" (Alberta Education, 2012, p. 38) for all students, including sexual minority (non-heterosexual or gender non-conforming) students.

The Catholic School Teacher Dilemma

Catholic school teachers are in a unique position in Alberta. They are tasked with educating students by delivering the various programs of studies from a Catholic perspective. On the surface, that sounds fairly straightforward, but, if we dig deep to examine the issues at play in the schools, there are several challenges, contradictions, and moral dilemmas that Catholic teachers face. Not only do teachers themselves have to navigate the conflicting realities of the teachings of the Catholic Church and the expectations of the secular world, they also have to help their students to do so. These teachers are guided by policy that has contradicting messages; in an educational culture that does not talk about tough issues, teachers are left to navigate such contradictions on their own, without clear direction, and without a safe place to freely discuss these challenges. Mixed messages are being sent to teachers and students, and it is not surprising that students and staff continue to experience discrimination in schools (Callaghan, 2012).

Bullying and Belonging: A Brief LGBTQ[1] Student Perspective

A Canadian study found that LGBTQ students experience five to six times more bullying in the form of verbal harassment about their sexual orientation than heterosexual students (Taylor & Peter, 2011). Catholic schools, ostensibly religious retreats, where LGBTQ students were asked to be open and share their feelings, were described as being particularly difficult, and students felt unsafe. In religion class, if homosexuality was ever discussed it was done so in a negative way. For these reasons, the majority of LGBTQ students finished high school with an intense anger towards religion (Maher, 2007). There is research that indicates that victimization experienced during secondary school has negative effects on adolescents that continues into young adulthood; adolescent gender non-conformity is a source of significant risk in the lives of young people, especially LGBTQ and gender non-conforming youth (Russell, Ryan, Toomey, Diaz, & Sanchez, 2011). There is a disconnect between the inclusive messages conveyed by official Catholic church doctrine, explaining that homosexuals must be accepted with respect, compassion,

---

[1] LGBTQ is a commonly used acronym for lesbian, gay, bisexual, trans-identified, transsexual, two-spirited, and queer identities. Sexual minority is a synonymous term (ATA, 2006, p. 5).

and sensitivity, and the heteronormative discriminatory realities of life within Catholic schools (Love, 2013).

Gay-Straight Alliances (GSAs)

Gay-Straight Alliances (GSAs) are school-based groups that promote welcoming, caring, respectful, safe, and inclusive learning environments for sexual and gender minority students and their allies (Alberta Education, 2014). GSAs are touted as critical change agents to help create safe and caring school environments for LGBTQ students and their allies (ATA, 2006). They are peer support networks to help students overcome feelings of isolation and alienation that are a result of homophobic and transphobic bullying (Alberta Education, 2014).

A recent Canadian study has concluded that schools that have had both explicit anti-homophobic policies and GSAs in place for three years had lower odds of sexual orientation discrimination, suicidal thoughts and suicidal attempts in both heterosexual and non-heterosexual groups as compared to schools without such policies and groups (Saewyc, Konishi, Rose, & Homma, 2014).

In 2014, then Education Minister, Jeff Johnson stated in a letter to School Board Chairs that the government supports GSAs, but did not want to overstep school board autonomy in legislating them. Specifically, he called on school board trustees to "review your local policies regarding gay-straight alliances to ensure they are in the best interest of the students you are elected to serve" (Johnson, 2014).

In 2014, it was estimated that there were over 40 GSAs in Albertan schools; however, there were no GSAs in Catholic schools in Alberta at this time. Do note that in Alberta there are two dominant forms of publicly funded schools – one where roughly 65% of students attend school known as the public school system, and a faith based system supporting Roman Catholic Church teachings where approximately 30% of students in the province attend.

Catholic Church Position

Catholic bishops believe GSAs are in conflict with Roman Catholic values (Saewyc et al., 2014). The Archbishop of Edmonton, Richard Smith, does not appear to support segregating or labeling students by establishing GSAs. He is quoted as saying:

Our context generally is love, acceptance, support, but obviously as anyone would suspect, and certainly as parents would expect, sending children to the school we will do this in in accordance with the principles of the Gospel, of love, accompaniment, and so on (CTV News, 2014).

Catholic School Community of Caring Program

As a result of Minister Johnson's position, several Catholic schools established Community of Caring programs. These programs were designed to foster school environments that are safe, caring, and celebrate diversity.

> "Rather than form kind of reductionist view groups, we look at the holistic picture and educate people through awareness weeks and things like that," said Tania Younker.

> "We have what's called a Catholic Community of Caring, and that [has built] unity through community. [What] that looks like in our schools is we are supportive, we are welcoming, [and we are] inclusive, a culture of respect [is building] and everybody has a place at our schools'" (Mertz, 2014).

Relevant Legislation

Recently in Ontario, the government passed Bill 13, an anti-bullying act which stipulated that "neither the board nor the principal shall refuse a pupil to use the name gay-straight alliance or a similar name" (Saewyc et al., 2014, p. 100). In Alberta, Motion 503, a private members bill that would make it mandatory to allow GSAs, was defeated in the legislature in April 2014. At this time, there was no provincial policy to mandate GSAs in Alberta schools; it had been left up to individual school jurisdictions to approve or deny the requests of students to establish GSAs.

The Case

School Context

You are the principal at Holy Smoke Catholic High (HSCH). HSCH is a large, metropolitan, Catholic school with a population of approximately 1500 students and 50 teachers. This school has a diverse demographic, with families across the range of the social-economic spectrum, as well as from a number of cultural and ethnic backgrounds.

The Question

An excellent teacher in your school has been working for some time with a diverse population of students, and offers tremendous support to them as they are coming to terms with their identity and place in the world. This teacher approaches you, as some of these students wish to establish a gay-straight alliance (GSA). The teacher explains the role of a GSA to be one to confront homophobia in the school, as well as to provide an opportunity for sexual minority students and their allies to provide a safe space to discuss inclusion and belonging in the school community and to build resiliency.

Your Response

You take some time, working with your teacher to gain a deeper understanding about the role of a GSA. You understand the GSA will not be a counseling group and that the work will not be in conflict with the teachings of the church. Initially, you tell the teacher that the students can meet as a group; however, they are neither allowed to advertise nor can they call the group a GSA. You begin the process to work with your district leaders to formally approve the student group.

Initial Impact

The limitations imposed resulted in the greater student body not knowing about the group meetings. Only a small friend group of the student who initially asked for the GSA seemed to be aware of the existence of the group. The meetings did not meet the stated goals, as the group seemed to "dance" around important topics. The students and staff members were unclear on what they could discuss, and there was some fear expressed by a couple of staff members that they would get into trouble professionally. The teachers you are working with let you know that they are having difficulty getting the word out to the student body to participate in this unnamed student group, and participation remains lower than anticipated.

District Response

The district denies your request to allow the formation of a GSA. An official from the school district's Central Office tells you that GSAs are not allowed.

Continued Efforts

After the summer break, students again asked for the creation of a school-based GSA. Goals, and the failings of last year's quasi-GSA, were again presented for your review. Despite the failings of the previous year's efforts, you only give permission to do what had previously been done (i.e., no GSA name, no advertising), because your request to allow a GSA was denied by Central Office.

You communicate this information to the lead teacher and the students. Both the students and teachers are disappointed, feel let down, and lack a clear understanding as to the rationale for the decision. In fact, you also do not understand the decision. A meeting is arranged with three supporting staff members, you, and district leaders.

The meeting between you, your staff members, and a Religious Education consultant, is arranged to clarify the expressed goals and to review the research that clearly indicates the benefits and protective factors of school-based GSAs. The goals are not in conflict with Catholic teaching. The decision to not allow school-based GSAs was upheld on the grounds that the school and district are an inclusive community that does not single out specific groups of students. You find the rationale interesting and ironic, given that you belong to a district that values and celebrates extra and co-curricular activities for specific groups of students (athletes, cultural groups, and language clubs, etc.), and offers services to select students based on strict criteria (First Nation, Métis, and Inuit populations, English Language Learner students, new immigrants, etc.). Also of note, the GSA proposed was open to everyone: sexual minority youth and adults, as well as heterosexual youth and adults.

The optics of the situation appear to be political in nature; one where the decision is made to appease people *other* than the students involved. You cannot help but think this is a decision where students were not at the center of the process, and now you feel that you are not meeting the needs of all learners in your community.

You continue to work with teachers to help support this group of students. You give permission to develop a staff and student working group for a school-wide Week Against Homophobia. You give permission to advertise weekly meetings for the group, and turnout among students and staff is very good. The staff/student group meets weekly over the course of two months, but discussion during the planning is largely impersonal (i.e., it is task-oriented re: the Week). Both students and staff express appreciation for the meetings, but also highlight the greater need for more work and awareness. Students again speak of their desire for a GSA.

Student Advocacy?

The students and staff who did participate in the anti-homophobia campaign want to build upon the success of the week, and again are requesting the formal recognition of a GSA. They clearly articulate that by not being allowed to form a GSA the perception of students and staff is that LGBTQ persons should continue to remain in the closet; they are fearful that the culture of "don't ask, don't tell" will continue, and the safety of a vulnerable population will continue to be jeopardized. Without explicit positive, inclusive messages about LGBTQ persons, LGBTQ youth will continue to experience the "oppression of silence" – silence that comes in the form of avoidance of discussion of LGBTQ issues, avoidance of positive education and images of LGBTQ persons and same-gender parents (ATA, 2006).

Case Analysis Questions for Discussion

1. Was your response in the beginning reasonable in the light of the fact that you believed it might be difficult to get Central Office permission for the formation of GSA?
2. Was your decision to allow the formation of an anti-homophobia week reasonable, responsible, and appropriate?
3. How can Catholic school principals and district leaders best advocate for the needs of LGBTQ youth?
4. How do Catholic school leaders build bridges with the LGBTQ community to ensure that Catholic schools are truly inclusive *and* mindful of Church teaching?
5. What would you have done if you were the principal of this school?
6. Given the recent research of the benefits of GSAs, including the reduction in suicide ideation among youth, do you think that districts (or the ministry) will be held liable for neglect of care in lawsuits filed by the families of LGBTQ youth (i.e., suicide) if GSA requests were denied?
7. Discuss conflicting rights in this case; specifically, human rights of LGBTQ persons and institutional and constitutional rights of Catholic organizations.

References

Alberta Education. (2012). *Education Act*. Edmonton Alberta: Alberta Queen's Printer. Retrieved from http://www.qp.alberta.ca/1266.cfm?page=e00p3.cfm&leg_type=Acts&isbncln=9780779769346.

Alberta Education. (2010). *Inspiring education: A dialogue with Albertans. Steering committee report*. Edmonton, AB: Government of Alberta.

Alberta Education. (2014). Welcoming, Caring, Respectful and Safe Learning Environments.

ATA. (2006). Gay-straight student alliances in Alberta schools: A guide for teachers.

Callaghan, T. (2012). *Holy homophobia: Doctrinal disciplining of non-heterosexuals in Canadian Catholic schools*. University of Toronto, Toronto, Ontario.

CTV News. (2014). Catholic archbishop speaks against GSAs in schools. from http://edmonton.ctvnews.ca/video?clipId=379068

Johnson, J. (2014). Motion 503 and Gay Straight Alliances. A Letter from the Minister to Board Chairs. April 14, 2014. Government of Alberta.

Love, B. (2013). Go underground or in your face: Queer students' negotiation of all-girls Catholic schools. *Journal of LGBT Youth, 10*(3), 186. doi: 10.1080/19361653.2013.799901

Maher, M. J. (2007). Gay and lesbian students in Catholic high schools: A qualitative study of alumni narratives. *Catholic Education: A Journal of Inquiry & Practice, 10*(4), 449-472.

Mertz, E. (2014). Alberta legislature votes down Gay-Straight Alliance bill Retrieved July 16, 2014, from http://globalnews.ca/news/1258107/alberta-legislature-votes-down-gay-straight-alliance-bill/

Russell, S. T., Ryan, C., Toomey, R. B., Diaz, R. M., & Sanchez, J. (2011). Lesbian, gay, bisexual, and transgender adolescent school victimization: Implications for young adult health and adjustment. *Journal of School Health, 81*(5), 223-230. doi: 10.1111/j.1746-1561.2011.00583.x

Saewyc, E., Konishi, C., Rose, H., & Homma, Y. (2014). School-based strategies to reduce suicidal ideation, suicide attempts, and discrimination among sexual minority and heterosexual adolescents in western Canada. *International journal of child, youth and family studies, 5*(1), 89-112.

Taylor, C., & Peter, T. (2011). 'We are not aliens, we're people, and we have rights.' Canadian human rights discourse and high school climate for LGBTQ students. *Canadian Review of Sociology, 48*(3), 275-312. doi: 10.1111/j.1755-618X.2011.01266.x

Case # 6

Including Homeless Children in an Elite School: Arzoo's Story

Divya Murali, Sveta Davé Chakravarty, & Shashi Mendiratta

The Challenge

In a socioeconomically and culturally stratified society, how can schools serving mostly privileged communities implement a new education policy requiring inclusion? How can they address the challenge of including the most-marginalized students, students with diverse backgrounds and ways of life? This case study follows the experiences of Aarzoo, a child living in a non-custodial home for former street children in Delhi. It narrates the efforts of a school—and her classroom in particular—to bring these hardest-to-reach children into school, create an inclusive learning environment, and ensure that each of them is learning.

Context

The Right to Education Act-2009 (RTE) was landmark legislation in India that provided for free and compulsory, quality education for *all* children between 6 and 14 years of age. When the Act came into force in 2010, India became one of 135 countries to make education a fundamental right for every child. Subsequently, India made formidable strides in expanding access to primary education; however, quality suffered. Children were enrolled in government schools, but absenteeism was high and many dropped out. Students remained disengaged and learning levels were abysmally low. Quality concerns in government schools led to a burgeoning of better-equipped private schools, claiming to provide higher quality education and catering to the middle and upper classes.

The inequity in the provision and utilization of educational opportunities mirrored the traditional socioeconomic and cultural divides based on caste, class, religion, etc. in a highly stratified society. Then, in a bold move, the Right to Education legislation mandated that private schools reserve 25% of all seats for children from economically weaker sections of society (the EWS category) as a measure to topple hierarchies and make schools more inclusive.

In a display of deeply entrenched prejudice, the provision met with stiff resistance from private schools, who took the matter to court and argued that including EWS category children would dilute the quality of learning and of discipline in the school, that their own children would learn "bad habits" and abusive language, and that the "EWS" child would not be able to adjust and cope with studies and would would face stigmatization. However, the courts upheld the provision and ruled that private schools must implement the Act.

The provisions of the Act also paved the way to bring the "hardest-to-reach children"[1] within the ambit of formal education. One such group of children are the homeless children living on the streets of urban centers, like Delhi. Attempts to provide education to these children led to the realization that the needs of a child were indivisible, and providing education to street children first entailed providing shelter, food, and healthcare. This led to the establishment of residential homes for street children and homeless children.[2]

---

1 Children living in conflict areas, homeless children living on the streets, children of sex workers and parents with HIV/AIDS etc. are categorized as "hard to reach" as there are multiple barriers in ensuring access to education for these children.

2 We make a distinction between "homeless children"—on the streets, but living with their families—and "street children," children *of* the streets, who typically have run away from dire poverty and/or abusive homes, often far away, and live without adult protection on urban streets. There are estimated to be some 50,000 in Delhi alone.

Overview

Augustus Schoo[3] is an elite private school in the heart of Delhi that has attempted to implement the provisions of the RTE, not just in letter but also in spirit. The school has a long tradition of catering to a diverse community of students. At all grade levels, classes include students with special needs: students with learning disabilities and/or physical impairment, students from lower-middle-class neighborhoods around the school, children belonging to some extremely marginalized social groups, as well as students from socioeconomically well-off and "elite" families. Under the EWS category, the school actively reached out to former street children living in non-custodial residential homes and enrolled them. While the school's willingness to open its gates to extremely marginalized students is in itself extraordinary, its experiences reveal the complexity of implementing the policy mandate, the everyday successes, dilemmas, and challenges of inclusion beyond "access"[4]

The Child - Aarzoo

This case follows 12 year-old Aarzoo who lives in a residential home for street children and attends the elite Augustus school. Her parents and two younger brothers live on the streets near the Jama Masjid in Delhi where her father works as a small street vendor and her mother does rag-picking. Aarzoo started living at the home for street children five years ago when her parents were unable to care for her. Contact with her family is limited to weekly phone calls, and visits during school vacations and some festivals. Teachers at the home taught Aarzoo basic reading, writing, and arithmetic. She was bright, quick on the uptake, and was enrolled in a local government school. Recently, under the new EWS legislation, Aarzoo was admitted to Class 6 in Augustus School, along with some other children from the home.

---

3   The name of the school, teachers, and children have been changed to maintain privacy.

4   While based on primary research and true events, several elements of the case study have been fictionalized to create a complex problem for the reader.

Aarzoo encounters Nina, her class teacher, on the first day of school. Nina is a young teacher in her 20s with a friendly disposition. Coming from an elite background, Nina had many pathways open to her but felt teaching was her calling. She had spent four years teaching at another elite private school without much diversity in the student population. The diversity of learners at Augustus, and its reputation as an inclusive school, motivated Nina to join the school. Having only been in this school for a few months, Nina feels as much of a newcomer as Aarzoo.

When Nina first encountered Aarzoo in her English class, she was sitting at the back of the classroom staring out of the window. The classroom was organized such that she could not walk up to Aarzoo, so she called out to her saying, *"pay attention"*. Aarzoo grudgingly complied but had a far-away look in her eyes. While Nina spent time dealing with forty students in her class, some with ADHD and other learning disabilities, maintaining discipline and struggling to complete the syllabus, the quiet Aarzoo occupied little mind space. While discussing EWS students in the various classes, Nina confidently told her colleagues, "the one in my class is so disciplined. She never gives me any trouble and listens quietly to my explanations. When I hear your descriptions of disruptive students, I feel blessed to have her. One less student to worry about!"

As Nina evaluated the results of the first English test, Aarzoo soon became a cause of concern. Aarzoo had left most of the test paper blank; she had only attempted two questions in broken English. Nina met Aarzoo in the staff room and, waving the test paper, demanded an explanation, "Why have you performed so badly? You are failing the test. If you did not understand you should have asked for help earlier!" Aarzoo responded in Hindi saying, "I can't speak well in English and you said we can only speak in English in class. Other kids would have laughed at me. They anyways don't talk to me. Only children from the home talk to me." Nina decided to test Aarzoo to determine her English proficiency levels. Aarzoo was very uncomfortable and felt agitated when she struggled to read a section from the book. She somehow managed to finish the tasks set by Nina.

Having seen the results of the proficiency test, Nina felt frustrated. She complained to her colleagues, "How do I deal with one student who is so far behind the others? She doesn't have any learning support at home either. The school should have enrolled Aarzoo in a lower grade and let her catch up." Nina felt sympathy for Aarzoo but felt quite clueless about helping her learn. She did not even know where to start. Nina learned that the school was conducting after school remedial classes in English for students who had a different mother tongue and no strong English speaking background at home. Nina recommended that Aarzoo be enrolled in the class, and soon Aarzoo also started attending the remedial class. Nina heaved a sigh of relief, reasoning that the remedial class would take care of the learning deficit and she would only have to make sure that Aarzoo was not failing. She discussed her topics and lessons with the remedial class teacher to ensure that they were being taken up in class, and that Aarzoo was being adequately prepared for exams.

Even though Nina's busy schedule rarely allowed for much one-on-one support, whenever possible she would sit with Aarzoo and explain the essays and poems in both Hindi and English. She would also give her extra practice questions as homework. Nina maintained a distant yet cordial relationship with Aarzoo, as she saw befitting of a student-teacher relationship. This provided her sufficient scope to discipline and reprimand Aarzoo when she did not do her homework or did not submit her notebook in class; when this happened Aarzoo would cite reasons such as she had lost her notebook or she hadn't found time to do homework. Nina thought these were just excuses.

In class, learning mostly took place through individual worksheets and assignments, Nina explaining and clarifying points to the class, recitation exercises, large group work and one mid-term class project involving small group work. In class, Nina rarely called on Aarzoo for answers, instead picking the more enthusiastic students who raised their hands. She wanted to give Aarzoo space until she felt more comfortable. Once, during an English grammar lesson, Nina wrote several fill-in-the-blank questions on the board and was calling on students to answer them. She called on Aarzoo as well. Aarzoo hesitantly walked up to the board and wrote 'hat' instead of 'that'. The whole class laughed. Nina told Aarzoo the answer was wrong and asked her to go back to her seat.

One day when Aarzoo was at Nina's desk, lice fell out of Arzoo's hair on to a notebook. Nina was aghast. She had received complaints from other students in the past about Aarzoo's lack of cleanliness. They had complained saying, "Ma'am have you seen her clothes? They are dirty. Sometimes she doesn't even take a bath and she smells. How can she come to school like this? How can we sit next to her?" Knowing that she couldn't access Aarzoo's parents and instruct them, Nina had let these complaints go. But this time around she took Aarzoo aside, told her that the school had certain standards of cleanliness and that she needed to abide by them. Aarzoo cried and said that there is often no water in the home, or if there is then the line is too long and she would be late for school if she waited to take a bath. Nina said she will complain to the home. And she did. However the staff at the home spoke of several constraints they had and their inability to control lice, as many children lived and slept together in close quarters. Nina felt helpless yet again.

Nina noticed that though Aarzoo spoke cordially to her classmates, none of them were friends. She rarely stuck around in class during lunch time. Nina often spotted her having lunch and chatting with other students from the home during lunch and other breaks. But when Kiya, a Burmese student, joined the class, Nina found that Aarzoo and Kiya often sat together, shared lunch, and were engaged in friendly banter. Curious to know how Aarzoo was doing, Nina asked Kiya about Aarzoo. Kiya said, "Ma'am. Aarzoo is very sad inside. She has a lot of pain in her. She opens up to me sometimes. She told me how she never had lunch with other students because they brought a variety of dishes from home and could also afford to eat in the canteen. But Aarzoo carries the same lunch of rice and lentils every day and is embarrassed. When she saw me carrying the same lunch one day, she felt comfortable talking to me and now we are friends. Ma'am, she is also a wonderful painter and expresses her ideas so well in her paintings. Have you seen them?" Nina had never seen Aarzoo paint; there hadn't been any such occasion in her English class. She also realized that Kiya had a very open, gentle, and welcoming personality and that had helped Aarzoo open up to her.

It was almost the middle of the school year, and thanks to the remedial classes Aarzoo's grade had improved from an F to a D; however, this was still far away from the C grade required for moving on to the next class. Given where Aarzoo had started, Nina considered it an achievement.

However, in the next few weeks Aarzoo's attendance started falling—and at some point Aarzoo stopped coming to school. Nina informed the school social worker, who followed up with the home. They informed the school that Nina's father had been arrested for theft and her mother was struggling to fend for the family. She no longer called Aarzoo, nor did she visit, and this had distressed Aarzoo beyond measure. After much coaxing and intervention Aarzoo came back to school.

Something was different about Aarzoo this time. She was irritable and angry. She did not want to be in school. She was rude and misbehaved in Nina's class and did not turn up for her one-on-one lessons. She had also joined a group of mischievous students in class and would often be disruptive, talking non-stop while Nina spoke and taking no interest in class activities, etc. Nina had no choice but to seat Aarzoo in the front where she could keep an eye on her, and she did not include her in large group discussions and class activities. Nina told one of her colleagues, "I am not sure how to deal with Aarzoo. Factors in her life are beyond my control. She has no respect. She disrupts the discipline in class and is also influencing others around her to play pranks and not pay attention. How can learning happen if there is no discipline? I have no choice but to separate her from the rest."

It is almost the end of the school year and Arzoo's academic performance has slipped further. Even the remedial class teacher is facing disciplinary issues with Aarzoo. In one of the last classes of the year, Nina is discussing a poem about a poor man begging on the streets and getting alms from a rich man. She hands out individual worksheets and asks students to fill them out. After they finish, Nina begins a large group discussion, going through all the questions in the worksheet. Nina finally asks, "What is more valuable? Wealth or Love?" Some students respond "wealth" and others say "love". Aarzoo is quiet and doesn't say anything. She looks down at her half-filled worksheet. Nina goes on to elaborate the importance of empathetic love versus sympathy and charity. Some of the students participate in the discussion, and Nina is satisfied that the students have understood.

After the class is over and students have left for the day, Kiya comes up to Nina and says, "Ma'am, did you know that Aarzoo has experienced extreme hunger and deprivation living on the streets, just like the beggar in the street? In fact, she told me that she used to take her little brother along to beg at the traffic signal when there was no food at home. Today Aarzoo was quiet and I kept wondering what she must have thought and felt. I wish there was a way for her to express her opinion in class so that we all could better understand the feelings of the beggar. I felt sad that all of us who are privileged could debate poverty, wealth, and love while Aarzoo kept silent." Nina explained to Kiya that this was a sensitive subject and perhaps it was best that Aarzoo did not speak. Kiya nodded but did not seem to agree; she left silently.

Problem Statement

Meanwhile, Aarzoo hasn't been able to score the required marks and will be repeating Nina's class next year. Given the uncertainties in Aarzoo's life, Nina can only wonder what will happen to Aarzoo academically.

Questions for Discussion

1. How would you evaluate Nina's relationship with Aarzoo? What do you think about the role of the teacher especially with students who come from low-income backgrounds and have difficult histories and emotional lives?
2. What kind of pedagogies and classroom environments can Nina use to foster an exchange of knowledge and experiences among students from diverse backgrounds, and to help Aarzoo find her voice and develop agency?
3. Do students living in poverty need something extra or different? Brainstorm the kind of mindsets Nina must cultivate, and strategies she must use, to ensure Aarzoo is learning in her class.
4. To what extent has the national education policy on "inclusion" been implemented? What in your view is the difference between inclusion and integration? What could be done to make the implementation of the policy more likely to be "in spirit," and not only in letter?

Case #7

"He's here everyday but, take him away!"

Chris Gilham

The administrators of a large, urban-based Canadian high school, in a socioeconomically and culturally diverse neighborhood, formally request school board support for a grade 10 student who is "at school most days, though not attending classes." Matthew is the school board consultant responsible for supporting the school's request. His primary role is to support the school with its job of facilitating the student's success at school. Matthew does not work directly with students; rather he supports school teams in their work with students. Matthew arranges a meeting with the assistant principal responsible for the student. Matthew knows this administrator well, from previous work together. They have a friendly working relationship.

In the meeting, Matthew learns that the grade ten student is Aboriginal, enrolled in a Learning Strategies course (a course intended to support struggling students with basic life and study skills), does not attend most of these classes - or any of his other classes - and spends most of his time around the outside of the school, smoking marijuana. The school resource officer (a police officer) has spoken with this student many times. No charges have been laid against the student. The assistant principal shares that the student has a highly dysfunctional home life. Attempts to contact the parents of the student have been unsuccessful. Despite the student not attending most of the Learning Strategies classes, Matthew asks if he may spend some time observing the student's particular Learning Strategies class, with the hope of learning more about how it supports struggling students. During his observation of the class, the student is not present.

Overview

Matthew receives over 100 requests per school year from schools seeking specific student support. In his role, he is also the gatekeeper for a variety of diagnosis-specific, specialized schools and classrooms throughout the school board. In the majority of requests, school administrators hope Matthew will place their student(s) of concern in a specialized setting. These requests far exceed the number of open placements in these specialized settings. Also, the majority of the students that schools request be placed in a specialized setting do not meet all the requirements for the specialized settings. In particular, though the student(s) may meet diagnostic criteria for the specialized setting (a diagnosis of Autism Spectrum Disorder, for example), the student's overall needs are not severe enough for the specialized setting. It is often the case that the school asking for this has not yet fully or properly accessed and implemented its resources, including school board and community supports. Before recommending placement in specialized settings, Matthew works to ensure that school teams fully support students. While this is often difficult and contested work, given that it can be at odds with the requests of school teams, Matthew does everything he can to support their efforts knowing that the final decision for placement requires his assent.

This particular case poses an immediate challenge for Matthew. Concerned about the lack of school engagement, even with the presence of the student 'around' the school, Matthew asks if there has been a review of the student's educational file. This has not been done by the school team. The thick file is brought to Matthew. He finds a standardized academic test commonly used to assess the basic academic skill levels of students entering high school. The assistant principal informs Matthew that every student in the school takes this test early in their grade ten year. This particular student's test reveals a reading level of grade two. A deeper exploration of the student's previous academic scores and grades confirms this reading level. The file contains numerous reports reflecting the student's long (since early elementary) and ongoing disengagement from learning in schools. The assistant principal shares with Matthew that there are many students at the school with very low reading levels. Most of these students are enrolled in the Learning Strategies class for support. The assistant principal shares his frustration with the increasing prevalence of largely illiterate students entering high school. He claims there is no funding to support non- or low-level readers in the school. Matthew shares with the assistant principal that of all populations of school students, Aboriginal students have the lowest high school completion rate, alongside students diagnosed with severe social and emotional disabilities. Often, Aboriginal students are identified with these severe disabilities.

Halfway through the meeting, the assistant principal asks Matthew to consider approving the removal of the student from the school in order to place him in an off-site, specialized setting for 'at risk' youth. He shares that school staff are frustrated with the student's lack of academic engagement. He believes that the school has done what it can for the student.

Matthew then observes the Learning Strategies class. The student is not present, as expected. He notes the teacher's use of a lot of print hand-outs, and that the teacher often asks students to read from the print hand-outs. During his observation, student engagement is very low, disruptions are frequent, and the teacher spends most of her time attempting to manage negative student behavior. Most students do not participate in the class. Matthew notes that many students constantly use their handheld devices to play games, watch music videos, or chat with friends.

Problem Statement

The Aboriginal student in question is on school grounds but not attending classes. He is enrolled in a Learning Strategies class intended to support his academic challenges. He is not disruptive, but spends his time wandering outside the school smoking marijuana. Academically, he is best described as a non-reader.

The administration of the school wants him placed in a specialized setting, effectively removing him from his community high school. Matthew is asked to approve this, but he is not able to meet with the student or observe him. Matthew's observation of the Learning Strategies class reveals a teacher pedagogy that relies on photo-copied worksheets and student reading competency. There also appears to be no guidelines on the use of handheld technology in the classroom.

Matthew has good information but not as much as he would like.

Discussion Questions

1. What can you say about the situation based on the information Matthew has gathered?
2. Given what Matthew knows already, what should he ask or do next? What should he recommend? Why?
3. What are the broad issues raised by this case? What are the issues of equity and social justice raised by this case?
4. Are there pedagogical issues raised by this case? If yes, explain.
5. Are there issues raised by the case that you are unsure about?
6. In this case study, I am uncomfortable with…
7. Through this case study, a specific topic I would like to learn more about is…

References

Sensoy, O. & DiAngelo, R.(2017). Is everyone really equal? An introduction to key concepts in social justice education. Teachers College Press, Columbia University. New York.

Case # 8

Negotiating and Navigating Disability in Inclusive Settings

Melissa K. Driver

Introduction

Hayden is a 6th grade African American female student with a specific learning disability. Her special education teacher, Ms. Fields, a first year teacher, collaborates with multiple general education content teachers throughout the school day to provide all of Hayden's special education services. By the end of the first quarter, Ms. Fields is concerned by Hayden's lack of progress in the general curriculum. She is also concerned with several of her co-teaching relationships, particularly her relationship with Hayden's English teacher.

Overview/Analysis

Hayden, who attends Meadows Middle School (MMS), was diagnosed in fourth grade with a specific learning disability after failing the state test and being retained for one year. She now attends a public middle school and receives special education services in her general education classroom. MMS is on the state watch list for failing schools, and serves a large number of historically underserved students of color and students receiving free or reduced lunch.

Hayden's special education teacher, Ms. Fields, is a first year teacher.

As a recent graduate from a dual-certification special and general education program, Ms. Fields was excited to obtain a position as a special education teacher working in inclusive classrooms. In her role, Ms. Fields co-teaches with the 6th grade English and Mathematics teacher and provides consultation support to the Social Studies and Science teacher. While excited to collaborate with other teachers, Ms. Fields is overwhelmed with how to effectively co-plan with each of her co-teachers in order to meet each of her students' individual needs across several content areas, and keep up with the paperwork and legal requirements of being a special educator. Balancing all of these responsibilities has made it difficult for Ms. Fields to feel fully involved in any of her collaborative relationships. Often she feels more like a teaching assistant in someone else's classroom than a certified educator. Ms. Fields is solely responsible for delivering all the special education services listed on Hayden's Individualized Education Plan (IEP), as well as the other students with disabilities in the 6th grade.

According to Hayden's IEP, she has difficulty with reading fluency, reading comprehension, written expression, mathematics calculations, and mathematics problem solving. According to the school-wide literacy progress monitoring, Hayden began her 6th grade year at a 2.5 grade reading level. Hayden is very shy and withdrawn in her classes. She is hesitant to participate in both academic and social activities. Hayden's parents were unable to attend the "Welcome Back" night hosted by MMS and have had little contact with any of her teachers.

Ms. Fields and her general education co-teachers are concerned about Hayden's progress in her current setting. In particular, her English teacher is convinced that an inclusive classroom is not the best fit for Hayden. Hayden's English teacher has expressed frustration about, "being held responsible for her test scores". She continually suggests that Ms. Fields should consider rewriting the IEP to include reading instruction in a special education classroom (i.e., resource/pullout or self-contained). Hayden struggles to read and understand grade-level text. The English teacher is frustrated because she believes Hayden should be in a remedial class instead of wasting her time falling further behind on grade level material. Her Social Studies and Science teachers both agree that her difficulties reading grade level informational text are their biggest concern. However, in comparison to other students, who are demonstrating disruptive behaviors in their classes, these teachers are less concerned about Hayden. In mathematics, Hayden's teacher is unsure about the best way to address significant gaps in her mathematical understanding while still keeping the class on pace with grade level material. He is unsure of what additional supports he can provide other than allowing Hayden to use a calculator, as stated in her IEP accommodations. The Mathematics teacher is the most welcoming when it comes to collaborating with Ms. Fields, but unfortunately they do not share common planning time and he needs to leave right after school to pick up his children.

The school-wide October benchmark testing revealed that Hayden was making limited growth in the areas of reading, writing, and mathematics. In addition, she did not meet the 1st quarter benchmarks aligned to her annual IEP goals. Ms. Fields has also noticed a change in Hayden's classroom demeanor. While still compliant, Hayden has begun expressing apathy towards classroom assignments, muttering comments such as "I don't care" or "this is stupid". After reflecting on Hayden's limited progress and newfound behaviors, Ms. Fields reached out to her parents to arrange a parent-teacher conference.

In her meeting with Hayden's parents, Ms. Fields realized that her parents have felt intentionally left out of the process and were unsure of how to best advocate for their daughter. They relied heavily on the school's expertise in elementary school. Her mother shared that Hayden was always a good student, receiving A's and B's in all subject areas, and enjoyed attending school. Hayden's cumulative files confirm this was indeed the case. Hayden's mother said that she was shocked to receive the 4th grade test scores and deferred to the school's recommendation for Hayden to repeat the 4th grade. Throughout the following year, Hayden's teachers expressed some concern about her reading abilities, but mostly praised her compliant behavior. After failing the state standardized assessment for a second time, the school recommended initiating the identification process for special education.

Problem statement

Ms. Fields is unsure how to best support Hayden's needs across each of her different content areas. She is most concerned with Hayden's progress in her English class and with her relationship with this teacher. As a first year teacher, Ms. Fields is unsure of the best way to address the concerns of the other teachers. Ms. Fields does not know what to do to improve the situation and meet Hayden's needs.

Case Problems

1. What are the issues surrounding Hayden's identification? Discuss the contextual factors that contributed to Hayden's placement in special education.
2. What should Hayden's identification and delivery of services have looked like?
3. What factors contributed to the perceived lack of parental involvement? What were the implications of this perception?
4. How has student behavior influenced school concerns (or lack of concern) regarding Hayden's academic difficulties?
5. How have Hayden's educational circumstances influenced her motivation over time?
6. What evidence of culturally relevant pedagogy is presented in this case study? What is lacking? What should be improved?
7. Should Hayden be pulled out of the general education classroom for her Reading/English instruction? Why or why not? What are the benefits and disadvantages of this instructional model?
8. Consider the staffing structure in the 6th grade at MMS. What is effective and ineffective about having one special educator for each grade level? What other models might the school use? Reflect on the advantages, disadvantages, practicality, and feasibility of your recommendations.
9. What were the perceptions of Hayden's teachers on educating students with disabilities inside the general education classroom? How might these perceptions have influenced their educational decision-making?

10. Reflect on the intersection of race, culture, socio-economic status, and ability presented in this case. How did each aspect of Hayden's identity impact her educational opportunities and outcomes?

Teaching Strategies

As you reflect on the questions presented in this case, consider the following evidence-based approaches and whether or not they might help Ms. Fields and Hayden. Full citations for journal articles are provided in the Reference list.

- **Explicit Instruction.** Explicit instruction is an evidence-based approach to teaching students with learning disabilities, and is applicable for all content areas. Explore this website on explicit instruction (the videos are particularly helpful) to learn more and see explicit instruction in action: http://explicitinstruction.org/. You can also learn more about applying this framework to address students' literacy needs by reading the Vaughn & Roberts (2007) article on reading interventions for secondary students.

- **Data-Based Decision Making.** An important aspect of designing effective instruction for students with disabilities involves collecting and using data to inform decision-making. Danielson and Rosenquist (2014) describe this process in their introduction to a special journal issue on this topic.

- **Culturally Responsive Teaching.** Throughout this case, many contextual factors work together to create challenges and solutions. The role of student identity, culture, and community is critical to understand for all educators. Kozleski (n.d.) explains what culturally responsive teaching is and why it matters. You can also explore more on this subject by visiting the Equity Alliance website: http://equityallianceatasu.org/

- **Building Relationships with Parents/Guardians.** A very important aspect of culturally responsive teaching is building authentic and strong relationships with students and their parents/guardians. In their articles, Edwards and Da Fonte (2012) and Matuszny, Banda, and Coleman (2007) provide plans for building relationships with parents/guardians.

- **Co-Teaching.** As observed in this case, co-teaching can be a complex and challenging phenomenon. Murawski and Dieker (2004; 2008) provide practical suggestions for building, maintaining, and improving co-teaching relationships.

References

Danielson, L., & Rosenquist, C. (2014). Introduction to the TEC Special Issue on Data-Based Individualization. *Teaching Exceptional Children, 46*(4), 6-12.

Edwards, C. C., & Da Fonte, A. (2012). The 5-Point Plan: Fostering Successful Partnerships with Families of Students with Disabilities. *TEACHING Exceptional Children, 44*(3), 6-13.

Kozleski (n.d.). Culturally Responsive Teaching Matters! Retrieved from http://www.equityallianceatasu.org/sites/default/files/Website_files/CulturallyResponsiveTeaching-Matters.pdf

Matuszny, R. M., Banda, D. R., & Coleman, T. J. (2007). A Progressive Plan for Building Collaborative Relationships With Parents From Diverse Backgrounds. *Teaching Exceptional Children, 39*(4), 24-31.

Murawski, W. W., & Dieker, L. A. (2004). Tips and Strategies for Co-Teaching at the Secondary Level. *Teaching Exceptional Children, 36*(5), 52-58.

Murawski, W. W., & Dieker, L. (2008). 50 Ways to Keep Your Co-Teacher: Strategies for before, during, and after Co-Teaching. *Teaching Exceptional Children, 40*(4), 40-48.

Vaughn, S., & Roberts, G. (2007). Secondary Interventions in Reading: Providing Additional Instruction for Students At Risk. *Teaching Exceptional Children, 39*(5), 40-46.

Case #9

Inclusion to Prevent Exclusion: A Tale of Two Schools

Louise Gazeley

Introduction

This case study focuses on Kyle's experiences of inclusion and exclusion as viewed from the perspective of his foster carer, Martha. It focuses on the disciplinary processes of schools, and the potential for these to either strengthen or ameliorate social inequalities. Kyle's contrasting experiences at two state secondary schools - Fairfields Academy and Coalville Community College - draw attention to differences in the micro-practices of individual teachers, differences that are linked to the institutional cultures established at leadership level. They raise fundamental questions about the purpose of education, the wider systems in which schools' disciplinary practices are located, and what it means to be a successful school.

Overview/Analysis

There are noted variations in the disciplinary practices of schools. In England these have evolved into complex processes, with the head teacher, in extreme instances and/or where all alternative strategies have failed, retaining the power to formally exclude a young person on disciplinary grounds. Young people in public care, and those with additional learning needs, are disproportionately affected by this sanction. There are also strong intersections with gender, socio-economic status, and ethnic background. Pressure has been exerted on schools to reduce such inequalities, leading to an increased focus on monitoring, early intervention, and targeted support. Experiences of inclusion and exclusion have therefore become increasingly closely intertwined.

Martha, a school governor, foster carer, and former teacher, discussed the case of Kyle, a 14 year old boy in her care with a long history of disciplinary exclusion. This had contributed to a pattern of disrupted attendance that appeared to have compounded weak literacy skills and low levels of motivation and self-confidence. Martha explained that she had been comparatively ignorant of the systems designed to keep children like Kyle in school, up until the point when she left teaching to become a foster carer. She felt that her role as carer included making sure that staff working with Kyle were aware when he was feeling more than usually unsettled, and that knowing this would allow them to deal with him a bit differently. She did not see this as being about allowing Kyle to "get away with things," but as about having "that knowledge, and that understanding, that you need to have in dealing with people who are delicate already." Martha maintained that it is possible to treat people equally while also recognising that they are not the same.

Martha described Kyle's most recent school experiences. Until recently he had been a student at Fairfields Academy, a school with a very good academic reputation that was located in an affluent suburb of the city. At Fairfields it was considered necessary to exclude young people at times in order to ensure a safe and conducive learning environment for others. Children like Kyle were in a minority; Martha felt that some staff struggled to understand him "because he doesn't fit the box that they're used to." She identified a lack of resources, experience, and flexibility, and thought that this had prevented the school having "the things in place to catch him when he falls." Martha described a series of micro-instances that culminated in Kyle being formally excluded once again:

> Kyle was supposed to be isolated for the day, although we were never made aware of that. They don't have an isolation

room, because children don't need them at that school. He was supposed to spend a day with the deputy head, who got distracted, and was busy, so he went to lessons. Already set up to fail, in my opinion, Kyle did fail and then was excluded for half a day.

Kyle was subsequently offered a managed move to Coalville Community College, another school in the city, with a view to him making a fresh start.

Coalville Community College was located in a diverse and very socially disadvantaged area, and it had a highly transient population. Martha knew that other local parents were reluctant to visit the school, let alone send a child there, and she attributed this to its historic reputation and current low academic performance. Nevertheless, Martha considered Coalville to be highly inclusive in its ethos, attributing this to leadership practices that she described as being based on a commitment that went "beyond having to." Staff were challenged to adopt a "never give up on you approach" and disciplinary exclusions were both a last resort and viewed as a failure. Martha felt that Kyle was well-supported at Coalville and that his particular needs were being pre-emptively addressed. In addition to receiving additional personalised support, time was spent anticipating likely challenges:

Kyle doesn't cope well with change, and they'd already got things ready so that instead of being in lessons which might be slightly different to normal, they'd got something planned and he knew about it at the beginning of the week.

Reflecting on Kyle's experiences in the two schools, Martha suggested that education does not necessarily suit boys, and that what happens in the classroom is what matters most. She thought that while some teachers were very receptive to implementing creative strategies to support young people struggling to maintain themselves in education, others were so resistant that they became an additional barrier. She questioned the extent to which differences in needs and circumstances inform current understandings of the purpose of education and what constitutes success:

It's not always about the final outcome, and if you look at the make-up of the school, of course, some of the children are not going to meet minimum academic standards, but really is that what school is all about - or is there more to school than that?

Martha considered all schools to be equally responsible for all children in their communities, and that "every staff member needs to send out the message that they are wanted and that they want to keep them."

Problem Statement

There is currently a strong focus at the level of international policy on the importance of doing more to disrupt a continuing cycle of inter-generational social disadvantage and 'school failure'[1]. This agenda has yet to be adequately informed by an understanding of how involvement in the disciplinary processes of schools feeds into the macro-level data generating these concerns. Despite their relative invisibility, the micro practices associated with disciplinary processes are powerful in strengthening or reducing pre-existing inequalities precisely because they impact disproportionately on the least educationally and socially advantaged. That they vary between schools and across contexts points to the importance of differences that are not readily reducible to single factors. The interplay between policies, localities, and practices (institutional and individual), feeds into differences in empathy and ethos that reflect different understandings of inclusion and exclusion, and the balance to be struck between the two.

Discussion Questions

1. How does Kyle's case challenge our understanding of what it means to be a successful school?
2. What does Kyle's case suggest about how the understandings needed to work inclusively and from a position of empathy are acquired?

---

[1] Defined as not having attained national minimum standards at the point of leaving compulsory education

3. Martha feels that Kyle was "set up to fail" at Fairfields. Where does responsibility for this rest: with class teachers, school leaders, teacher educators, or wider educational, social, and political systems?

Teaching Suggestions

1. Discuss the different forms of inclusion and exclusion experienced by Kyle, and produce a visual mapping of these.
2. Annotate your visual mapping to show the individuals and experiences that you feel have been most influential.

Suggested Readings

Barker, J. Alldred, P. Watts, M. and Dodman, H., (2010). Pupils or prisoners? Institutional geographies and internal exclusion in UK secondary schools, AREA, 42, 3. pp. 378-386.

Gazeley, L., Marrable, T., Brown, C. and J. Boddy, (2015) Contextualising inequalities in rates of school exclusion in English schools: beneath the 'tip of the ice-berg,' British Journal of Educational Studies, 63 (4). pp. 1-18.

Harris, B. Vincent, K. Thomson, P. and Toalster, R. (2008), Does Every Child Know They Matter? Pupils' Views of One Alternative to Exclusion, Pastoral Care in Education: An International Journal of Personal, Social and Emotional Development, 24, 2, pp. 28-38.

Case #10

Brentwood High School

Lynn Butler-Kisber

Introduction

The case study focuses on issues of inclusion and equity at Brentwood High School in the suburbs of a small city in Ontario. The case examines the challenges and the issues that the vice-principal, Mrs. Clarke, needs to address in her second year at the school. Up until ten years ago, the school had enjoyed an excellent reputation in the school system, in both academic rankings and extracurricular activities/sports. Changing demographics in the school population have been attributed to a change in the reputation of the school. There has been some talk, however, among certain educators in the School Board that a deficit lens may have eroded the reputation of Brentwood and contributed to the absenteeism and to the apparent lack of interest in participating in the school on the part of family members. To this small group of educators, it does not appear that the school, and at least some staff members, are understanding the needs of the students and the community and adapting to them in ways to meet the changing demographics of this community and the economic demands many families are experiencing.

Overview

Brentwood High School (BHS) is located in the suburbs of an urban centre in Ontario with a population of approximately one million. The school itself is situated on a large tract of land that includes a school yard, a track and field area and a parking lot that can accommodate approximately 75 cars. Not more than a block away is a small, strip shopping mall, a pizza parlour, a gas station and a small number of other commercial buildings. The housing in this area is varied and consists of single dwellings, semi-detached homes, condominiums and government subsidized apartment buildings. The neighborhood which was originally made up of white, middle-class families has changed rapidly in the last 10 years with a large influx of immigrants from East Africa, Pakistan and the Middle East. Currently, the neighborhood is both visually and economically very diverse.

The population of BHS is approximately 600 students, 60% of which are from immigrant families, which is a far cry from the very homogenous student body of a decade before. The decreasing numbers have opened up space within the school, but the declining youth population in the school system has resulted in budget cuts and increased workloads for teachers.

There is a staff of 58 teachers organized into 11 departments, one for each of the high school subject areas, plus a principal, vice-principal, one librarian and a school custodian. The teaching experience of the staff represents the range of early, middle, and late career professionals, some of whom have been there for at least 20 years. A large proportion of male teachers make up the late-career group, while the opposite is true in the early-career group. Informal conversations in the staffroom among veteran teachers frequently revolve around "retirement plans" and "the good old days." Recent budget cuts have resulted in a reduction of what had been two vice-principals and two librarians. Teachers now take turns helping the librarian as part of their workloads.

In recent years the school's reputation has suffered, traced at least in part to an altercation several years ago that occurred a few hundred feet away from the school among four or five male students from BHS and several other non-BHS males. It had been broken up by police, garnered negative media attention, and as a result of the incident, the school had acquired a bad reputation. Reports of the altercation had not been treated kindly in the press, and rumors were that the school was a violent place and should be avoided.

Mr. Bill Johnson, the Principal, has been in education for 35 years. He has been at BHS for 12 and has witnessed the changing demographics in this suburban area and the increasing diversity in the student body. His career began as a physical education teacher and some of the skills that he acquired in the gym have helped him to relate to the students, to appreciate the value of extracurricular activities and to emanate a no-nonsense approach to student behavior. He is affable and friendly with students and staff and has a strong desire to make the school as successful as it was twenty years ago, which he hears it was, over and over again, from his friends in the community and from his professional counterparts.

The vice-principal is Mrs. Helen Clarke. It is her second year in this role. Prior to that she was head of an English department in another local high school for over a decade. Her roots in education, however, were in elementary school and her experiences with younger children occurred both in Ontario and Trinidad and Tobago, her country of birth. A relatively new addition to BHS is the Cultural Liaison Officer, Mr. Simon Oaks, who was assigned to BHS and three other schools by the School Board to help immigrant students to transition into their new environments. Mr. Oaks grew up in this city in Ontario and was a former student in the system. Mrs. Clarke and Mr. Oaks are the only visible minority professionals on the staff.

When Helen Clarke came to BHS, she was assigned responsibility for student behavior and class scheduling, typical roles among other duties for vice-principals within this large school board. During her rounds, she quickly became aware of how the informal social interaction among the students occurred largely along cultural lines even though home classes were assigned alphabetically and were culturally diverse. For example, it was noticeable in the hallways how homogeneous groups of students stayed in close proximity and were impervious to other groups. In the cafeteria unspoken rules prevailed. Certain tables were for certain groups of students and these implicit rules were understood by all. Unless seats were assigned by the teacher in classrooms, these groupings of students were replicated there. An interesting thing had happened, though, when class time was extended from 60 to 75 minutes, ostensibly to allow for more hands-on, inquiry-oriented student work. In spite of the lengthening of the time in each period, a number of teachers stopped and even went to sit at their desks when 60 minutes had elapsed and allowed more informal interaction among students. From an academic standpoint, this negated what the extra time was for, but Helen Clarke noticed that some of the barriers among different groups broke down and informal conversation did occur in these lingering few minutes between students in different groups who normally would not be have been involved in exchanges. Furthermore, extracurricular activities (sport teams, student clubs, and school dances), were all poorly attended. Absenteeism from classes was at a high, although it was apparent that many students had family or economic responsibilities in addition to attending school. Helen Clarke wondered in her first year why a strategic plan had not been developed to reduce absenteeism and slowly came to the realization that even if one had been created, it would have lacked traction among a number of staff. Family participation at BHS was consistently low. There was an enthusiastic and energetic student council but markedly drawn from the white student population at BHS. When she had a chance to speak with two girls from Somalia about why they didn't run for student council in spite of their scholastic and leadership abilities, they indicated they were not attracted to solo leadership roles, but would have jumped at the opportunity if they had been able to run for election as co-presidents All of these issues troubled her, particularly because they were not issues that she heard raised at staff meetings, or even informally, at any time during her first year and she wondered why.

As a new member of staff, for the first year of her tenure, Helen Clarke decided to carry out her duties conscientiously, and to gather informally information about the issues that she felt were contributing to absenteeism and the lack of involvement in extracurricular activities, as well as scarce family involvement. She realized, from previous administrative experience that "a new kid on the block" should take some time getting to know the staff and student body before embarking on efforts to institute change. She was, however, determined that in her second year she would initiate changes. She began this process by arranging to meet with Bill Johnson as her first academic year at BHS came to a close.

Case Questions

1. What are the issues or challenges that Helen should discuss with Bill? Based on the information in the case, what are some possible challenges that could arise from this discussion?
2. What steps/strategies should Helen Clarke take to counter the issues BHS faces, and why?
3. With whom should Helen Clarke meet and how, when and why?
4. What might some of the short and long-term challenges be that Helen will face and what cautionary advice should she be given?

Case #11

RACE: A Polarizing Force

Philip McAdoo

This case highlights race as a polarizing cultural force in education.

Problem Statement

Students, faculty, and staff had a wide range of responses to Trayvon Martin, whose death by a white police officer in the United States sparked outrage across the county. On your campus, there was a huge racial divide. Black students, for the most part, were engaged and frustrated, while most of the white students felt like race was not a factor in the death of the black teen. There were lots of questions and comments that mirrored the racial divide in the news and around the country.

Diversity is about difference, and being open to other ways of thinking and being. As Director of Diversity, you have the responsibility of addressing diversity in an independent school, in the southern United States, with a longstanding history of privileging sameness. Your job is to reach out to diverse populations to encourage potential students, families, and staff to view the school community as a responsive environment that is open to change, difference, integration, global studies, and cross-cultural communication as well as identify, research, and foster new ties to develop partnerships, recruitment, and funding opportunities.

Race: A Polarizing Cultural Force

As Director of Diversity, you are committed to valuing diversity; you believe that this should be a key principle of major institutions. In schools, diversity has become fundamental to students' character development and to the quality and depth of the education they receive. A basic tenet of diversity is that differences have value that should be sustained throughout our educational practices. The overarching goal should be to produce students who have a better understanding of the complexities of an ever-changing world.

The foundation of your leadership practice in diversity is acknowledging that we are a global society of differences. It is imperative that we accommodate varying value systems through a lens of critical understanding with a focus on sustainability. The critical understanding of difference should be based in engagement with various religious, ethnic, social, and other groupings. You believe that directly experiencing different points of reference is the ultimate expression of humanity, which opens up students to genuine human relationships as they seek to understand and see their stories reflected in the lives of others.

With no established program to build upon, you sought to create a framework for growing diversity within the social construct of education in a white, southern conservative community. Your objective was to facilitate conversations to cultivate continuous improvement in an environment where there was a commitment to the idea that we should live in a colorblind society. Your intention was to present diversity as an extension of the school's sustained identity of excellence in education by actively engaging the school in comprehensive, encompassing and relevant initiatives that would counter the current, routinized culture; however, this culture was long-established, and there were very different perceptions of diversity.

The news of Trayvon Martin was everywhere. From t-shirts to Facebook posts, the image of Trayvon's face was news spanning the world. Neighborhood watchman George Zimmerman shot the 17-year-old Martin to death in Sanford, Florida. Zimmerman followed the teen, who was wearing a hooded sweatshirt, after telling 911 operators that

Martin looked "suspicious." Citing Florida's Stand Your Ground self-defense law, Zimmerman was not immediately charged with a crime. As the story unfolded, thousands of protesters wore hoodies to deplore the death of the black teen.

While these protesters chanted Trayvon Martin's name, students felt silenced. It was not uncommon for students to wear bracelets to support a cause, or add their voices via social media to massive outrages. This was the same campus that had rallied behind a group of white students to show a film calling attention to the abducting, killing, and displacing of innocent children at the hands of a brutal warlord in Central Africa. There was an assembly, students bought t-shirts, and for a whole day the community felt good about their contribution to global justice. But in the case of Trayvon Martin, the response was different.

Grief and outrage from black students and black teachers slowly intensified as they brought their emotions to school, with no place to unpack them. The position held by most whites on campus was, "What does Trayvon Martin have to do with me?", while most black teachers and black students frantically searched for validation. They started to look to you, as Director of Diversity, for guidance. After all, it was your job to hold us to our policy, outlined in the diversity strategic plan that "promotes the free flow of ideas" and "introduces our students to a wide variety of thought."

It was difficult to convey the reality of the violence that black boys face in this country, and the impact it has on the lives of black students. This was the first time black students had reached out to you directly for help. They shared stories of their white classmates' galling ignorance and bold indifference to what had happened. They congregated in your office to report a teacher's aggressive stance, calling Trayvon Martin a thug and declaring that he deserved to die. They pointed in frustration to their friends in other area schools who were being encouraged by their teachers and administrators to talk about racial profiling, and to participate in open forums about race on their campuses, while we maintained silence.

The issue of Trayvon Martin highlighted the personal and institutional impact of race in an inflexible educational setting. As an educator, you worked hard to be a resource for the school community. You drew from your personal experiences as a gay black man, and your early professional challenges, to conscientiously teach students and colleagues alike about the experiences that minorities often face. You arrived in a community that had been built on a sense of white being superior and anything else being inferior. The atmosphere of racial superiority made change difficult.

The academy branded itself as a "neighborhood school," governed by a board of current and past parents. In the culture of the wealthiest, whitest suburb, it was difficult to convey the reality of the violence that black boys face in this country, and the impact it had on the lives of black students at the school. The headmaster repeatedly and publicly acknowledged that parents were "the heart of the school" and key to the school's success, especially financially. "We do not spend around $25,000 per year for a school where these kinds of issues are allowed or supported," exclaimed a parent. She stated that the school should not take a stand to support "these kinds of social issues, especially with regards to blacks vs. whites."

More disturbing than the e-mails and feedback from parents and teachers was the administration's response to the student-led initiative to address issues of race. Many wanted to know what the decision process was for the school forum, and the head of the school pointed to a lack of communication. You reminded him that we followed the typical protocol for student activities by posting the announcement in the school's internal, web-based portal, and obtaining the proper permit. He went on to say that he was left at a loss for what to tell faculty and the board. You highlighted a copy of the school's board-approved strategic plan on diversity and shared it with him. The plan stated:

> We acknowledge and respect the differences of opinion that exist around political and social issues in our community. Therefore, the academy promotes the free flow of ideas and will introduce our students to a wide variety of thought while avoiding bias in all school programs and functions.

Problem Statement

Students, faculty, and staff had a wide range of responses to Trayvon Martin. Black students for the most part were engaged and frustrated, while most of the white students felt like race was not a factor in the death of the black teen. There were lots of questions and comments that mirrored the racial divide in the news and around the world.

Discussion Questions

1. As an educator charged with diversity and inclusion efforts, how do you respond to this case?
    a. What is your obligation to students, faculty, staff, board?
    b. Whose needs are met first?
2. As you begin to learn more about the case, you are aware how much race will play a role in how people will respond. How do you meet the needs of the community?
    a. Does race become a factor in how you approach the work?
3. The black students, faculty, and parents have given you a charge: be responsive. How do you convey those concerns to a board of mostly white, southern, men?
4. A prominent donor in the school community is outraged that the school would take on such a subject. They called to meet your boss, and have suggested that if you continue to spread your "propaganda" they will no longer give to the school.
    a. How do you manage the conversation with your boss?
    b. What is your approach moving forward?

Case #12

Including Sophie:
Autism, Dyslexia, and Mental Health

Jenn de Lugt

Introduction

Sophie, a ten year old girl with autism, struggles socially, and has severe sensory and fine motor concerns. She began school eager to learn, but it was challenging. Although she showed signs of having dyslexia in Grade 1, it wasn't until Grade 3 that she was formally tested. Sustained and repeated failure with reading through the years eroded Sophie's self-esteem to a point where severe anxiety developed into withdrawal and depression, and finally an attempt to take her life.

Overview/Analysis

"How many eight year olds want to kill themselves..." exclaimed Sophie's aunt, holding back the tears and anger lingering just below the surface. Patty was Sophie's aunt, but Sophie called her "mom." Five years previous Patty agreed to raise her sister's daughter, Sophie, as this was her sister's second child with autism, and, as a single parent, she was struggling. Sophie is now ten years old and in Grade 5; she was held back a year in Grade 2. Sophie is intelligent and creative, and can communicate well orally. She enjoys "writing" stories by dictating them to Patty, who writes them out for her. She loves anything and everything related to animals, according to her aunt, and volunteers at the local Humane Society every second Saturday morning. Sophie's current teacher describes her as being tall, bright, very imaginative, and very creative. She also described Sophie as having "extremely high" anxiety, and, although she has not seen it herself, she is aware that in the past Sophie has screamed, yelled, and hidden under the furniture. She felt that Sophie's autism and anxiety were so intertwined it was impossible to tease the two apart.

Sophie's story is a complicated one, and as early as Grade 1 Patty realized that Sophie was struggling academically. Sophie had started Kindergarten eager to go to school, and excited to read. Sophie had severe fine motor challenges and soon found writing impossible. She responded by not writing when asked to do so. As a result, she lost her snack, she lost her recess - teacher responses that cumulatively reinforced her sense of failure. By the end of Grade 1 Sophie was barely writing anything; she didn't recognize any words even simple, high frequency words such as "the" or "at and barely even her own name. Patty went on to say that by the end of Grade 1 Sophie didn't know the alphabet, and by the end of Grade 2 she still hadn't learned it. Although Patty pushed for a Psychoeducational Assessment in Grade 1, Sophie wasn't assessed until two years later. According to her classroom teacher, this assessment indicated that Sophie had such severe dyslexia that she would never be able to read, and that reading and writing were not going to be a part of Sophie's reality.

As Sophie's schooling continued, her self-efficacy for reading deteriorated; according to Patty, she began to lose all interest in reading, she didn't even want to look at a book, she didn't want anyone to read to her, and she certainly wasn't willing to try reading herself. Patty recounted how Sophie would call herself "stupid," how other kids called her "dummy," and how the Resource Teacher called her "lazy" and "unmotivated." Patty found this attitude to be both confusing and upsetting, as she couldn't see how someone would believe that a child would willingly sit in a classroom and be totally different than everybody else.

Sophie learned to hate school. Patty described a typical school day; it started first thing in the morning with fighting, kicking, scratching, and spitting. Patty described these mornings as "horrible" because Sophie was so desperate not to go to school. In pure survival mode, Patty learned to dress her when she was just waking, before Sophie realized that it was another school day. When they eventually managed to make it outside in time to catch the school bus, Sophie would bolt as soon as she saw the bus round the corner. At school Sophie would often become aggressive; she would kick things and tell her teachers she was going to kill them. She ran and hid in the bathroom when it was time to read, and started leaving the school property as well.

For Grade 2, Patty and her sister decided to enrol Sophie in a specialized, self-contained class for students with autism, an intensive language and social skills program. Although they were initially optimistic, as the year progressed Sophie started to display signs of extreme anxiety. She would cling to the doorway of the classroom, not come inside the school after recess, and would frequently hide under her desk. Her classroom teacher didn't recognize the anxiety behind these behaviours and viewed them as purely delinquent. As the reading and writing demands increased, and without the proper supports in place, Sophie was asked to do things that were impossible for her. Patty described how over time things just went from bad to worse. She felt that these repeated and sustained failures were completely eroding Sophie's self-esteem, her sense of self-worth. It was in December of that year when Sophie came home one day and "just snapped." According to her aunt, something literally broke, describing it in this way: Sophie wouldn't get out of bed for three months; she would only get up and go to the bathroom; she hardly ate; all she did was scream and cry.

Following a five month hiatus, and with the help of a psychologist and a specialized transition program at the city hospital, Sophie was ready to try reintegrating into the public school system.

Problem Statement

With the trauma of Sophie's breakdown still too clear a memory, Patty was determined to do everything she could to ease Sophie's transition back into school. The initial days and weeks would be critical, and Patty was keenly aware that, with Sophie's fragile sense of self, without some proactive and sustained changes a recurrence would likely be imminent. Patty and her sister decided that the first step would be to enrol Sophie in a new school; although it was slightly further away, they felt a fresh start was important.

Patty arranged to meet with the school principal, Ms. Sanchez, two weeks before classes were due to start. During the meeting, Patty provided a detailed account of Sophie, including her history, her challenges, her strengths and interests, and the findings of the reports provided by Sophie's psychologist and the director of the hospital transition program, believing the more information the principal had regarding Sophie, the better.

When the door closed, Ms. Sanchez felt completely exhausted and more than a little overwhelmed. Although she had been a principal for five years, she had never encountered a case as complex and as dire as Sophie's. To complicate things further, with the cuts announced only yesterday, she wasn't sure they would even have the resources to successfully provide the requisite accommodations. The multiplicity of Sophie's needs were beyond any simple solutions, and, frankly, she didn't know where to start...

Case Problems

Discuss the following:
1. Considering her internalizing and externalizing behaviour concerns, as well as her learning challenges, and the interrelatedness of both, how should Sophie's needs be prioritized? Who should be involved, and in what ways?
2. In creating a transition and intervention plan for Sophie, identify the immediate, short- and long-term goals that would best ensure her successful integration back into the school system.
3. Should Sophie be in a segregated class for students with autism? Why, or why not?
4. When upset, Sophie exhibited both physical and verbal aggression. With a philosophy of inclusion, what can be done to support her in an inclusive setting keeping in mind her safety and well-being, and that of her classmates?

5. To get the support Sophie needs to address her dyslexia, Patty and her sister had to find, and pay for, a private program. Consider the following:
    a. Could anything have been done differently in the classroom or school setting?
    b. What system changes might need to be considered?

Teaching Strategies

Children and youth with multiple exceptionalities clearly present the greatest challenges to educators and administrators. Effective program development and delivery should consider the following:

- The whole student: their physical, cognitive, and socio-emotional strengths and challenges
- The interrelatedness of mental health and learning needs
- The critical role of relationships
- Social as well as academic inclusion

References

Autism Speaks http://www.autismspeaks.ca/ The Canadian Research Centre on Inclusive Education http://www.inclusiveeducationresearch.ca/ Understood: For learning and attention issues https://www.understood.org/en

de Lugt, J., & Hutchinson, N. (2017). Unpacking the relationship between learning to read and mental health: using an ethnographic case study approach. *Computer Supported Qualitative Research, 71*, 95-103.

Dods, J. (2013). Enhancing understanding of the nature of supportive school-based relationships for youth who have experienced trauma. *Canadian Journal of Education, 36*, 71-95.

Lane, K. L., & Menzies, H. M. (2010). Reading and writing interventions for students with and at risk for emotional and behavioral disorders: An introduction. *Behavioral Disorders, 35*, 82-85.

Leach, D. and Duffy, M. (2009). Supporting students with Autism spectrum disorders in inclusive settings. *Intervention in School and Clinic, 45*, 31-37.

Case #13

Wendy or Chad?
Supporting Transgender Youth in Elementary Schools

Bud Harrelson & Kathleen Brown

Introduction

Chad is a transgender fourth-grade student. During the summer, his parents met with the principal of Cambridge Hills Elementary to inform her that Chad had begun to transition from female to male, and would fully present as male when school re-opened in the fall. This case explores the decisions and actions taken by the principal to create a welcoming and inclusive learning environment for Chad. Even though the principal worked to create a safe space for Chad at Cambridge Hills, she encountered resistance and challenges within the school, and from district leadership.

Overview

Chad is a transgender boy in the fourth-grade at Cambridge Hills Elementary School. When Chad was in the second and third grade, he communicated to his parents that he was a boy. Chad expressed himself as a boy by wearing stereotypically masculine clothes, wearing his hair short, and playing with stereotypically masculine toys. Even though his teachers at school called him by his birth-name, Wendy, he often introduced himself as Chad and asked his peers to call him Chad.

Chad's parents both identify as cisgender and heterosexual. They, like all parents, want what is best for their child. In an effort to support Chad's gender identity at home, they refer to him as Chad and use male pronouns. They purchased stereotypically male clothes and toys for him. At the same time, to minimize Chad consistently encountering gendered activities, they registered him for the co-ed t-ball league. Chad also participates in weekly individual tennis lessons.

In the spring of his third-grade year, Chad's parents sought the guidance of a psychologist on how to best support Chad's gender dysphoria. In accordance with the American Psychological Association's (2015) guidance, the psychologist recommended that Chad be allowed to fully live his life in accordance with his gender identity, which is male. In addition to adopting a masculine name and using masculine pronouns, this includes fully expressing himself as male in public – wearing stereotypically masculine clothes, adopting a stereotypically masculine haircut, and using gender-segregated facilities that align with his gender identity (e.g., using the boys' restroom at school). Chad's parents embraced the psychologist's recommendations, and made an appointment with the Cambridge Hills Elementary principal to inform the school of Chad's transition and create a support plan for Chad.

The Cambridge Hills principal was very supportive of Chad and his family; she was committed to creating a safe learning environment for Chad. After meeting with Chad's parents, she began to formulate a support plan for Chad.

Cambridge Hills is located in a progressive school district. Even though the district identifies itself as progressive, it has yet to tackle the issues that arise in schools when a person's gender identity does not match their sex assigned at birth. The district has not adjusted its written policies or provided professional development on the needs of transgender people. All of the high schools and middle schools in the district host a Queer-Straight Alliance club. Meanwhile, in a neighboring district to the east, school security officers threatened to strike if transgender students were allowed to use the bathroom that aligns with their gender identity. Likewise, in a neighboring district to the west, an assistant principal and a third-grade teacher resigned after protests about the teacher reading *Morris Micklewhite and the Tangerine Dress* to his students and talking about bullying.

Problem Statement

The principal sets out to create her support plan for Chad. Without district policies or guidelines to follow, she does some initial research about how to support transgender students in elementary school. She discovered several help resources on GLSEN's webpage (2017). She also referred to the American Psychological Association's recommendations for supporting transgender youth.

The principal selected a fourth-grade teacher for Chad that she knew would be supportive of Chad's transition. The fourth-grade teacher referred to him as Chad and used male pronouns during class. However, because the family had not legally changed his name from Wendy to Chad, she could not update the student data management system to reflect his new name. As a result, everywhere else in the school Chad was known as Wendy. When he checked out books at the library, he had to do so as Wendy. The librarian even referred to him as Wendy and with female pronouns. This distressed Chad. Chad's parents asked the principal to address the issue with the librarian. The librarian responded that her religion did not recognize transgender people, saying that "God made boys and girls. You cannot pick your gender." Ignoring the principal's directive, the librarian continues to refer Chad as Wendy.

The librarian's use of Wendy confuses Chad's classmates. A few students shared with their parents that a girl classmate was coming to school as a boy and using the name Chad. These parents requested a meeting with the principal to discuss why they were not notified that a transgender student was in class with their children.

The principal called the assistant superintendent to help her prepare a response to the parents' request for a meeting to discuss a transgender student at Cambridge Hills. The assistant superintendent asked how the principal was accommodating the transgender student's needs. She shared hand selecting his teacher, referring to him by his male name and with masculine pronouns, ordering a few picture books with transgender characters to include in the teacher's classroom library, and allowing him to use the boys' restroom. The assistant superintendent reminded the principal that state legislature recently passed a law that does not permit a school to allow students to use a gender-segregated facility that aligns with their gender identity. Chad may no longer use the boys' restroom. He also asked if the picture books she had ordered were approved by the district's curriculum committee and aligned with the fourth-grade curriculum.

Teaching Strategies

1. Role play the conversation between the principal and the librarian addressing the librarian's refusal to refer to Chad by his chosen name.
2. Role play the conversation between the principal and assistant superintendent in response to the assistant superintendent's news that Chad can no longer use the boys' restroom.
3. Role play the conversation between the principal and Chad's parents where the principal must deliver the news that Chad can no longer use the boys' restroom and that the school will not be able to include books with transgender characters in the classroom library.
4. Have students draft a response to the parents who were concerned that they were not informed about a transgender student being assigned to their children's classroom.
5. Brainstorm with the students how the principal and district might have been better prepared to meet the needs of transgender students, especially those who transition while in school?
6. Brainstorm with students how this scenario might have been different if the student was in middle school or high school.
7. After learning that Chad can no longer use the boys' restroom, his parents decide to remove him from Cambridge Hills. Brainstorm, with students, what alternatives the parents might explore to meet Chad's needs.

a. Exploration Questions: At the time of Chad's transition, no federal or state laws provided protections for transgender students in schools. However, the Obama Administration had released guidance to schools explaining how Title IX protects transgender students via the U.S. Department of Education's *Dear Colleague Letter on Transgender Students* (Lhamon & Gupta, 2016). What federal and state legal protections do transgender students currently have in schools?

b. According to Payne and Smith (2014), elementary teachers exhibit fear and anxiety in response to the presence of a transgender student in their classroom. A teacher's emotional response limits the school's ability to affirm the student's transgender identity. Fortunately, Chad's fourth-grade teacher fully welcomed him into her classroom and took the appropriate steps to create a welcoming and supportive classroom learning environment. However, what might have happened had the teacher been fearful or anxious of Chad being assigned to her classroom? What steps might the principal have taken to remedy the situation had the fourth-grade teacher(s) not fully affirmed Chad's transgender identity?

c. The principal desires to conduct school-wide professional development on how to support transgender students in the elementary classroom. What resources might the principal use to prepare for the professional development?

d. Initially, Cambridge Hills allowed Chad to use the boys' restroom. Brainstorm with students Chad's possible responses to no longer being able to use the boys' restroom and the requirement that he use the single-use restroom in the nurse's office.

References

American Psychological Association. (2015). Supporting transgender and gender diverse students in schools: Key recommendations for school administrators. Washington, DC: Author. Retrieved January 3, 2017 from https://www.apa.org/pi/lgbt/programs/safe-supportive/lgbt/school-administrators.pdf

GLSEN. (2017). Retrieved from www.glsen.org

Lhamon, C., & Gupta, C. (2016). *Dear colleague letter on transgender students.* Washington DC: U.S. Department of Education & U.S. Department of Justice Retrieved January 3, 2017 from http://www2.ed.gov/about/offices/list/ocr/letters/colleague-201605-title-ix-transgender.pdf

Payne, E., & Smith, M. (2014). The big freak out: Educator fear in response to the presence of transgender elementary school students. *Journal of Homosexuality, 61*(3), 399-418. doi: 10.1080/00918369.2013.842430

Additional Resources

Picture Books for Use with Fourth Grade

These picture books either include gender nonconforming characters or discuss gender stereotyping. They are age–appropriate for elementary school students. As curricula vary from state to state, you may want to confirm that the picture books are aligned with your state's fourth-grade curriculum.

Allen, D. (2001). *Brothers of Knight*. London: Puffin Books.

Baldacchino, C. (2014). *Morris Micklewhite and the Tangerine Dress*. Toronto: Groundwood Books.

Bradley, S. (2015). *Henry Holton Takes the Ice*. New York: Dial Books.

Curry, T. (2015). *A Peacock Among Pigeons*. Herndon, VA: Mascot Books.

Fierstien, H. (2005). *The Sissy Duckling*. New York: Simon & Schuster for Young Readers.

Hall, M. (2015). *Red: A Crayon's Story*. New York: Greenwillow Books.

Herthel, J., & Jennings, J. (2014). *I am Jazz*. New York: Dial Books.

Hoffman, M. (1991). *Amazing Grace*. New York: Dial Books.

Hoffman, S., & Hoffman, I. (2014). *Jacob's New Dress*. Park Ridge, IL: Albert Whitman & Company.

Tucker, K., & Lin, G. (2003). *Seven Chinese Sisters*. Park Ridge, IL: Albert Whitman & Company.

Walton, J. (2016). *Introducing Teddy: A Gentle Story about Gender and Friendship*. New York: Bloomsbury USA Childrens.

Protecting a Student's Gender Identity – Title IX and FERPA

For guidance on a school's legal obligations to protect a student's gender identity, see the Privacy and Educational Records section (p. 4) of U.S. Department of Education's *Dear Colleague Letter on Transgender Students*. For additional guidance on a school's legal obligations to transgender and gender-nonconforming students see the U.S. Department of Education's *Resources for Transgender and Gender-Nonconforming Students*.

Lhamon, C., & Gupta, C. (2016). *Dear Colleague Letter on Transgender Students*. Washington DC: U.S. Department of Education & U.S. Department of Justice Retrieved January 3, 2017 from http://www2.ed.gov/about/offices/list/ocr/letters/colleague-201605-title-ix-transgender.pdf

Office of Civil Rights (2016). *Resources for Transgender and Gender-Nonconforming Students*. Washington, DC: U.S. Department of Education. Retrieved January 17, 2017 from https://www2.ed.gov/about/offices/list/ocr/lgbt.html.

Organizations

Gender Spectrum www.genderspectrum.og

GLSEN www.glsen.org

Human Rights Campaign – Welcoming Schools www.welcomingschools.org

Lambda Legal www.lambdalegal.org

National Center for Transgender Equality www.tranequality.org

PFLAG www.pflag.org

Safe Schools Coalition www.safeschoolscoalition.org

Teaching Tolerance – Diversity, Equity and Justice www.tolerance.org

Case #14

Including Older Pupils With Challenging Behaviour:
A Case Study Within a Secondary School in England

Carl Parsons

Context

The Royal Boulevard Academy, Ullbridge, is a grand name for a school situated across two mainly social-housing estates on the edge of this market town, 35 miles north east of London. It has 960 students. The original building was opened by Princess Margaret in 1966, hence the 'Royal'. The current school, which has been subject to many 'improvement efforts' over the years, is the result of a recent amalgamation of two secondary schools; it is housed in new buildings and on two sites. The Upper School, for 300 students from ages 14 to 18, is on the site of what was historically the most difficult school in the area and had the lowest examination results. The new building, renaming and amalgamations can do nothing for the deprivation on the local estate though. Suffering through the closing of major manufacturing and a decline in ferry port activity, unemployment is high and there are significant social and family challenges: four times the national percentage of households claiming housing or unemployment benefit; incapacity benefits at three times the national rate; and assessed achievement of five year-olds entering primary school is already very low—the same applies at age 11 when they enter secondary school and at age 16 the percentage achievement of GCSEs (General Certificate of Secondary Education) stands at a little over half the national average. The author has written about one such school and its environment (Parsons, 2012).

Lynsey Hanley writes that, in England, "Council estates are ... a physical reminder that we live in a society that divides people up according to how much money they have to spend on shelter", and that living on a social housing estate (housing project) "is a lifelong state of mind .... the wall in the head" (2007, p4).

The upper school has a unit, the Achievement for All (A4A) centre, across the playing field at some distance from the main site, and this is where the problem lies. A4A caters for up to 30 problematic 14-16 year-old students. It was inherited from before the amalgamation and has been seen as a way of coping with some of its most challenging and troubled older students. Sally, the head teacher, with qualifications in social work and experience in both therapeutic education and in schools with a significant number of challenging pupils, is concerned that this centre, though *containing* students and *protecting* the rest of the upper school from disruption may be 'ghettoizing' (her word) those students. There is opposition from significant, long-serving staff in the main school about making changes, and also from the A4A staff who are a caring, cohesive, and determined work unit who want to be there and work hard to ensure that their students want to be there and are prepared for the next stage post-16.

The Problem

Sally wants the centre to be more integrated with the main upper school, for there to be more lessons in mainstream classes, and more organized transition so that some students might move back to mainstream classes full-time and benefit from the better academic outcomes achieved there. This principled, inclusion position is opposed by most staff in both the main school and in A4A, as well as the students in A4A. Voluble staff have complained publicly about how their lessons would have to be more controlled and didactic, would probably be disrupted any way, that they were there to teach their subject, had never been equipped to teach 'special' students, and had no desire to acquire those skills. The A4A students have experienced rejection from, and feel antagonism from, main school staff whenever they appear there. A4A centre staff sympathise with their students and are protective towards them. Sally, with a small team sympathetic with her goal, is still pondering how far to extend the school's reach to effect meaningful, sustainable change in the young people and the school organization which she wants to serve them.

The A4A centre clientele, staff and activities

The centre staff try to address the multiple overlapping problems of low attainment, poor attendance, and behavior and mental health difficulties ranging from ADHD through Aspergers to quite serious social deprivation and mental health conditions. Beyond having diagnostic and therapeutic abilities, the A4A staff are determined and committed, with great empathy for troubled students. The social problems of the residential area reinforce their problems, and are part of the 'ecology of deprivation and despair' (Sally's words again), which have to be taken into account if meaningful solutions are to be found.

Students in A4A attend from 9am until 1pm rather than for the full school day. However, optional activities are timetabled for the afternoon, and there are arrangements made with other education providers, including the Further Education College (FE Colleges cater mostly for post-16 students for vocational courses); small groups go there to do Health and Beauty or Construction. There are also work experience opportunities where students can have a placement that might be part of a route to an apprenticeship or employment. In order to use the resources in the main school, groups are regularly timetabled there for ICT.

The Centre's students' problems are exceedingly varied, but in educational terms are to do with oppositional behavior, a failure or unwillingness to conform to school rules and classroom expectations; sometimes it is accompanied by the use violence or threats to teachers and other students (Mattys & Lochman, 2017). This is not the inevitability of education for estate young people; however, the world over, they occur disproportionately where poverty levels are high. Three examples are given briefly below.

Peter was picked up by the police in the town centre, and found to have a quantity of cannabis; it was judged to be too much for his own use and therefore he was considered to be dealing. He was also brought home after midnight, after being among a crowd of young people in town where fighting broke out: he said, 'It was nothing to do with me'. In the classroom he was referred to as 'a nightmare', refusing to work, annoying others, throwing things, and walking out. A4A admitted Peter, after long discussions with him and his father. There was an offer of counselling, which was refused, although in an informal way Special Needs staff did counsel him. Like all the other 14 to 16 year-olds in the unit, Peter has a personalized curriculum, usually taught in groups of about five. Most of the English, maths and humanities subjects are taught in this way. Peter is actually keen to get a good grade in maths, and is aware that the examination course is better taught in the main school. A number of others join mainstream classes for specialisms that they have a particular interest in or talent for - music and IT are examples.

In Alice's final year in the lower school she began to withdraw to the extent that she hardly attended; she then was referred to a Pupil Referral Unit (PRU) as a school refuser, where, perhaps both predictably and ironically, she attended for only 50% of the time. She finds A4A better, as proven by her current attendance at the Centre of 100%. Alice's home life is not regarded as satisfactory; her mother has left and she lives with her father and two brothers, both older, and does lots of skivvying.

From A4A she goes to college every Tuesday with five other students doing health and beauty. The Centre manager accompanies them in and stays for the first hour. It has made a difference to Alice, and the staff are flexible in supporting her. Alice does not like crowds, and does not take well to any sort of rebuke or punishments like a detention or losing a break for infringements. However, with the work they have put in, staff are confident Alice will be able to cope; she's been to the college, knows the routines, and has been set up to succeed. Staff at the Centre have helped her to apply for college for the following year and will accompany her to the open days.

Bert would prefer to be in school for just one hour a day. He is reported to display oppositional behavior in classroom for anything outside sport and music, subjects at which he excelled and impressed. He reported quite openly that he never concentrated for all the other subjects and 'just mucked about'. He judges that many of the students in the Centre would not be at school at all if it were not for the provision of A4A. Bert is relatively unsupervised at home, fends for himself in terms of food (which he does quite sensibly), 'sofa-surfs' such that his whereabouts are often unknown to his mother and step-father.

It is common to situate a unit like the A4A, for students judged disruptive, away from the main teaching block, thus keeping 'problematic' students away from others. It is also common to find Units like the A4A poorly maintained; damage, graffiti or breakages are only slowly fixed. The students had negative comments to make of both the state of the A4A building (broken windows, chipped paintwork) AND the unwelcoming reception they got when going up to the main school for occasional lessons. Added to this, they felt that the assistant head responsible for special needs visited seldom. It is interesting, if not unusual, for them to list complaints regarding the school without reflecting back on *their* responsibility for anything (e.g. the broken window, which was Peter's doing). A4A staff feel that this is the best setting for many of these students, concur with students' complaints about the state of the building and the lack of welcome from staff in the main school, but are also sympathetic with the position and attitudes of their mainstream colleagues.

Problem Statement

Sally wants to ensure that students in A4A are integrated at certain points with the mainstream students but has significant resistance to this from all school participants.

Questions

1. In reflecting on possible reorganization or resitting of the A4A, Sally (head teacher) thinks about selling the 'inclusive' change to staff. How could Sally address the staff resistance to the inclusion plan, and what would her first steps be? Would she need to address the staff at the Main Site differently than those in A4A?
    i   How could Sally address how students in A4A are feeling about the inclusion plan?
    ii How could Sally address the A4A students' negative feelings and beliefs about school?
2. There is a plan to review the staff expertise mix across the spectrum of student need.
    i   Is there enough counselling, mentoring, psychotherapy, and mental health inputs (in the UK - CAMHS Child and Adolescent Mental Health Service)?
    ii Should a school 'buy in' or 'make its own'?
3. The students' problems, in Sally's view, are rooted in the students' wider 'ecology'. What does this mean? Are there solutions to be realistically identified and addressed in the wider ecology and if so what staffing and funding are needed?
4. What are the quick wins Sally can bring about in one term and what should she aim to celebrate communally at the end of one year?

References

Hanley, L. (2007) *Estates: An Intimate History*, London: Granta.

Matthys, W. & Lochman, J. E. (2017) *Oppositional Defiant Disorder and Conduct Disorder in Childhood*, Chichester UK: Wiley.

Parsons, C. (2012) *Schooling the Estate Kids*, Rotterdam: Sense Publishers.

Case #15

The Complexity of Curriculum Decision-Making:
Defining a Strategic Course for Student Achievement in light of School and District Policy

Lindsay Kwock Hu

Abstract

This case study illuminates the complexity that surrounds a decision regarding the curriculum used to facilitate learning for students who attend a failing school according to the results of the recent State Standardized Test. The faculty at Wilson Middle School (WMS) is struggling to identify an English Language Arts curriculum that will improve low student performance and equip students with 21st century skills, and, as a result, has spent countless hours debating the curriculum that should be used to support their students. In addition, the sudden involvement of the school district has complicated this matter, compelling a faculty typically open to new ideas into reluctant compliance. Thus, potentially circumnavigating administrative curriculum policy carries with it political, social, and academic consequences. Teachers must weigh their curriculum decision within this context in order to determine what is ultimately most strategic for student learning.

Background and Problem Statement

Wilson Middle School (WMS) is located in an urban school district with a high number of visible minorities living in poverty. WMS serves 296 students in grades 6-8, and it is significant to note that 20% of the student body identifies as Black or African American and 80% identifies as Hispanic or Latino. Also, 97% of students receive a free and reduced price-meal.

WMS is a historically failing school. Since the school opened its doors in 2006, it has struggled to gain traction and improve student performance. The 2016 administration of the State Standardized Test for English Language Arts (ELA) revealed that less than 15% of students tested at a proficient level and only 6% met proficiency in math. The school district has discussed making dramatic changes to the school, including changing the leadership team, but so far has not acted upon such discussion. In addition, the lack of teacher support and high teacher-to-student classroom ratios have created an environment that has resulted in high teacher turnover every year. Building a school community focused on student learning has been nearly impossible, and has left school resources strained and morale down.

In response to this underperformance, the school district has issued a pacing plan based on the district-adopted ELA curriculum. The pacing plan stipulates when lessons and literacy assessments are to be implemented, and provides no alternative instructional plan to students who may require differentiated support. In addition, the school would receive the support of a district literacy coach. The coach's responsibility would be to ensure that teachers implement the pacing plan with fidelity, as well as provide individualized instructional coaching to teachers and oversee the collection and analysis of assessment data to help teachers identify the most strategic instructional support. Overall, teachers are surprised a traditionally hands-off district has stepped in to provide such support, and it has created consternation amongst the instructional staff.

But the faculty attributes low student performance to a different factor. They believe the lack of student performance is a direct result of the district-mandated curriculum. For one, every lesson within the curriculum is prefaced on a teacher-driven model, where teachers dominate the majority of the instructional conversation, and every lesson culminates in the completion of a worksheet that asks a series of low-level comprehension questions. In addition, students complain that the curriculum is "boring" and "irrelevant," and as a result lessons are routinely punctuated by student disruptions. For faculty, continuing a disengaging curriculum and adhering to such a rigid curriculum pacing plan, would only exacerbate disengagement and low student performance.

Furthermore, a few weeks ago, faculty members attended a professional development day at a local university that focused on problem-based learning (PBL). PBL is an inquiry-based format that enables students to develop academic skills by investigating a problem and proposing a solution. Studies on PBL have shown that the format does have some promise, particularly for historically low-performing students (Belland, 2010; Tate, 1995). Tate (1995) argues that problem-solving, grounded in culturally relevant material, provides students the opportunity to exercise reading, research, and writing skills, amongst other higher order thinking skills, within a meaningful problem that traditional curriculum may not be able to offer. In addition, students are empowered to design a solution to a problem afflicting their environment. As such, most faculty are convinced that this format of curriculum may be the engaging, challenging curriculum their students have been yearning for.

But changing the curriculum carries with it multiple risks. For one, the principal, who has been at the school since its opening, has made it clear that she does not support such a move, and has already begun walking around to classrooms to share this opinion. According to the principal, "Doing so would severely compromise the one window of opportunity the school has to significantly raise test scores." Her actions make clear to teachers that she is not willing to negotiate this point.

Also, not every teacher is enthusiastic about moving to a PBL curriculum, especially given that there is no guarantee that doing so will result in increased student learning. Changing the curriculum means teachers would now be responsible for developing, designing, and culling instructional materials to facilitate the solving of a problem. The most vocal dissenter, a veteran teacher who is also the teacher's union representative, is concerned about the potential ramifications from the district. Openly circumnavigating a curriculum policy that the district has put into place for the express reason of raising student learning is risky; they are unsure of what the consequences would be, and many are reluctant to find out.

What should teachers do?

Case Study Questions

1. Describe the motivations of the principal, school district and teachers to act in the way they do in this case.
2. What are the benefits and risks of following the district pacing plan? What are the benefits and risks of implementing PBL?
3. If you were a teacher at this school, how would you influence the principal to act upon and support PBL? How would you influence the district to act upon and support PBL?
4. Prepare a report for how this situation could be remedied from the district's perspective, the principal's perspective, or the teacher's perspective.
5. What does a PBL curriculum look like, particularly in a low-income, low-performing school? Provide an example.
6. How does student discourse—the discourse expected when solving a problem—enhance the development of higher order thinking skills? What additional 21st century skills are developed in problem-based learning?
7. Create a problem-based learning unit outline based on your students' needs and interests. What problem would be most interesting to your students that could still be used to develop research, reading, writing, and other academic skills?

References

Belland, B. R. (2010). Portraits of middle school students constructing evidence-based arguments during problem-based learning: the impact of computer-based scaffolds. *Educational Technology Research and Development, 58(3)*. 285-309.

Tate, W. F. (1995). Returning to the root: A culturally relevant approach to mathematics pedagogy. *Theory into Practice, 34(3)*, 166-173.

Case #16

Unexpected Bus Duty:
Lessons on Inclusion from a Field Trip

Steve Sider

Introduction

This case considers a secondary school setting in a school board that has espoused an inclusion model for students with special education needs. In this model, elementary and secondary schools were directed to integrate students with a wide range of special education needs into the regular classrooms to the greatest degree possible. This case examines the experience of a school administrator who had to respond to a situation that involved a student on the Autism Spectrum who had an unexpected behavior problem on a class field trip.

Overview and Analysis

"Mr. Stephenson, we need you to come to the bus drop-off area immediately."

The message caught me off-guard because it was only 1:50 p.m.. As one of the vice-principals at Clé Secondary School, I normally took the afternoon bus duty but typically the buses didn't start loading until 2:35 p.m., the end of the school day.

I quickly grabbed my phone, headed out of my office, and ran to the bus loading area. Within seconds of arriving I could see that this was clearly not a problem with the regular bus routines at the end of the day.

Instead, I came across a crying, moaning, and rocking student in the middle of the sole school bus that was in the parking lot. It was Graeme, clearly upset and inconsolable.

Graeme was a well-liked Grade 10 student. He is also on the Autism Spectrum. As a high functioning student with Autism, he had been included in almost all of the same high school courses as his peers, with accommodations from teachers and the occasional "check-in" with the Student Success Teacher.

I quickly asked Pamela Ibrahimovic, the teacher in charge, where they were coming from. She indicated that they were returning from a Grade 10 History field trip to the local science and technology museum. Pamela quickly filled me in.

Everything had progressed smoothly and the 3 hour visit and tour had gone exceptionally well. Then, on the 45 minute return bus ride, the students had gotten increasingly loud. Some things had been thrown about and the bus driver had warned the students to sit in their seats.

The noise and commotion had clearly impacted Graeme.

Pamela reported that he started crying and rocking, then shouting. He then struck one of the female students in the seat beside him. The other students were shocked because they had never seen this behaviour from Graeme before. The students on the bus quickly became quiet except for Graeme's crying and moaning.

The bus had only been minutes away from the school and Pamela had phoned the school to alert the office that she and the other supervising teacher needed help. As soon as the bus pulled into the school parking lot, Pamela had all of the students get off the bus to return to the classes in which they would finish the day. She talked quickly with the girl who had been struck, and, although not hurt, Pamela had asked her to go to the office so one of the administrators could document what happened from her perspective.

I looked at Graeme who remained inconsolable in the middle of the bus.

I approached him and sat in the seat across from him. Graeme continued to moan and rock.

"Where do I begin?" Our school had prided itself on integrating students with all types of exceptionalities and diagnosed conditions into regular classroom settings. We had seen significant benefits, both for the students and their peers. Graeme had been one of the students who had been able to keep up with much of the work in his "applied level" courses and who had been cheerfully greeted in the hallways by students and teachers alike. Although often by himself, he had not exhibited any kind of anti-social or problem behaviour. At that moment, it dawned on me that he was not one of the students who normally took a bus to school.

I continued to sit quietly by Graeme, wondering again how and where to begin.

Problem Statement

I had two immediate problems that would require a quick response, and a third problem, with longer term consequences, was starting to percolate in my mind as well. On top of this, I knew that social media would soon be used, if it hadn't been already, to distribute various students' perspectives of what had happened.

My first problem was that I needed to calm Graeme so that we could discern what happened from his perspective. He was clearly upset and I would not be able to understand what had precipitated his behaviour in his current state. I knew that I had about 45 minutes to calm Graeme, and hopefully remove him from the bus, before 900 students (of our student population of 1,700) would be coming onto the buses. If it was noisy and confusing for Graeme before, it would only get worse.

I thought back to my experience as a special education teacher and tried to recall some of the techniques I had used to calm students who had experienced anxiety and anger. Certainly some of the work on theory of mind (Leslie, 1991), self-regulation (Shanker, 2012), and strategies for supporting students with ASD (Maich, Hall, & Sider, 2013) came quickly to mind.

My second problem, also requiring a quick response, involved the student that Graeme had hit. Although seemingly physically unharmed, she had been struck and that would automatically bring the situation to a discipline process. I was also concerned about the student's emotional well-being and needed to think about what steps I would take to support her in this area. Again, I thought of some of the recent professional learning that our board had undertaken in this area. In my mind, I could visualize resources on well-being in schools (Page & Page, 2014) and resilience (Truebridge & Benard, 2016).

A third problem, not necessarily requiring an immediate response but with the potential for longer-term and more wide-spread impact, was considering how Graeme's behaviour had been perceived by his peers and the wider school community. This to me was a bigger issue related to our school's value placed on inclusion. This problem was really about our school culture. Everyone, including Graeme and the girl he had hit, needed to feel safe and accepted.

"How am I going to rebuild trust and community with this group and Graeme?"

With that thought in mind, I quickly returned to the immediate challenges.

Case Problems and Teaching Strategies

Consider the following questions to help guide your learning from the case:
1. What are the key lessons that you have learned from this case?
2. What would be the immediate steps you would take to help calm Graeme? What next steps does Mr. Stephenson need to consider after Graeme has calmed down?
3. What would you advise Mr. Stephenson to do with the issue of restoring trust and community between Graeme and his peers?
4. What do you see as the potential antecedents to Graeme's behaviour? How could they have been avoided or minimized?
5. What role did Pamela and the other teacher have in either abating the situation or quickly responding to it? What could Mr. Stephenson and the school staff have done to minimize the potential of this situation from happening?
6. What communication should be considered with parents/

guardians? With the school bus driver? With teachers? With the students who were on the bus?

7. What aspects of inclusion are particularly challenging for secondary school settings?
8. How do school leaders foster a healthy, inclusive school culture for students with special education needs?

Consider the following web resources for supporting leaders in inclusive schools:

Canadian Research Centre on Inclusive Education: http://www.inclusiveeducationresearch.ca/

Engaging All Learners: http://www.engagingalllearners.ca/il/school-leadership-and-inclusion/

Inclusive Schools Network: http://inclusiveschools.org/category/resources/leadership-for-inclusive-schools/

Ontario Principals' Council: https://www.principals.ca/stream/video/launch-Vid.aspx?vidID=17

References

Leslie, A. M. (1991). Theory of mind impairment in autism. In A. Whiten, Ed., Natural theories of mind: Evolution, development, and simulation of everyday mindreading. Cambridge, MA: Basil Blackwell.

Maich, K., Hall, C. & Sider, S. (2013). Learning people skills: Social literacy for people with Autism Spectrum Disorders. Education Canada (53)2, 21-23.

Page, R. M., & Page, T. S. (2014). Promoting health and emotional well-being in your classroom (6th Ed.). Burlington, MA: Jones & Bartlett Learning.

Shanker, S. (2012). Calm, alert, and learning: Classroom strategies for self-regulation. Toronto: Pearson Education Canada.

Truebridge, S. & Benard, B. (2016). Reflections on resilience. Educational Leadership (71)1, 66-67.

Case #17

Facing High School:
A Mother Reflects on Her Son's Journey Through Inclusive Classrooms

Diane Linder Berman with David J. Connor

Introduction

My son Benny has been included successfully for nine years, and has surpassed all expectations by leaps and bounds. It is his very accomplishments that bring us to the point where we now face new, daily challenges that plague me day and night. At the same time, Benny has learned to accept that with his disability comes obstacles, and he seems to accept that he might have to work ten times harder at things than his non-disabled peers.

Overview/Analysis

Benny was a beautiful baby who did not meet any developmental milestone on time. By the age of three he amassed many labels, including Pervasive Developmental Disorder-Not Otherwise Specified (PDD-NOS), Attention Deficit Hyperactivity Disorder (ADHD), and extreme receptive and expressive language delays. After placement in an integrated pre-school where he made progress, I was adamant that he be educated alongside typical peers. However, the local education authority (LEA) where we lived insisted he be placed in the special education district, exclusively for children with disabilities, in a class with five other children with severe and/or multiple disabilities. I rejected this arrangement, and they agreed to place him at our local school in a class, still segregated from non-disabled peers, with 12 children with less severe disabilities. Benny's behavior was so erratic and impulsive, especially compared to those with lesser disabilities, that he "failed" in two such placements, and when the LEA threatened us with legal action, my husband and I decided to relocate within New York State and find an inclusive school (Berman, 2009).

We found one school with an accommodating principal, who promised me that he would make our situation work. The school had approximately 60 students per grade, was in a suburban area, with students walking or being driven to school. School staff created a community around Benny that went far beyond merely supporting him—it allowed itself to change as a result of Benny's presence. Subsequently, Benny's academic performance rose to grade level standards, and he began to write with fluency and beauty. He learned mathematics and science at the level of his peers. He formed friendships and joined performance groups, finding his talents for singing and dancing (Berman & Connor, 2017).

When the time came to graduate and to Middle School, we celebrated. Benny began with confidence, and we stopped worrying so much about him. He had his buddies from elementary school and seemed to be adjusting well to the academic demands of sixth grade. Benny's Individual Education Program (IEP) gave him extended time on tests, refocusing and redirection, two periods of speech therapy, and a social-skills group. He was still in the inclusion program, which meant all of his classes had two teachers, plus a daily period in the resource room working one-on-one with his specialist teacher.

In Grade 8, the district requires everyone take two high school level classes, culminating in the NY State Regents Exam in June. Benny enrolled in Algebra and Earth Science. Algebra went well from day one, but Earth Science was a challenge. While he could comprehend the material, Benny was overwhelmed by the onslaught of new vocabulary (the textbook glossary alone contained over 600 words). Although he did not pass one test in Earth Science, with all the excellent lab work and his attention to homework, he passed three out of four quarters. Nonetheless, his dismal result on the Regents Exam brought his yearly grade to a 62, making it the first class he had ever failed, devastating him. The unfortunate choice of the word "failure" made the blow even harder. Day after day he would ask me how it was that I was okay that he "failed" a class. I would tell him that it was fine, that it was not a measure of his ability, but just one test.

Benny's other grades fell as well. I began to question our decision to have him pursue a Regents Diploma required to graduate in NY State. I wonder if we had inadvertently tricked Benny. He had been in an elementary school that taught him through grand, differentiated activities, capturing his interest in education. We taught him that with hard work he could accomplish anything, and how to be attuned to his own progress. Then slowly through 6th and 7th grade the focus narrowed, and finally in 8th grade he found himself in a fairly constricted place, where education became almost exclusively bound to a paper and pencil test. We are now sending him off for four more years of school, where he will struggle day and night to achieve grades that are at best barely passing, or at worst leading to obtaining an inferior diploma. At this juncture, it seems Benny will be stripped of his dignity, and I wonder about his ability to face college—and the world—after coming face to face every day with more of his limitations and fewer of his strengths.

Problem Statement

We have a 9th grader who is facing the hardest academic challenges of his life. We have all worked hard through elementary and middle school to help Benny develop into a young man who wants to learn, and who cares deeply about his success. He is young man who *could* succeed in college and *could* have a career, but who has to first prove himself through a series of impossibly complex tests.

Case Problems

The questions to think about are as follows:

(i). Provide questions to support the process of analysis

Q: Can principles of inclusive education used in elementary and middle school be carried through to high school, or even college?

Q: What are some challenges in specifically creating high-school inclusive classrooms?

Q: How may the "one size fits all" Regent's diploma requirement in New York State impact the self-concept and self-worth of students with disabilities? What can schools, families, and students with disabilities do about this? In what ways might they work together to increase the likelihood of academic success of students in Benny's situation?

Q: What responsibility does a high school have to continue approaches and methods of inclusive education employed at elementary and middle school levels? How would this actually look in a high school? Where are some opportunities for this growth? Is the "opportunity" only associated with the disabled child[1] or is there room for all students (and teachers) to grow in this way?

Q: Given the narrow, inflexible criteria for graduation when we know so much about differentiation, what can teachers do that is in the locus of their control?

Q: On a philosophical note, where do the issues of human dignity come into play within educational policy? For example, is it "right" for state education policy to subject kids to repeated failure within mandatory schooling? What are some ways in which educators and parents can "talk back" to restrictive measures, and advocate for more flexible approaches to teaching, learning, and assessments?

---

[1] Note that the use of "disabled" is supported in Disability Studies scholarship, where the onus is shifted from disability being conceived as an intrinsic deficit to a set of social, cultural, and historical systems that created disabling conditions for individuals with impairments.

(ii). Specify individuals in the case study and identify the next steps

Q: How can Benny manage the academic demands placed upon him, and at the same time cultivate a positive disability identity?

Q: How can Diane and her husband find the "right balance" between advocating for and being supportive of Benny?

Q: Does it sound as if Diane is asking for more relaxed criteria for graduation, or that Benny is held to a lower standard? Does she want to "have her cake and eat it too"? In other words, should Diane be grateful that Benny is allowed to take the classes and not complain for questioning the rigorous standards?

Q: How can school personnel be proactive in their support of inclusion through classroom arrangements and maximizing expectations of all students?

(iii). Identify key decisions made in the case study and what choices could have been made instead

Q: Why did Benny's parents feel dissatisfied with his original elementary school placement in New York City schools? What drove them to find another school? If Benny had stayed in his originally determined, restrictive placement, only with children with autism, what might have been different about the outcomes of his parents' original decision?

Q: To what degree did Benny's parents assume that the skills he'd learned in elementary school would "carry him" academically and socially in middle school? Could anything have been done differently? If so, what?

Q: When Benny experiences a sense of failure due to not passing the Regents exam, his parents decided to share his educational experiences with him from their very inception. Was this a good decision? If so, why? If not, why?

Q: Diane notes that despite witnessing so much frustration in Benny, she also feels elation in seeing his strength and determination. Should she step back at some point and let the imperfect world in and accept the fact that for now, and maybe always, there will be enormous hurdles for Benny to navigate?

(iv). State how the situation should have been remedied

Given the nature of the problem is both personal and systematic, the assignment is in two parts.

Part A: Taking all things into consideration, what could have been done to better support Benny in elementary and middle school to prepare him for high school? Or, given the focus, drive, and beliefs of his parents, has Benny received the maximum support within his circumstances—and is actually doing fine when measured against himself rather than typical peers?

Part B: In some ways it can be argued that Diane speaks for numerous parents caught in the bind between what the state expects in terms of academic performance, and what children and youth can actually do. How might the issues she raises be used in writing a report to the state legislature? Based upon issues of individualism, mutual respect, and dignity, what could more equitable policies look like?

Teaching Strategies

Given space limitations, we have decided to focus upon increasing academic vocabulary, as it is a crucial skill at the high school level.

Teachers can teach vocabulary by:

- Including it in classroom expectations and routines, making it part of the everyday scenery of teaching and learning
- Actively using a student's background knowledge to chain new information with existing knowledge
- Helping students make new vocabulary connections to other information learned in class
- Providing strategies and opportunities to help students memorize vocabulary by storing and retrieving it
- Using a wide variety of approaches, from the simple to the complex (word walls, word work, read aloud, warm ups, concept mapping, etc.)

- Always making explicit the vocabulary connections across categories
- Consciously cultivating word consciousness within all students

Students can learn vocabulary by:

- Articulating or "owning" the targeted vocabulary word, through having time to practice and rehearse saying it out loud, saying to him or herself, saying it to others
- Practicing using targeted vocabulary in speaking and writing, and identifying it within listening and reading
- Consciously cultivating word consciousness within him or herself

References

Berman, D. L. (2009). *Beyond words: Reflections on our journey to inclusion*. Harrisburg, PA: White Hat Press.

Berman, D. L., & Connor, D. J. (2017). *A child, a family, a school, a community: A tale of inclusive education*. New York: Peter Lang.

Case #18

The Dilemma of Christmas in the Secular Public School

C. Darius Stonebanks

Introduction

As public schools across Canada continue to adjust from their traditional religious roots (Protestant and/or Catholic), to non-confessional orientations, the question of what practices should be continued is a concern to some teachers. Of all the customs and celebrations that have traditionally taken place in schools, perhaps Christmas is the most difficult to navigate. Deeply entrenched in the culture of the teaching profession, as well as the school, it is often difficult for educators to see its exclusionary nature. This case study asks the reader to consider who is and is not included in this annual event, and whether an individual teacher can shift perspectives amongst school community towards an otherwise accepted cultural norm.

Overview/Analysis

As a relatively recent teacher to Saint Anthony's elementary school, it had quickly become Mr. Hamza's custom to eat lunch with students in their cafeteria, instead of the staffroom. Although he told everyone that his reason for doing so was to develop better pedagogical strategies for his work as an educator working with at-risk children, secretly he knew that eating with the children was less stressful than a staffroom - especially considering the topic of conversation amongst his colleagues was the upcoming annual Christmas concert. Since the educational reforms in the province of Québec had changed public schools from confessional (Catholic or Protestant) to linguistic (French or English), he wondered how his colleagues would react to rethinking their traditional practices. Although the school was new to Mr. Hamza, for many decades it had functioned in close collaboration with both the local Catholic Church and the original Catholic, Christian community from predominantly Irish decent, for whom the school was primarily designed. However, the demographics of the area had already begun to change; Canadians of non-Christian decent moving into the neighbourhood, shifting the previously assumed homogenous cultural nature of the school clientele to a now diversified medley of students.

Mr. Hamza was beginning to understand that, for both the established teachers and the local traditional community, the Christmas concert was more than just a "busywork" activity; it was both a sacred event and something that reaffirmed the school's historic identity. Mr. Hamza, who was not from a European or Christian background, and who had himself attended a Protestant school in Montreal, had mixed feelings of the experience of participating in elementary school Christmas activities, remembering the awkward emotions of eternally being cast as a trembling shepherd in the Nativity play. Complicating matters, Mr. Hamza was new to the school, and was one of the few staff members who were not of a Christian background. So, he was unsure of how he would approach the discussion of Christmas planning, and was considering, given his newly arrived status among the staff, whether or not it would be better for him to allow more seasoned teachers to grapple with the dilemma.

As Mr. Hamza entered the student cafeteria, a table of grade five children excitedly waved him over, motioning to an empty seat they had seemingly reserved for him. The children sitting at the table of eight were all of South Asian ancestry, and when they found out months ago that Mr. Hamza was West Asian they began a tradition of asking their parents to pack extra lunch food for him as well. As Mr. Hamza sat, Dharish placed a vegetable wrap in front of him and playfully announced in a menacing tone, "My mom says this is way too hot for you and that you *won't* survive", evoking laughter from his peers. As they all ate, the conversation fluidly moved from one subject to another, home and school, and then one child, Shaaheen, mentioned Christmas class activities that had begun in her class. Mr. Hamza seized the opportunity to get a better understanding of the school culture and asked Shaaheen if celebrating Christmas was a big part of the upcoming month. Shaaheen excitedly said "yes", and went on to explain that a great deal of time and effort would go into decorating the gymnasium and preparing for the big spectacle. "Does everyone participate?" Mr. Hamza asked. "For sure", Shaaheen responded, "it's a big part of what we do in December. Everyone joins in". "Well, not *everyone*", Dharish said with a smirk, "Not if Lakshmin repeats what she did two years ago at *that* Christmas assembly". At the end of the table, Lakshmin mockingly threw her hands up in the air and said "you *always* bring this up", and proceeded to cover her face. From what Mr. Hamza knew, Lakshmin was an excellent academic student and always trusted by staff to perform any duty that required independent responsibility, so he was naturally intrigued as to what the children were talking about and asked for details. Lakshmin kept her face covered, and her friends laughed while loudly encouraging her to tell her story. Finally, Lakshmin brought her hands down from her face, revealing a smile along with a slight blush, and told *her* Christmas story.

Lakshmin explained that since kindergarten, as December would approach, all her teachers would talk about was how Santa Claus was going to bring presents to all the good little boys and girls. She would excitedly decorate the classroom, write letters to Santa Claus, and sing songs that varied from elves to Jesus Christ. But, each Christmas morning she would awaken to no presents. No amount of her participation would result with a Christmas morning miracle or magical act that resulted in presents. By the time grade three came around she began to question what was wrong with her, and why Santa had abandoned her. When the Christmas assembly arrived, she found herself sitting on the gymnasium floor questioning everything, and when from her vantage point she spotted "Santa Claus" through a hallway door that, despite being guarded by some teachers, allowed her to see that it was really a retired teacher she recognized putting on his red suit, she, in her own words, "flipped". "At that moment, I saw my little cousin in kindergarten, and she was getting so excited by the principal announcing that the school had a special guest and that Santa was coming to visit. I just looked at her and couldn't control myself. I stood up and yelled out, 'It's a lie! It's a lie! There's no such thing as Santa Claus!', and everyone went crazy". As she concluded her story, indicating that she got into a bit of trouble, her friends continued to laugh and, despite being noticeably depleted by reliving the moment, Lakshmin laughed as well. Mr. Hamza stood up from the table and said to Lakshmin, "You are very brave", and as he exited the cafeteria and thought about an upcoming staff meeting, wondered if he would be as well.

Problem Statement

The majority of Canadian (and the United States of America's) public schools are described as "secular", often through legal requirements (Bafesky & Waldman, 2006). In the case of the province of Québec, where "Mr. Hamza's" fictional school of "St. Anthony's Elementary" is located for example, its Ministry of Education uses the word "secular" when it defines its schools as being "... entirely non-religious" (MELS, 2007, p. 292). Still, despite what seems quite clear, teachers like Mr. Hamza must navigate the reality that many public schools that have switched from religious to non-religious in Canada, like Saint Anthony's, have roots deeply entrenched in religious practice and culture; therefore, the communities that existed previous to this change couldfeel personally compromised by losing what they consider to be historic norms. However, teachers like Mr. Hamza are equally aware that there is a growing body of research that indicates that "secular" schools in the Global North can and do enable religious (predominantly Christian) privilege. Much like the invisible advantages that are given to some students, administrators, teachers, and parents because of their Whiteness (McIntosh, 1998), public schools that are meant to serve a secular function bestow similar privileges to religious stakeholders over others (Schlosser, 2003). With these considerations in mind, Mr. Hamza knew that he needed to address how students in his school were feeling. He also knew that there were always opportunities at every staff meeting for staff members to add items to the "Business Arising" section of the agenda. In preparing for the upcoming meeting, what legal, professional, social, and natural justice considerations must Mr. Hamza grapple with before engaging with his colleagues?

Case Problems

1. To what extent can Mr. Hamza's dilemma be informed by recent and past religious struggles in Canada's public schools? For instance: the debate over "Samaritan's Purse", American evangelical Franklin Graham's Christian charity which openly advocates its purpose to proselytize, being used in Canadian schools; earlier experiences of other non-Christian religious minorities, like Jewish students (and teachers) in Canadian public schools between 1945 and 1999; the 2006 Supreme Court of Canada ruling on the so-called infamous "Kirpan Case" of Quebec; and, the manner in which non-Christian based observations, rituals, and holidays are actually included in school practices and curricula.

2. Can these prior cases guide and solidify Mr. Hamza's concerns that current practices should be examined for their impact on students (and perhaps teachers) who may not view school holiday practices (like Christmas) as being as truly universal and inclusive as some believe? In preparing for potential retorts to Mr. Hamza's dilemma, can it be argued that Christmas is actually a secular event in modern schools, devoid of religious connotations?

3. Are there examples of past religious holidays that have become truly open to all varieties of religious and non-religious worldviews? Moreover, assuming that Mr. Hamza's colleagues continue to carry out Christmas traditions, despite the prior response by Lakshmin, how may some of the teachers respond to his queries and justify these teaching practices?

4. Finally, if you were to assist Mr. Hamza in addressing his colleagues in a staff meeting, what would be the central concerns

you would include, what prior professional experiences would you draw from, and what suggestions would you consider, in which to move St. Anthony's to a more inclusive space?

References

Bafesky, A. F. & Waldman, A. (2006). State Support for Religions in Canada: Canada versus the United Nations. The Netherlands: Martinus Nijhof Publishers.

Ministère de l'Éducation, du Loisir et du Sport (2007). "Ethics and Religious Culture; Programme de formation de l'école québécoise : Éducation préscolaire, enseignement primaire", Québec, Gouvernement du Québec.

McIntosh, P. (1988). White privilege and male privilege: A personal account of coming to see correspondences through work in Women's studies. Wellesley, MA: Wellesley College Center for Research on Women.

Schlosser, L. (2003, January). Christian Privilege: Breaking a Sacred Taboo. Journal of Multicultural Counseling & Development, 31(1), 44-51.

Case #19

I Didn't See This Coming

Cindy Diehl-Yang & Nicholas J. Pace

Introduction

The case outlines the difficulties a mixed Asian-American family experiences as their visually impaired son adjusts to school in a small town. Complex, nuanced, and unexpected issues related to class, ethnicity, culture, and disability surface as questions about what constitutes appropriate educational accommodations, tradition, and power.

Case Overview

Martin Cho had made a name for himself in Atlanta advertising. Although he laughed at stereotypical portrayals of the Korean workaholic professional, he also knew it fit. Raised in Seoul and Stanford-educated, he was one of the most sought after ad men in the city. His wife Julie was his counterbalance; Midwestern, easygoing, and soft-spoken. Leaving Atlanta for their move to the Midwest meant a less hectic life for their family. The Chos bought a comfortable house in Pleasanton, a town of eight thousand, thirty minutes from the state capital and headquarters for Martin Cho's employer, Capitol Visions.

Julie accepted a part time teaching position at the local community college. This allowed her to attend to their two sons' adjustment to Pleasanton High School. Michael, a tenth grader, and Joel, a ninth grader, were the center of Martin and Julie's lives. Where Michael presented as a stereotypical Asian overachiever with a 4.0 GPA, advanced classes across the curriculum, and participation in multiple extracurriculars, Joel presented differently. When Joel was a baby he suffered a near-fatal daycare accident in which he aspirated applesauce and was without oxygen for several minutes. The staff's efforts to clear his airway resulted in a traumatic brain injury and bilateral retinal hemorrhages in both of Joel's eyes. With such unpredictable injuries, doctors informed the Chaos that Joel's prognosis was uncertain at best. Doctors prescribed extensive therapy to help him relearn how to sit up, eat solid food, and roll over.

Martin and Julie rearranged their lives to accommodate Joel's therapy—speech, physical, occupational, vision, and later counseling. With support, he progressed on a normal rate with his peers—walking, talking, drawing, and playing with others his age. When Joel was five years old he was diagnosed as being legally blind, which led to his first IEP (Individualized Education Plan).

Joel's IEP team initially recommended placement in the state residential school for the blind, five hours from the Cho's Atlanta home. The Chos refused to have Joel at school so far away. As a result, Joel's school began developing an IEP with accommodations and Joel began to flourish.

During sixth grade, Joel was tested for difficulties in his advanced classes. After two days of testing, officials determined that Joel presented with an uncommon learning disorder known as Dyseidetic Dyslexia, which is marked by difficulty visualizing symbols effectively. With Joel's visual difficulties and new diagnosis, it became apparent that he would never read at grade level in a manner that would allow him to keep up with his peers. The Atlanta school found auditory ways for Joel to process information and he continued participating actively in school.

Although the Cho's realtor had praised Pleasanton and Pleasanton High School, Joel's adjustment had been turbulent. Chipper and engaging, he had been socially connected in Atlanta. As a student, his determination and superior auditory skills had allowed him to compensate for his lack of sight. He had served as an ambassador for other students with disabilities, a student council representative, and held a position in the school closed circuit television show.

In Pleasanton, Joel was quiet, withdrawn, and reluctant to practice the self-advocacy and assertiveness his parents had instilled in him. The peer guide assigned to him faded away after a few days. Incredibly, to Martin and Julie, a few of Joel's teachers were unaware of his visual impairment, despite several family meetings with school officials at the start of the year and a video conference transition meeting with his support staff from the Atlanta school.

By the end of the first quarter, Joel's success in Atlanta was a distant memory. Julie, in her Midwestern style, had gone out of her way to be calm and congenial in her interactions with teachers and administrators, even as she tried to clearly communicate her concerns and frustration. She knew Joel's challenges represented new territory for Pleasanton High School. Additionally, Joel's half Asian heritage and newcomer status in the somewhat provincial Pleasanton further magnified the way he stood out. Teachers sometimes referenced Michael as they tried to figure out why Joel wasn't performing the same as his older brother. The comparison caused strife between the two at home. Where previously Joel looked to Michael for support and as a role model, he now pulled away so as not to be seen as competing with him. Joel was earning straight Cs and Ds, in stark contrast to his exemplary performance in Atlanta.

The relationship between the family and the school reached a low point on a Thursday in November. Joel failed another assignment, this time in Steve Hoover's science class, after his paraprofessional, Diane Lake, failed to read the test questions to him. Ms. Lake was Joel's third paraprofessional of the year and seemed to have difficulty understanding Joel's accommodations. Instead of reading the questions, Ms. Lake sat quietly when Joel asked her to read the questions. That night at home, Joel said abruptly "I'm *done*. I want to be homeschooled," tears streaming from his eyes.

Later, in a meeting with Principal Mark Richardson and two of Joel's teachers, Martin reached his breaking point. "Things worked fine in Atlanta! I can't decide if you people are actively sabotaging my son's education or just incompetent. I wonder if my attorney could help us figure out which it is."

Principal Richardson immediately apologized. "Clearly we have some work to do," he said, trying to salvage the meeting.

Two days later, the superintendent called Principal Richardson. He could sense the superintendent's anger through the phone line. "Well, Mark, I heard the meeting with the Chos didn't go so well. You've gotta make this go away. I just had an email from Capitol Visions. Their hundred thousand dollar pledge to the technology wing of the high school is on hold."

Principal Richardson's heart rate jumped. He was in his first year at Pleasanton High School and his fourth year as a principal. He knew the superintendent sometimes seemed autocratic and heavy handed, but was respected as a deal maker who had significantly improved Pleasanton's school facilities and reputation.

The superintendent continued. "That damn Chink is gonna screw the whole thing up. And I don't think that kid needs a babysitter we can't afford. We've got to have that funding back for the technology wing. Don't you apologize to those entitled pains in the ass. Fix it and keep their attorney out of the building."

Principal Richardson wondered how he would navigate a path forward.

Problem Statement

How does a new principal ensure equity in a complex context?

Principal Richardson wrestled with several ideas on how to proceed. He wasn't sure why some teachers, particularly Steve Hoover, had so much difficulty following the accommodations on Joel's IEP. Granted Joel had a rare form of dyslexia, and teachers lacked experience with visually impaired students, but was it really that much different than other accommodations? As often as the Chos had been frustrated with the school, wouldn't most teachers make extra effort to not screw up simple accommodations? Perhaps Hoover and other teachers had philosophical objections to accommodations in general. But, he said to himself, the law is the law.

Principal Richardson also wondered why the paraprofessional

would have sat silently and let Joel flounder on the test? Was the paraprofessional training program that inadequate? Was the para intimidated by the teacher and afraid to advocate for Joel? On top of that, what could he could do to get paraprofessionals to stay in their jobs when they could earn a better wage at the grocery store?

Principal Richardson also wondered about the Chos' role in all this. Self-advocacy was one of Joel's IEP goals. Why hadn't Joel spoken up when he couldn't read the assignment? Finally, Principal Richardson wondered how to move forward with the superintendent, who seemed to question - or not understand - the legal responsibility the school had for Joel's accommodations. Principal Richardson wanted to make the situation right, while the superintendent seemed to be focused on restoring Capitol Vision's contribution to the technology wing. Finally, the superintendent's ethnic slur angered Mark deeply, but, given the power differential, he wondered how to address it with his boss.

Discussion & Reflection Questions

1. If the adage that "an ounce of prevention is worth a pound of cure" is accurate, what might have prevented the situation with Joel from getting to this point?
2. Place yourself in the meeting when Martin Cho wonders if he needs an attorney. Evaluate Principal Richardson's response. What should he do next?
3. Place yourself in Principal Richardson's shoes when the superintendent calls. How would you have responded?
4. Imagine Principal Richardson asks two colleagues for advice on how to handle the superintendent. One responds, "I know the superintendent says some inappropriate things, but he's really harmless. Let it go and just deal with the issues at hand. Trying to change him won't help and might make things worse. You can't control his outdated attitude."

   The other colleague advocates a different approach. "You can't separate what he said from the larger situation. That can't be allowed, no matter who said it. You're selling out unless you say

something. You've got to speak truth to power."
Which colleague offers better advice, in your view?
5. Outline the goals of Principal Richardson's coming conversations with Mr. and Mrs. Cho, Mr. Hoover, and Ms. Lake. Describe how he should approach each.
6. How should Principal Richardson address the paraprofessional's inaction related to Joel's accommodations? What should an effective training and retention plan for paraprofessionals include?
7. What role, if any, do you believe race/ethnicity plays in the case? How might the dynamics of the case change if the race/ethnicity, class, sexual orientation, immigration status, language, etc. were different?

Teaching Strategies

1. Identify the key issues in the case, in order of importance. Do you see issues as being moral/ethical, legal, professional, or something else? How do the key issues you identify reflect your experience, philosophy, and/or potential biases? If collaborating in a group, compare your answers to another group and ask for clarification of their reasoning.
2. Most complex leadership dilemmas hinge on complicated factors that could go in one direction or another, and have a significant impact on the situation. Collaborate with a team to write two alternative endings to the case.
3. Principal Richardson's head is full of questions about how to move forward. Prioritize the order in which he should address these issues by constructing a three-column table labeled "Immediate," "Near Future," and "Longer Term." Place the issues into the column that you believe is most appropriate. Then offer suggestions for addressing each.

References

Accelify. (2016, January 25). 3 ways educators can close the achievement gap for students with disabilities. Retrieved from https://www.accelify.com/accelify-blog/2016/01/25/3-ways-educators-can-close-the-achievement-gap-for-students-with-disabilities/

Berry, A. B., & Gravelle, M. (2013). The benefits and challenges of special education positions in rural settings: Listening to the teachers. *The Rural Educator, 34*(2).

Berry, A. B., Petrin, R. A, Gravelle, M. L., & Farmer, T. W. (2011). Issues in special education teacher recruitment, retention, and professional development: Considerations in supporting rural teachers. *Rural Special Education Quarterly, 30*(4), 3-11.

Braden, J. P., Schroeder, J. L., & Buckley, J. A. (2000). Secondary school reform, inclusion, and authentic assessment. RISER Brief #3. Madison, WI: Wisconsin Center for Education Research, Research Institute on Secondary Education Reform for Youth with Disabilities. Retrieved from http://archive.wceruw.org/riser/Brief%203%20text%20only.pdf

De Fina, P. A. & Feifer, S. G. (2002). *The neuropsychology of written language disorders: Diagnosis and intervention.* Middletown, MD: School Neuropsych Press.

Landsman, J. & Lewis, C. W. (2011). *White teachers/diverse classrooms: Creating inclusive schools, building on students' diversity, and providing true educational equity.* Sterling, VA: Stylus Publishing.

McCray, C. R. & Beachum, F. D. (2013). *School leadership in a diverse society: Helping prepare all students for success.* Charlotte, NC: Information Age.

Case #20

Is This Inclusion?

Linda Chmiliar

Introduction

The following case study takes a brief look at the very complex case of a six-year-old First Nation boy, Elvis, experiencing challenges in his grade one class. The case describes the initial incident where Elvis's situation first came to light on Feb. 1, 2017, and reports on the school's response.

Overview/Analysis

This case takes place in a school in a large urban city in Western Canada. The school is situated in a low socioeconomic area of the city; the neighborhood consists primarily of low rental and subsidized housing, mixed in with single family dwellings. The community population is very diverse. The school consists of 14 classrooms of kindergarten to grade six students. There is also a part-time special education classroom in the morning where students who are having significant, fundamental difficulties with learning receive support. These students are included in their home room activities in the afternoons.

The focus of this case study is a six-year-old First Nation boy named Elvis, enrolled in one of the grade one classrooms in the school. On February 1, Mrs. White, the grade one teacher, arranged a noon hour meeting with the principal to talk about her concerns regarding Elvis. She indicated that Elvis was always late for school, arriving anywhere between 30 minutes to 2 hours late for class every day. Mrs. White's response to this behavior was to send Elvis out to a chair in the hallway, as his arrival was always disruptive to her lessons and the other children. She had Elvis sit and wait until she was free to talk with him. Mrs. White said that she had sent notes home with Elvis, and had tried to phone the mother using the phone number provided on the intake form, but at this point in time she had not heard from the mother.

The principal, Mr. Jackson, was very concerned about the information that Mrs. White reported to him. Not only was he worried about Elvis's school attendance and late arrivals, and the fact that the teacher had not yet been able to contact the mother, but was also troubled about his perception of Mrs. White's attitude toward Elvis and her discipline of his behavior. After his meeting with Mrs. White, Mr. Jackson quickly walked down the hall to the counsellor's office to get her feedback. They both felt uncomfortable with the situation, and they determined that the counsellor, Miss Abbott, would observe the situation the following day.

The next day Miss Abbott stationed herself in the hallway down the hall from the classroom with a pad of paper and a pen. At 9:45 Elvis came through the door and proceeded to his locker. He took off his coat, placed it in the locker, put the travel mug he was carrying into the locker, and closed the door. Elvis gave Miss Abbott a big grin as he opened the door to the classroom and walked in. Immediately, Miss Abbott could hear Mrs. White's raised voice coming from the classroom door. Within a minute or two Elvis emerged from the classroom. He went to his locker, retrieved his travel mug, sat on a chair outside the door, and proceeded to drink from the travel mug. Curious, Miss Abbott approached Elvis, and asked, "Elvis, how are you this morning? Your drink smells great, what are you drinking?" Elvis indicated that he was fine and that he was drinking "Indian coffee." Surprised, Miss Abbott asked to see the mug and found that in fact Elvis was drinking very strong coffee. In further conversation, Elvis indicated that he had got himself up, made himself a cup of coffee, and came to school. He had stayed at his "Auntie's house" with his mother. About 15 minutes later, Mrs. White emerged from the classroom to talk with Elvis about arriving late for school. He had finished his coffee by then and had returned the mug to the locker.

Miss Abbott returned to her office, and at her first opportunity to talk with Mr. Jackson she reported her observations. They had a quick meeting and decided that Miss Abbott would ask to meet with Elvis the following day to explore the situation further. Over the next few days Miss Abbott met with Elvis in her office, and, with the help of the special education teacher, had Elvis complete a brief education assessment. The counsellor was also able to contact Elvis's mother regarding this situation.

The education assessment revealed that Elvis was able to read words, sentences, and comprehend passages at a grade 3 level. This far exceeds what would be expected six months into the grade one school year. However, Elvis exhibited difficulties with a pencil grip, and was only able to print his name. He was very reluctant to even try to print other simple words and had difficulties copying simple sentences. Elvis could recognize numbers up to 10 and could count to 20, but was not able to demonstrate ability to complete simple addition. Elvis's oral language was not assessed at this time, but his communication with the counsellor and special education teacher appeared to be appropriate for his age.

A meeting between the mother and Miss Abbott revealed that Elvis, his mother, and younger brother had just moved to the city. They had left the family home and Elvis's father due to marital difficulties and were now staying with extended family. Elvis's mother indicated that she often worked late at night, so Elvis and his brother had to periodically stay with a relative overnight.

After hearing the information regarding the education assessment and Elvis's home situation, Mr. Jackson felt that immediate action was required. He talked with Mrs. White about being more supportive of Elvis and approaching his late arrivals to class in a different way. Mrs. White was adamant that she was dealing with the behavior in an appropriate way and declined to change her approach. Mr. Jackson then approached Mrs. Seeth, the special education teacher, to see if Elvis could move to the morning special education class on a temporary basis. As there were several grade one students already attending the class, the special education teacher felt that it might be very comfortable for Elvis to come to the class.

Problem Statement

In classroom observations, it was clear that Elvis was also demonstrating difficulties with attention, staying on task, completing work, following classroom rules, and managing his behavior. Elvis continues to be sent to the time-out chair in the hallway outside of his grade one classroom when he is late for class, unable to complete assignments, does not stay in his desk, or talks out of turn. The principal and counsellor are very concerned about Elvis, and think that he may be in crisis in his current situation. There is a special education classroom in the school where students attend for the morning, and they return to their regular classrooms in the afternoon. This class is attended by 13 students from grades one through six, and the teacher, Mrs. Seeth, and the classroom assistant, have all of the students work at their own level and pace on language arts, mathematics, self-management, and behavior. Mrs. Seeth has indicated that she would be willing to work with Elvis. The principal is considering sending him to the special education class in the mornings while working on a long term solution to this situation.

Questions and Teaching Strategies

1. In your opinion, what are the three most critical concerns in this case?
2. Which concern requires the most immediate attention?
3. Examine actions and decisions made by each of the individuals in this case. For each individual, indicate if you would have responded differently in this situation, and how you would have responded.

   Grade 1 Teacher Mrs. White
   Principal Mr. Jackson
   Counsellor Miss Abbott
   Special Education Teacher Mrs. Seeth
   Elvis's mother
4. In Canada, considerable effort is being put into addressing the Truth and Reconciliation Commission report calls to action. The

commission was established to examine the history and legacy of Canada's residential school system. In an executive report to government, it was indicated that, "First Nations and Canadians have a collective public responsibility to ensure a high quality system of education for First Nation students in both First Nation and provincial schools. We have a duty to do better and an obligation to protect and support the rights of First Nation children to a good education that builds a strong First Nation identity, language and culture and ensures that these students are learning and achieving at the same level as non-First Nation students."

In your opinion, does the school's response to this situation match the spirit of the quotation above for education for First Nation students? What elements are missing?

How can these elements be applied to Indigenous students in other countries?

5. Develop a plan for the school to address the issues you have identified that provides Elvis with a healthy, safe environment where he is included in the classroom in a way that supports his cultural, emotional, behavioral, and academic needs. Make sure your plan includes all of the individuals in this case.

Reference

Nurturing the Learning Spirit of First Nation Students: The Report of the National Panel on First Nation Elementary and Secondary Education for Students on Reserve. Retrieved February 2017 from https://www.aadnc-aandc.gc.ca/DAM/DAM- INTER-HQ-EDU/STAGING/texte- text/nat_panel_final_report_1373997803969_eng.pdf

Case #21

Linguistic Exclusion From Above

Eleni Oikonomidoy

Introduction

This case study is based on the experiences of linguistic and social exclusion of a newcomer, immigrant student, within the context of an ELL (English Language Learners) classroom in the United States of America. Her peers' and her teachers' use of Spanish in class result in her linguistic exclusion in both academic and social spaces.

Overview/analysis

Maria[1] has been in the U.S. for the last six months. A native of the Philippines, she joined Lakeside High school mid-year and was placed in the ELL (English Language Learners) track. Although she couldn't understand why she was placed in ELL (she thought her English was quite good, as she had studied it back home), she did not think that it was her place to challenge her school. She was grateful for the opportunity to study in the U.S., despite the fact that she found that the curriculum was not at her level. She had completed advanced studies in the Philippines and she found some of the material redundant and boring.

---

1 All names and locations are fictitious.

While her native language was Tagalog, she did study English at school and she had completed advanced study in math. She thought that in a way she was being excluded from the advanced-level classes that some of her native-born peers had access to. She was certain that the one good thing about her placement in the ELL class was that she would be among other students who were not U.S.-born, and she would be able to share experiences with them about both the challenges and wonderful opportunities presented when living in the U.S. Although she sensed that the "American Dream" as it is presented in the movies was not true, she still hoped that there were parts of it that could be actualized. For instance, she would be able to go to college and study medicine.

Maria had heard of whole schools that were created for newcomers, but such were not available in her city. On the contrary, her school provided 'special' classes for newcomers. In her initial transition, she felt that developing relationships with U.S.-born peers could be challenging. First, although she spoke English, her confidence in conversing with native speakers of the language was limited. In addition, she had heard from her cousins who had been in the U.S. for a couple years that U.S.-born peers had negative views of newcomers (oftentimes making fun of the way they dressed and talked), and preferred to not associate with them. Nevertheless, she believed that she would have common ground with her fellow newcomers because they had similar experiences. They were all from different countries and they were just now learning how to navigate school and life in the U.S.

However, once she entered her ELL classes, she found out that the majority of the students were Spanish speakers and could easily converse with one another. She tried to break the linguistic wall and engage in conversations with them, but many times such efforts were both exhausting and a waste of time. Her peers oftentimes ignored her and continued to speak in Spanish to one another, making her feel unwelcomed. This situation was not limited to social encounters. The linguistic exclusion with the use of Spanish took place during small group work as well. She was also concerned that her peers were gossiping about her. What made things even more challenging for her was that her English ELL teacher, Mr. Lopez, was bilingual in English-Spanish. Although this helped all those who were Spanish speakers, Maria felt excluded. Sometimes, her teacher engaged in lengthy conversations with her Spanish-speaking peers in Spanish. During those times, she experienced double-exclusion: exclusion from the mainstream curriculum due to her perceived limited academic English knowledge, and the exclusion within the ELL class when her peers and teachers spoke in Spanish.

She wished that she had a teacher who spoke Tagalog. But then she considered whether she would feel comfortable speaking in another language in front of her peers given that there were only a handful of students at the school who spoke her language.

She liked her teacher, and was also certain that Mr. Lopez tried his best to translate and present information in both languages. However, when he and her classmates spoke in Spanish for long periods of time she didn't know what to do. She looked away, she pretended to read her book, and she acted as if she was taking notes but... still... she felt isolated. She knew that her teacher wanted to help her peers. She also sensed that the fact that he spoke Spanish empowered her peers in a strange way. Because they knew that their teacher spoke Spanish, they (she thought) didn't even try to converse in English in the classroom. For instance, during small group work, her peers spoke to her in Spanish, a behavior that had become normalized in the classroom, despite the fact that they knew that she could not understand. She felt very frustrated and, despite enjoying the idea of group work, she often gave up trying to work with them, even if she knew the answers.

She had heard from other ELL students at the school that they also felt the dual exclusion. However, she didn't know what to do about it. She couldn't talk to her teachers, as she felt intimidated. She would never be able to 'question' a teacher's behavior. She knew that she had to respect all of her teachers' choices. She felt that no one could understand her. She tried talking to her parents but they both seemed to be uncertain as to what the issue was. They told her to listen to her teachers and all would be fine.

One day, she decided to confide to one of the ELL aids in the class, Mr. Carter. This aid had been very nice to her from the beginning of her transition. Maria just wanted to hear another perspective on the situation.

She didn't want to get in trouble though. She had contemplated about doing it or not for weeks, and had lost sleep over it.

That day, during lunch, Mr. Carter came to check in with her. She found that this was the perfect opportunity! She shared her dilemmas and asked for advice: Mr. Carter was very reaffirming, which made her feel much better. He listened to her, and then he shared that he would talk to the ELL coordinator about it.

Problem Statement

The ELL aid shared Maria's concerns with the ELL coordinator, Mrs. Martinez, who was bilingual in Spanish and English. The coordinator seemed to genuinely care about the issue; however she felt that the use of the two languages was critical for the Spanish-speaking newcomers. She was unsure about how to address Maria's feelings of exclusion.

Case problems

Here are some questions to consider:
1. Do you find Maria's feelings of exclusion justified or exaggerated? Explain.
2. If you were a bilingual teacher, like Mr. Lopez, wouldn't you be inclined to use L1 for support of your students? Do you find anything problematic with this approach?
3. What are the limits of inclusion/exclusion within the context of an ELL class? Could it be that spaces of inclusion always result in spaces of exclusion, in this and other contexts?
4. If you were the ELL coordinator, Mrs. Martinez, what would you do to help Maria? Would you involve the principal in the identification of a possible response or would you allow the ELL team to present a "solution" to you? What may be pros and cons in each one of these approaches?
5. What type of relationship between the school and the parents do you think may have allowed for a different response from Maria's parents?

6. What may be additional forces of exclusion that newcomer ELL students face and never bring to teachers' attention?

Recommended activities

1. In small groups, create a script and role-play the interaction between the Spanish-speaking peers, the Spanish-speaking teacher, and Maria. Debrief, paying attention to the body language and emotions of all those involved.
2. Write a report stating how the situation should be addressed, using support from the literature on intergroup dialogue. Who would you involve in the decision-making? Why? What would be the desired outcome?
3. In small groups, write, and then present, monologues that describe the following actors' thought process in relation to the issue at hand: Mr. Lopez, Mrs. Martinez, Maria, & Maria's parents.
4. Consider the meaning of culturally responsive teaching (Gay, 2010). Identify three theoretical insights that could help inform the situation at hand.
5. Li (2010) writes, "In a mainstream system, the stories of newcomer students are rarely heard because they are the least powerful stakeholders in the Canadian educational hierarchy" (p. 120)
    a). Consider the implications of this quote within the context of your respective educational system (from national to local).
    b). Contemplate ways in which this reality could change. How could both newcomer students and parents be included in educational policy and practice?

Recommended Readings

Aldana, A., Rowley, S. J., Checkoway, B., & Richards-Schuster, K. (2012). Raising ethnic-racial consciousness: The relationship between intergroup dialogues and adolescents' ethnic-racial identity and racism awareness. *Equity & Excellence in Education, 45* (1), 120-137.

Allen, D. (2007). Just who do you think I am? The name-calling and name-claiming of newcomer youth. *Canadian Journal of Applied Linguistics. 10* (2), 165-175.

Barillas-Chon, D. W. (2010). Oaxaqueno/a students' (un)welcoming high school Experiences. *Journal of Latinos and Education, 9* (4), 303-320

Bennett, J. (2012). Care and advocacy: Narratives from a school for immigrant youth. Charlotte, NC: Information Age Publishing.

Franquiz, M. E. & Salinas, S. S. (2011). Newcomers to the U.S.: Developing historical thinking among Latino immigrant students in a Central Texas High School. *Bilingual Research Journal, 34* (1), 58-75.

Gay, G. (2000). Culturally responsive teaching: Theory, research and practice. New York: Teachers College Press.

Griffin, S. R., Brown., & Warren, n. m. (2012). Critical education in high schools: the promise and challenges of intergroup dialogue. Equity & Excellence in Education, 45(1), 159-180.

Hsin, J. & Tsai, C. (2006). Xenophobia, ethnic community, and immigrant youths' friendship network formation. Adolescence, 41 (162), 285-298.

Kanno, Y. & Kangas, S. E. N. (2014). "I'm not going to be, like, for the AP": English language learners' limited access to advanced college-preparatory courses in high school. American Educational Research Journal, 51 (5), 848-878.

Lopez, G. E. & Nastasi, W. (2012). Writing the divide: High school students crossing urban-suburban contexts. Equity & Excellence in Education, 45 (1), 138-158.

Miyazawa, K. (2013). Dreaming and surviving in heterotopia: First-generation immigrant girls' pursuit of the American Dream in New York City. Taboo: The Journal of Culture and Education, 1, 63-76.

Nilsson, J., & Axelsson, M. (2013). "Welcome to Sweden.": Newly arrived students' experiences of pedagogical and social provision in introductory and regular classes. International Electronic Journal of Elementary Education, 6(1), 137– 164.

Peguero, A. A. & Bondy, J. M. (2011). Immigration and students' relationships with teachers. Education and Urban Society, 43 (2), 165-183.

Willoughby, L. (2009). Language choice in multilingual peer groups: insights from an Australian high school. Journal of Multilingual and Multicultural Development, 30 (5), 421-435.

Case #22

Donna Becomes Don:
A Call for School Districts to Better Serve Transgender Youth

Nan Stevens

Introduction

Donna becomes Don is the story of a courageous young person who begins the journey of transitioning while still in elementary school (age 12, grade 7) within a conservative school district that has next to no resources. The intent of this case is to stretch the thinking of those teachers and administrators who are uncomfortable, or who have not worked, with transgender youth before, in hopes that they will be more prepared and open when the occasion presents itself. Don's story serves to illuminate the changing needs of students on the margins. Teachers and school administrators need to gain awareness, and develop skills and professional qualities, which will better serve the youth for whom they are caring.

Overview/Analysis

I have known Don since he was born. His birth date is four months before that of my first son. His mother and I enjoyed visits at Starbucks to nurse our babies and talk about our changed lives. I have known Don his entire life, and I am honored that he wanted to share his story with teachers and teacher educators. He said, of being interviewed for this chapter, "if it can help other kids like me, I am all for it."

For as long as she could remember, Donna did not want to be a girl. This inner conflict existed throughout her childhood development. Donna resides in a rural area and excels in sports, many of which are male dominated, such as mountain biking, skiing, snowboarding, and dirt biking. Although she self-identified as a tomboy, everyone assumed she was a boy.

At the age of 12, Donna happened upon a video online of a female youth's story of transitioning to a male. Seeing this video opened up Donna's world to the reality that gender re-assignment was a possibility for her. Donna's disclosure to her parents and extended family was met with support from some, and resistance from others.

Donna attended a French Immersion elementary school within an interior region of British Columbia, Canada. The school demographic is comprised of middle class families, with traditional values, taking advantage of the opportunity for their children to learn French from an early age. Donna started at the school in Grade 1, and established a nice social group of friends who were progressing together as a cohort through their primary and intermediate years. This narrative is a result of interviews with Don, which were conducted to help identify the issues and problems that he faced as a transitioning youth in the public school system in a small city in central BC.

Donna had known from a very young age ("all my life") that he was born into the wrong gender. "I always dressed boyish and acted boyish. I called myself a tomboy and so did everyone else." In the summer before grade 7, Don was browsing the internet. He came across a video of a girl transitioning into a boy. Don never knew this was possible until he saw the video. He learned that such a transition could occur for him. The idea of being born into the wrong body was validated when he learned that there were others besides himself with similar thoughts and feelings. It was very liberating for Don to see this story online.

Don disclosed to his parents first about his wish—and need—to transition. When Don returned to school in grade 7, he became more public about his wishes and needs. Having a transitioning youth in their classrooms was extremely new for the teaching staff. According to Don, "They were trying to accommodate me, but they did not know what to do." What Don was seeking from his teachers and principal was a resolution to where he might go to the bathroom, and how gym class was going to play out. These were the logistical and practical things that needed to be resolved. At the same time, he was seeking support and resources from the school staff that had known him for seven years. The teachers and administrator in the school simply did not know how to manage Don's requests and needs.

At times, Don felt isolated and excluded, yet never wavered from his commitment to his personal journey. There was "really not anywhere to go for support at school." His parents were his greatest advocates, and they approached the school to try to come to a working solution for their son. The bathroom was the biggest challenge. Don didn't feel comfortable using either the girls or the boy's bathroom at this point in his transition, so it was decided that Don would use the custodian's bathroom. Yet, the problem with having a separate bathroom from all the others kids was that Don was ostracized, and had to be stealthy in his bathroom visits so that he wouldn't be seen entering and exiting that bathroom by other students.

Some of Don's peer group still referred to him using the "she" pronoun. It was taking some time for his friends to get accustomed to the change. One of Don's best friends in grade 7 came from a religious background where Don was only allowed to be called 'she'. Don accepted that.

Don described his Grade 7 year. "The teachers were old fashioned, with old fashioned ways of thinking. The teachers did not know how to deal with things, especially the principal." Typically, counsellors are not part of the staff at the elementary level; however, Don had the chance to work with an 'area counsellor' in the district. They never did meet.

For the years since Don's disclosure, his greatest supports have included his parents, friends, and outside agencies or groups who walk alongside individuals who are transitioning. His schools were not places of support. For youth in transition, the education system needs to be more responsive in its concern and care for transgender individuals.

Schools are a place where students need to feel safe amongst their peers, where they can be themselves, take risks, and find their authentic path. The experience that Don had with his elementary school teachers and principal was problematic, and needs to change.

Problem Statement

Gender dysphoria is a general term used to refer to an individual's discontent with their assigned gender. People with gender dysphoria may be very uncomfortable with the gender they were assigned, sometimes described as being uncomfortable with their body (particularly developments during puberty), or being uncomfortable with the expected roles of their assigned gender. The term, transgender, refers to the broad spectrum of individuals who transiently or persistently identify with a gender different from their gender at birth (Parekh, 2016).

The prevalence of gender dysphoria in teenagers is on the rise. Transgender youth are presenting at clinics for treatment related to gender dysphoria in higher numbers than previously seen (de Vries & Cohen-Kettenis, 2012). Similarly, at the Children's Hospital in Vancouver, BC, the clinic has seen a dramatic increase in the number of teenage patients from 2006-2011 (Khatchadourian, Amed, & Metzger, 2014).

Transgender and gender non-conforming youth face challenges at home, at school, in foster care, and in juvenile justice systems. (National Center for Transgender Equity, 2017, para. 1). The National Survey of School Culture found that 75% of transgender youth feel unsafe at school, and those who are able to persevere had significantly lower GPAs, were more likely to miss school out of concern for their safety, and were less likely to plan on continuing their education. (National Center for Transgender Equality, 2017, para. 1). When Don was asked what could have been done differently during his elementary school days, or what can teachers learn from the experiences they had with him, he replied, "They could have been more supportive, more open. There was so little emotional connection for me with the teachers." This chapter poses the question, "Do you see a role in teacher education courses, or training, in addressing this issue?"

Few providers (including educators) feel knowledgeable and comfortable enough to treat transgender people, and even fewer feel comfortable treating [working with] transgender youth (National Center for Transgender Equality, 2017). As teachers may be the first point of contact for a youth (besides their family members), it is essential that teachers prepare themselves for supporting individuals who may be in their direct care. Teacher education programs, and in-service professional development, provide opportunities for instilling knowledge and developing comfort for teaching professionals.

Teaching Strategies for Pre-service and In-service Teachers

A number of teaching strategies are recommended to assist teacher educators in the preparation of pre-service teachers for working with transgender students. Additionally, the following strategies are instructive for assisting practicing (in-service) teachers and educational leaders in their personal and professional development:

1. Small group discussions using case studies of fictional transgender youth, followed up with a larger group discussion in which a reporter from each group shares each case and the group's steps to help facilitate support for the student;
2. Role playing is an effective way to 'act out' the scenarios presented in #1. For example, individuals in each group can take on specific roles, such as the transgender youth, teacher, administrator, school counsellor, and/or parent. Through role playing the group members may gain a better understanding of the lived experience of the student, and the need for empathy and support;
3. An exploratory assignment where pre-service/in-service teacher or administrator interviews a transgender youth in their community; or interviews a service provider who works closely with a transgender youth;
4. A panel of guests (e.g., transgender youth, service providers, parents/guardians, siblings, and allies) is an effective way to present a number of perspectives at the same time, with a chance for questions and discussion following;

5. Conducting a literature review in response to targeted questions is another way to gather current information, statistics, and best practices for supporting transgender youth;
6. Use of small and large group discussions with key questions is a strategy that may be used to guide learning. Examples of key questions are provided below:
   i   What do you think teachers and school administrators can do to become more supportive and open towards transitioning youth?
   ii How can teachers and school administrators access opportunities for growth and development in this specific area of inclusive education?
   iii What are the key gaps regarding lack of support areas in this case study, and what choices, by teachers, parents, administrators, the student, or other, could have been made instead?
   iv Can you identify any outside school resources that could support the school staff in a case such as Don's?
   v   How would you transfer your learning from this case to other cases of exclusion in elementary and secondary schools?

Summary

The case study presented in this chapter enables teacher educators and developing teachers and administrators to see the need for personal and professional growth when working with marginalized youth. As the transgender population continues to increase (particularly in teenagers), so must the knowledge, skills, and understanding of those who are responsible for serving them. Diversity has become the norm in our schools and in society. Teaching to diversity is the only way our schools, and the educational system within which we teach, will be responsive and responsible to today's youth.

References

de Vries, A., Cohen-Kettenis, P. (2012). Clinical management of gender dysphoria in children and adolescents: The Dutch approach. Journal of Homosexuality 59(3):301-20. DOI: 10.1080/00918369.2012.653300.

Khatchadourian, K.; Amed, S.; & Metzger, D.L. (2014). Clinical Management of youth with gender dysphoria in Vancouver, BC. Journal of pediatrics 4(4). 906 -11. DOI: 10.1016/j.jpeds.2013.10.068

National Center for Transgender Equality Website. (2017). Issues: Youth and Students. Retrieved from http://www.transequality.org/issues/youth-students

Parekh, R. (2016). What is gender dysphoria? American Psychiatric Association. Retrieved from https://www.psychiatry.org/patients-families/gender-dysphoria/what-is-gender-dysphoria

Case #23

Punthea's Father:
A Study in PTSD

Robert E. White

The following case portrays staff and parental responses to an incident that occurred in an inner city daycare centre. The scenario underscores the challenges involved at all levels of society during emotionally intense, divisive instances when individuals display elements of post-traumatic stress disorder (PTSD). Questions challenge readers to identify responses to PTSD. Teaching notes are included to assist readers in deciding how to proceed in the face of complex and competing perspectives relating to this anxiety-based disorder.

Overview

Punthea sat quietly at her little table. Her snack sat before her, untouched. At four years of age, Punthea was a quiet child by nature. While she was born a Canadian citizen, her parents had emigrated a few years previously from their home in Cambodia. Her mother, Sita, was studying at the nearby university to upgrade her teaching credentials, while her father, Narin, worked at a local computer software company. Although finances were strained, the cost for Punthea to attend the daycare was not of great concern.

As children ran past, playing during the morning break, Punthea remained in a contemplative pose. Suddenly, a child ran into her chair. Punthea lurched forward and almost fell from her perch. She turned to face the child, a friend of hers named Millie, gave her a stern look and returned to her thoughts. The teacher, Ms. Madison, saw the interaction and thought little of it except that Punthea was unusually quiet, even for her.

As the day progressed things did not improve. At 4 p.m., when her mother came to pick her up, Punthea burst into tears. As her mother dressed her in her outdoor clothing, the tears turned into screams. Her mother, alarmed at this unwarranted behaviour, paused to ask her what was wrong. Punthea continued to scream.

Ms. Madison and the teaching assistant came over to see what was the matter. Upon questioning, both people claimed that nothing amiss seemed to have happened that day, although they had both noticed that Punthea had become less outgoing over the course of the term. They asked if everything was all right at home. Sita, Punthea's mother, said that she could think of nothing that would have set her child off like this. She also confided that Narin had just been laid off and was searching for a new job.

Two days later, Punthea arrived at daycare with a swollen lip. When Ms. Madison voiced concern and empathy, Sita looked away and said that she had hurt her lip when she fell down on the pavement the previous day. Punthea's behaviour again seemed uncharacteristic, as it had for some time now. Ms. Madison decided that this might just be a phase that the child was going through. Following this, on a daily basis, Punthea would cry and begin to scream when one of her parents came to pick her up to take her home.

The following week, when her father came to pick up his daughter from daycare, Punthea ran away and hid in a pile of stuffed toys. Her father, Narin, picked her up and unceremoniously dumped her in her stroller and made for the door. On instinct, Ms. Madison met him at the door as he was leaving and attempted to engage Narin in conversation about his daughter's unusual behaviour. Narin seemed to be in a hurry and did not wish to talk. He claimed that his daughter's crying was a usual occurrence and he hoped she would grow out of it soon. He intimated that it bothered him a lot and gave him a headache.

Ms. Madison decided to approach the mother and ask about conditions at home, as she could think of nothing that would set the little girl off like this at daycare. During the conversation, Sita admitted that Narin was the disciplinarian in the family. He had been raised in a very authoritarian household, whereas Sita described her own family of origin as kind and loving. She evinced some concern over Narin's parenting methods and Ms. Madison suggested that Sita see a counsellor at the University's Student Services Centre.

After discussing her concerns in a meeting with a university counsellor, Sita became convinced that her husband, who had been a child during the Cambodian civil war, suffered from post-traumatic stress disorder (PTSD). It was this reaction to stress, and the subsequent anxiety, that caused him to discipline his daughter too harshly. Her swollen lip had been caused by Narin. He had force-fed when she refused to eat her dinner when she would not eat her dinner, cramming so much food into her mouth that she could neither chew nor swallow. His perseverance resulted in her swollen lip, the result of his holding her jaw open while he fed her more rice.

Sita had not born witness to these events as they had actually occurred, as she had left Narin in charge of the little girl while she went to do errands. Apparently, Punthea was not comfortable being left alone with her father and she began to cry. Narin admitted that, after the crying began, he admonished her to stop. This resulted in more histrionics until he finally snapped and shouted at her. The power struggle continued until Sita returned to see her daughter, eyes filled with terror, unable to eat because her mouth had been so crammed full of rice.

As they discussed this turn of events, Narin admitted that he felt that his actions were inappropriate. He admitted that Punthea's crying was as if an explosion had gone off in his head. When this happened, he said he could not remember things clearly – that all he could think of was to stop the crying. Narin was ashamed of his treatment of his daughter and agreed to meet with the university counsellor in order to get help. Eventually, Narin was diagnosed with post-traumatic stress disorder. He continues to receive counseling in an attempt to deal with his family in more appropriate ways.

Problem Statement

How can schools and Early Childhood Educational facilities support students who are exposed to post-traumatic stress disorder? How can these institutions help families where PTSD is a reality? What strategies, policies or procedures can support children and families who are experiencing post-traumatic stress disorder?

Discussion

Hopefully, this case study content will encourage delving more deeply into information about PTSD. Following are some resources that may facilitate teaching strategies:

Resources

Alat, K. (2002). Traumatic events and children: How early childhood educators can help. Childhood Education 79(1), 2-8. http://www.tandfonline.com/doi/abs/10.1080/00094056.2002.10522756?journalCode=uced20

Church, D., & Feinstein, D. (2013). Energy psychology in the treatment of PTSD: Psychobiology and clinical principles. In T. Van Leeuwen, & M. Brouwer. (Eds.), Psychology of trauma (pp. 211-224). Hauppage, NY: Nova Science Publishers.

Gorman, J. (2003). PTSD. Lansing, MI: National Alliance on Mental Health.

Gyurko, P. (2015). Post Traumatic Stress Syndrome. Retrieved, January 2, 2017 from https://tackk.com/kujz58

Kirsch, V., Wilhelm, F. H. & Goldbeck, L. (2011). Psychophysiological characteristics of PTSD in children and adolescents: A review of the literature. Journal of Traumatic Stress 24(3), 370–372. http://onlinelibrary.wiley.com/doi/10.1002/jts.20620/full

Rolfsnes, E. S. & Idsoe, T. (2011). School-based intervention programs for PTSD symptoms: A review and meta-analysis Journal of Traumatic Stress 24(2), 155-165. http://onlinelibrary.wiley.com/doi/10.1002/jts.20622/full

Van der Kolk, B. (2015). The body keeps score: Brain, mind and body in the healing of trauma. London, UK: Penguin Books.

Teaching Strategies

The case above describes some of the challenges involved in identifying and diagnosing PTSD. While it is widely accepted that educators are in no way prepared to treat students for symptoms of PTSD, they tend to be the first line of defense when it comes to the best interests of their students. Oftentimes, it is the teacher who is the first person to recognize that something is amiss. While PTSD requires therapy, it is the educator who can contribute significantly to the prognosis by providing a safe and secure environment for students, particularly during intense periods of anxiety. The teacher may find him- or herself working as much with the parents as with the student to fashion a smooth transition for the student from the roller coaster of unpredictability to a somewhat smoother passage. These teachings offer opportunities for readers to unpack some of the intricacies associated with post-traumatic stress disorder.

Activities

The following activities are intended to prompt reflection, dialogue, and modeling of skills and actions that educators may utilize in responding to potential causes and effects of PTSD in the students under their care.

1. Explore how to build a strong school climate by providing learning opportunities to increase awareness of post-traumatic stress disorder.
2. Investigate the origins of post-traumatic stress disorder and identify various names that have referred to PTSD in the past.
3. Describe a situation that you may have experienced that might have led to post-traumatic stress disorder. Did you develop symptoms? If so, what were they? If not, why do you think this to be so? Can you identify any supports that helped you through this time?

Questions for Further Study

The following questions may be used to further consider aspects of the case above:

1. How could Sita and Narin work together to minimize effects of his post-traumatic stress disorder?
2. How did the daycare personnel interrupt the cycle of abuse that so frequently accompanies post-traumatic stress disorder?
3. How would you develop a program to deal with the potential appearance of post-traumatic stress disorder in your classroom? Who would you involve? What resources would you require?
4. If you were to make a policy recommendation to your school board about post-traumatic stress disorder, what would you do?
5. How would you implement a post-traumatic stress disorder policy or program in your school? In your classroom?
6. How would you go about educating your community with respects to the effects of post-traumatic stress disorder?

Case #24

Looking at the "Big Picture" and Long-term Outcomes:
Partnering with Parents and Self-Advocates to Ensure Quality Outcomes for Students with Intellectual Disabilities

Lynne Sommerstein & Diane Lea Ryndak

Schools and parents sometimes disagree over service delivery for students with disabilities. This disconnect can lead to inappropriate services for the student, alienation of the parents, conflict within the school, and/or additional costs of independent evaluations, due process hearings, or mediation. When such situations arise, schools often take disparate stances, ranging from appeasing the parents by providing what they ask, to escalating to due process hearings. This case study focuses on how educational services will impact a student's long-term outcomes, and makes us ask how we can partner with parents and self-advocates to tailor their future.

Overview/Analysis

Elizabeth Craig, 15, attends a self-contained special education class with 12 students who have intellectual disabilities, taught by a teacher and a paraprofessional, at Crestwood Middle School. She receives the services of a speech pathologist, occupational therapist, and an additional

1:1 personal instructional assistant. Elizabeth is integrated in art, music and chorus, all in which she is socially appropriate and passing.

She had attended an inclusive pre-school with speech therapy twice a week. Her mother indicates Elizabeth was reluctant to cooperate in 1:1 speech therapy until her mother brought children from the pre-school into speech therapy sessions. Elizabeth continues to attend dancing, soccer, religious school, and Girl Scouts with peers without disabilities. Elizabeth is a polite, well-groomed young woman. She has strong social skills, and fitting in with her typically developing peers is important to her. She often watches them and does what they do.

On her current evaluation with the Wechsler Intelligence Scale for Children-Revised (WISC-R), Elizabeth scored within the moderate range of intellectual disabilities, with a 20-point difference between verbal and performance scores. Her sub-scores on the WISC-R ranged from 1-6, with relative strengths in the performance areas. Elizabeth tested at a 2.5 grade level in reading, with strengths in receptive comprehension. She had a 3.5 grade level performance in math.

Her parents engaged an independent evaluator, believing that Elizabeth's abilities were greater than standardized tests showed and that expectations for her were too low. An independent ecological evaluation indicated Elizabeth's receptive reading was closer to eighth grade. She had a significant expressive language delay, with severe articulation and word retrieval difficulties. Elizabeth was attentive and made eye contact, except when she was under stress. Concurrently, Elizabeth was diagnosed with a significant Central Auditory Processing disability, taking almost seven seconds to process auditory information, and was determined to be a visual learner. Data showed that her behavior corresponded to that of her typically developing peers in inclusive settings.

Upon review of Elizabeth's placement for the next academic year, the Crestwood Multidisciplinary IEP Team recommends a more restrictive self-contained special education class, comprising six students served by one teacher and one paraprofessional. They indicate that Elizabeth's needs are too intense for her to receive services in general education classes, because she cannot keep up with the students who are her age and needs instruction in functional activities. They note that Elizabeth has made little progress this year and has been exhibiting some disruptive behaviors in her self-contained class, such as inattention, talking out of turn and kicking a boy that she likes. Mr. and Mrs. Craig have been cooperative in correcting their daughter and giving her consequences for her behavior. They observe that Elizabeth demonstrates no inappropriate behaviors outside of her self-contained class, outside of school, and at home.

Elizabeth's parents have requested a due process hearing under the Individuals with Disabilities Education Improvement Act (2004), citing inappropriate placement that did not reflect Least Restrictive Environment (LRE), and inappropriate curriculum that did not meet their daughter's needs. They request that their daughter be placed in an age-appropriate, general education class with the support of a special education teacher, speech therapist, occupational therapist, and paraprofessional. They argue that their daughter's curriculum is not age-appropriate or challenging, and focuses on developmental and functional skills that she already has achieved. In addition, they argue that Elizabeth's inappropriate behavior is her way of communicating her frustration with both the self-contained class and curriculum.

Problem Statement

There are discrepant perceptions about two issues: (a) the educational setting that would be most beneficial for Elizabeth, resulting in outcomes that match the values of Elizabeth and her family; and, (b) the curriculum content that would be most important for Elizabeth to learn so she can participate in meaningful ways with her peers, family, and community members.

Case Problems

Consider the following key issues, and complete the problem-solving activity below.

Case Problem #1: What are the Least Restrictive Environment (LRE) issues?

> **Setting Issue:** How can Elizabeth's academic instructional needs (individualized, alternate/functional content) be met in general education classes?
>
> **Interventions and Supports Issue:** How can Elizabeth's behavior issues be addressed in the general education class?
>
> **Instructional Content Issue:** How can Elizabeth participate in a general education class if she needs a modified curriculum?
>
> **Values Issue:** How do you explain Mr. and Mrs. Craig's expectations for their daughter and why those differ from those of education team? What does the term "big picture" mean for Elizabeth and other students?
>
> **Problem-solving Activity:** As a team, students should write about the following.
>
> A. How could the school district and IEP Team work with Elizabeth and her parents to respect the point of view of all team members, and embrace the idea of looking at Elizabeth's "big picture"?
>
> B. Identify the next steps that will be taken to resolve the conflict.
>   Step 1.
>   Step 2.
>   Step 3.
>   Step 4.

Case Problem #2: What responsibility does the district and the IEP Team have to respect and follow the parents' request?

Issue with Priorities: Consider this observation about lifespan priorities: "One of the most commonly reported challenges in rearing children with disabilities is a feeling of a loss of control" (Edwards & Da Fonte, 2012). How can the IEP Team make Elizabeth and her parents feel in control of their futures?

Issue with "Primacy of Professional Decision-making" (Taylor, 1988): Why do so many schools uphold the professional perspective over the family perspective when they disagree? Who has the greatest stake in the decision-making process?

Issue with Collaborative Decision-making: When parents disagree with existing resources and instructional issues (e.g., instructional content; location of services), how can district personnel, school personnel, and IEP team members tailor their professional judgment to merge with the perspectives and beliefs of Elizabeth and her parents?

Problem-solving Activity: As a team, students should write about how THEIR TEAM would address the issues of Priorities, Decision-making, and Collaboration in relation to Elizabeth's educational services.

A. What decisions could your IEP team make that would demonstrate collaboration with Elizabeth and her parents related to setting priorities for Elizabeth's desired outcomes?

B. Identify the next steps that will be taken to develop a collaborative approach that demonstrates respect for the parents' perspective on the "big picture."
   Step 1.
   Step 2.
   Step 3.
   Step 4.

Case Problem Remedies (To be reviewed after the activities have been completed)

Case Problem #1: What are the Least Restrictive Environment (LRE) issues?

How the situation was remedied: Students should compare their answers to the actual resolution and steps completed (see Ryndak, Morrison, & Sommerstein, 1999; Ryndak, Ward, Alper, Montgomery, & Storch, 2010). After Mr. and Mrs. Craig prevailed in a due process hearing, the school district was instructed to place Elizabeth in general education classes with same-age classmates, with the support of a special education teacher, paraprofessional, speech/language pathologist, and occupational therapist. They were expected to collaboratively provide instruction on appropriately modified grade-level curriculum to facilitate Elizabeth's engagement and progress in the general curriculum with her classmates, along with instruction on individualized functional skills identified through an ecological assessment of the contexts in which she participated. Several steps were completed in relation to Elizabeth's educational services, including:

A. The school principal and district administrators identified and provided professional development activities, including outside technical assistance during classes to ensure the education team implemented evidence-based instructional practices in general education classes.

B. The school psychologist conducted an ecological assessment to determine Elizabeth's performance and learning needs across settings, addressing both curricular content and instructional processes.

C. The special education teacher provided ongoing consultation to the general education teachers to provide effective instruction on the modified general curriculum and functional contents during their general education instructional activities.

D. The speech/language pathologist identified supportive contexts with typically developing classmates for speech services.

Case Problem #2: What responsibility does the district and the IEP Team have to respect and follow the parents' request?

How the situation was remedied: Students should compare their answers to the actual resolution and steps completed (see Ryndak, Morrison, & Sommerstein, 1999; Ryndak, Ward, Alper, Montgomery, & Storch, 2010). The hearing officer directed the IEP Team at Crestwood Middle School to develop a collaborative relationship with Elizabeth and her family by using self-determination, person-centered planning approaches in the development of Elizabeth's short- and long-term academic and functional goals. The IEP team was told to work with Elizabeth and her parents in relation to setting, curriculum content, and instructional practices to meet their expectations for services and outcomes, both now and in the future. Similarly, the hearing officer encouraged Elizabeth and her parents to work with the IEP team to investigate grade-level curriculum and class settings to determine modifications to the general education curriculum and instructional activities, as well as supports and interventions, that would facilitate achievement of her short- and long-term goals. Several steps were completed in relation to the involvement of Elizabeth and her parents in making decisions about her educational goals and services needed to be implemented during her transition years and beyond, including:

A. The IEP team directed the special education teacher and/or the district transition specialist to work with Elizabeth and her parents to develop Elizabeth's plan for transitioning to adult life, ensuring that it reflects self-determination and person-centered planning approaches, as well as the values and vision held by Elizabeth and her parents.

B. Elizabeth, her parents, and the special education teacher and/or the district transition specialist, identified adult service providers to facilitate Elizabeth's desired outcomes, and met to determine how they would create services that match said outcomes.

C. Elizabeth, her parents, the special education teacher and/or the district transition specialist, and adult service providers developed, implemented, and monitored the first steps in a transition plan that matched her desired outcomes.

References

Edwards, C., & Da Fonte, A. (2012). The 5-Point Plan Fostering Successful Partnerships with Families of Students with Disabilities. *Teaching Exceptional Children, 44*(3), 6-13.

Individuals with Disabilities Education Improvement Act Amendments of 2004, Pub. L. No 108-446, 118 Stat. 2647.

Ryndak, D. L., Morrison, A. P., & Sommerstein, L. (1999). Literacy prior to and after inclusion in general education settings. *Journal of the Association for Persons with Severe Handicaps, 24*(1), 5-22.

Ryndak, D. L., Ward, T., Alper, S., Montgomery, J., & Storch, J. F. (2010). Long-term outcomes of services for two persons with significant disabilities with differing educational experiences: A qualitative consideration of the impact of educational experiences. *Education and Training in Autism and Developmental Disabilities, 45*(3), 323-338.

Taylor, S. (2001). Caught in the continuum: a critical analysis of the principle of the least restrictive environment. In D. Fisher & D. L. Ryndak (Eds.), *The foundations of inclusive education; A compendium of articles on effective strategies to achieve inclusive education* (pp.13-25). Baltimore: TASH.13-25. (Reprinted from *Journal of the Association of Severe Handicaps, 13*(1), pp. 41-53, 1988).

Case #25

Katie's Dilemma

Cam Cobb

Introduction

Katie found herself learning a new position and receiving conflicting requests from the Vice-Principal and Principal at her school. It all happened in a whirlwind shortly after New Year—but it all began in September, near the start of her third year with the school board ...

As autumn fast approached, Katie began to prepare for her new position. She set up her classroom, which was a space to provide support to learners with different sorts of needs. While her new role was to focus on special education, Katie would also provide informal support to learners identified with special needs as well as those who have not been identified. She wanted the room to be something more than a room for special education support—she wanted it to be a space for everyone. A sort of drop in. The day after Labour Day, Katie began her first year working as the lead special education teacher at Village Green Community School. Still very early in her career, it was a new world for the young teacher. She had taught Grade 6 the previous year, and Grade 4 the year before that.

Overview/Analysis

Built in the early 1920s, Village Green serves a diverse community in the downtown core of a busy city. The school has over 500 students, 100 of whom were on an Individual Education Plan (IEP). Seventy-five of these students have been identified as learners with exceptionalities through the Province of Ontario's formal identification process—the Identification Placement Review Committee (IPRC).

It is the first day of autumn. Although it is cool outside the sun shines brightly in the cloudless sky. It shines through a small glass ornament that hung on the main office window, casting a bright orange glow on a small section of the floor. It is nearly four o'clock and a bustling Friday was finally winding down at Village Green Community School.

Katie steps into the office. The sign on one of the office doors reads: "Dana Dewey, Vice Principal."

The door is ajar. Gingerly, the young teacher steps forward and gently knocks a few times.

"Do you have a minute?" Katie calls out.

"Of course, Katie. You know, we really appreciate how you've stepped in and taken on your position this year. I knew you could do it and I'm here to help anytime you need it."

Katie smiles. "Thanks. I think now's one of those times."

"Of course. How can I help you?" replies Dana.

Slowly, Katie steps into the room and sits in one of its empty chairs. "It's the meetings for the Individual Education Plans—the IPRC review meetings," she says. "I know these are basically review meetings for all of the students who are on an IEP. And, in the meetings we review things like placement and support."

"Yes."

"Well—I've been in these meetings before, but always as a homeroom teacher. Never as the lead special education teacher at the school. And, now my role is a bit different."

"Of course."

"And—well—it's just ... I'm just not sure how to get everything started. I know I should begin with the Grade 8 students, but there are quite a few to hold."

"Try to get as many parents to come out as possible. Even if the placement or the main content of the IEP isn't going to change. You know, it's always nice to have a chance to talk to parents about a child's learning plan and placement options. Just make sure that you start with the Grade

8 meetings in January because we need to get everyone ready for their high school placement and registration. And, we need to make sure they get the IEP as soon as possible."

Katie nods.

Dana's cellphone rings out and Katie instantly looks at it.

"Sorry," Dana smiles, reassuringly. "Just ignore it." After pausing for a moment, Dana continues, "Anyway, that's my advice. Meeting with parents is one of the most important things we do. So, we need to encourage as many parents to come out as possible. From my experience, it's the best way to approach these IRPC review meetings. When I worked as a special education teacher, and later, as a consultant, that's how I always approached it."

As time passes, Katie settles in to her new position. She approaches her work energetically, and thoroughly.

In December, Ben Windu, the school principal is transferred to another school, and the day before the winter holidays begin, Don Ewing, arrives at Village Green. New to the position, Don sashays around the building, exuberantly announcing to everyone: "Hi, I'm Don Ewing, I'm the rookie in charge here!"

Don Ewing waltzes into Katie's classroom in the late afternoon and introduces himself. Katie is working with a small group of learners on a project they are completing.

"We need to talk about the IPRC reviews," he announces. "I'll come back."

In the rush at the end of the day the two miss one another and throughout the holiday Katie wonders what Don was going to tell her.

Before continuing with Katie's narrative, we might review some of the special education parameters in the province. In Ontario, special education support is a right for those who have been formally identified. And every learner with an exceptionality has an IEP, which sets out the student's placement and learning plan. While IEPs must be updated at regular intervals, the details of the IEP are to be agreed upon by parents (and guardians), teachers, consultants, school administrators, and other school professionals. Schools must hold (or at least offer to hold) an IRPC review meeting every year, which parents may waive if they so choose. These meetings are usually held between January and March.

It is early January and school has just returned from the winter holidays. The days are short and cold. By this point, Katie has been working in special education at the school for four months. And while she knows many of the 75 identified students with an IEP, and she knows some of their parents, there are many students and parents with whom she is unfamiliar.

Katie knows the task that lies before her. First, she needs to determine if parents want to hold an IPRC review meeting for their child. Second, she needs to schedule meetings at times that work for teachers, parents, consultants, psychologists, social workers, and so on. Third, she needs to arrange supply teacher coverage for these meetings. Everyone needs to prepare for each of these meetings so they will be able to discuss the placement and learning plan options for each student. In terms of scheduling, she does not know exactly how to budget, or where to begin.

The following morning Katie steps into the office to retrieve her mail. Don saunters of his office carrying a cup of coffee.

"Oh, Katie, I'm glad I saw you."

"Yes?"

"About those IRPC review meetings."

"Yes?"

"Let me give you some advice, Katie. Well, it's also a plan. Make sure you dissuade parents from coming to these meetings. It costs far too much to pay for all those supply teachers to come in. You need to get as many parents as possible to sign those waiver forms for their meetings. I've only set aside one supply teacher day for your January IRPC review meetings anyway. You know, I may just be a rookie principal, and I may just be new to the school, but I know a tight budget when I see one. And, this is one place where we can save some money for the school. We've got to pull together as a team Katie. I mean, these meetings are all just reviewing things anyway. What do you say?"

Surprised by what she has heard, Katie does not know how to respond. While IPRC review meetings are optional, she never expected to hear what the school's new principal has just said. She glances at the office door feeling uneasy.

Problem Statement

Katie is a beginning teacher at Village Green Community School. She has been tasked with the job of setting up 75 IPRC review meetings. She feels overwhelmed with the task. Don Ewing, the principal at Village Green urged her to dissuade parents from attending these meetings so that less money needs to be spent on supply teachers. Dana Dewey, the vice principal, has recommended that she encourage as many parents as possible to come to these meetings. Katie does not know what to do. What would you recommend?

Discussion Questions

1. What do we know about Katie and her role at Village Green Community School at the start of the story?
2. A new principal comes to Village Green in December. What can we say about the transition the school is currently going through?
3. Katie's Dilemma presents us with a complicated scenario. What are some of the key variables at play?
4. At the end of the narrative, Katie finds herself in a rather tricky situation. How should she respond? Why?

References

Bennett, S., & Dworet, D., with Weber, K. (2013). Special Education in Ontario Schools (7th edition). Niagara-on-the-Lake, ON: Highland Press.

Ong-Dean, C. (2009). Distinguishing Disability: Parents, Privilege, and Special Education. Chicago, IL: University of Chicago Press.

Slee, R. (2011). The Irregular School: Exclusion Schooling, and Inclusive Education. New York, NY: Routledge.

Case #26

Disrupting Expectations:
Challenges to Academic Inclusion in a "College For All" Culture[1]

Michelle J. Bellino & Nathan Phipps

Introduction

This case centers on Adam, a novice teacher of English as a Second Language (ESL) in an urban public school in the US. Many of the students in this class have had fragmented educational experiences in their countries of origin, and possess a wide range of literacy skills in English and their native language of Spanish. Adam struggles to balance everyday teaching responsibilities and classroom management with the desire to be culturally responsive to his students and encourage high aspirations for educational achievement and attainment. When Federico, an older student with erratic attendance and low academic motivation shows up in class, Adam questions his ability to effectively support his students' range of academic, emotional, and personal needs.

---

1   All names have been changed to pseudonyms. This case is based on an amalgam of teaching experiences.

Overview/ Analysis

A few minutes before class began, Adam looked up from his notes and noticed Federico at the door. It was a reunion of sorts when Federico showed up at class, and students rose from their seats to slap hands asking, in Spanish, what he had been up to. "Nice to see you," Adam said, smiling before gesturing to his forehead to signal that Federico remove his hat. Adam had to fight a feeling of slight panic when Federico showed up. On the rare occasions when Federico attended class, there was always a mixture of hope and fear—hope that this was the turning of a new corner and a signal of Federico's own interest in his education, and fear that, as was often the case, his presence would do more to disrupt and distract the class than further Federico or the classes' learning. Adam tried not to take it too personally, when Federico's desk remained empty most days.

Adam was one of several English as a Second Language (ESL) teachers at the school, and most of the students whose families moved mid-year transferred into his intermediate class, the smallest section of ten students. Adam taught reading and writing classes to these students, nearly half of their schedule in a given day. A few months into his first teaching position, Adam was beginning to feel close to these students, gaining a sense of their academic strengths and areas for improvement, as well as their unique talents and aspirations. There was Elvis, who had meticulous handwriting and recorded music in the school's modest studio after class; Miguel, who called him Mister and arrived early every morning; José, who had lost a limb to cancer and was easily distracted by drawing abstract tattoo designs in the margins of his notebook; and Blanca, the only female student in the class, who loved fashion magazines and often copied her friends' written assignments in hopes of impressing Adam with the right answer.

Adam was also building relationships with his students' families and deepening his sense of their lives outside of school. Often working through a translator, Adam's conversations with family members helped him understand that many of his students had fragmented experiences with school in their countries and communities of origin. In some cases, students had been chronically absent in order to contribute to the family income, or they had taken turns with siblings attending school sequentially, so that one child was always available to help at home. In other cases it was the teachers who had erratic attendance and little professional training. Some students endured strenuous travel to arrive at a school that was insecure, under-resourced, or in some cases even toxic. Now living in the U.S., some students and their families were content to be attending a school with a consistent schedule, trained teachers, and sufficient curricular resources. Others resented that they had been assigned to a school the state considered "failing," openly questioning their prospects for post-graduation education and employment.

At school-community events, parents often lamented that they could not be more helpful with their children's schooling and sought Adam's advice on films, songs, and books that would enrich their English language learning experiences. Federico's uncle was one of the only family members Adam had been unable to connect with. Adam left a dozen messages on what he presumed was Federico's Uncle Julio's cell phone and had made contact once, only to discover that Julio felt Federico was an adult and could make his own decisions about whether and when to attend school.

Federico struggled academically. But unlike other students in Adam's ESL classes, Federico had rudimentary literacy skills coupled with what seemed like low aspirations to improve them. On most days, Federico could hardly produce a coherent sentence in English without his classmates' assistance translating, a now routine interaction that Adam felt he had little control over. When Adam insisted that Federico complete his thought on his own, Federico grew frustrated and lashed out, or gave up, and explained he did not want to be bothered. Federico's writing was among the poorest Adam had seen, misspelled words strung together with little attention to sentence structure. Federico wrote small letters in light pencil, hardly legible, as if hoping Adam would fill in missing letters and words.

Much of this was not Federico's fault. At age twenty, Federico was one of the oldest students at the school, five or six years older than most students in the intermediate ESL section. Every student in the section was born in Puerto Rico or the Dominican Republic, comprising two of the largest student populations at the school. Federico was born in

El Salvador and moved to the US to live with his uncle and cousins. He already had a part-time job at an auto shop and occasionally missed school for work. Federico had only been at the school for a year but was already notorious. He had a reputation for being combative with teachers, and even the most experienced teachers were anxious that they "get him out of here," in part because teachers wanted to avoid legal implications if he began dating fellow students.

By the time Federico took a seat, Adam had mentally walked through the plan for the day and noted he would need to adapt several tasks since Federico had missed a number of prior classes and had unlikely read the assigned chapter. He would have the students work in groups, as planned, but spend additional time getting Federico up to speed. Perhaps he would have to walk him through a few of the exercises from earlier in the week before having him join in the group activity. Despite the difficulty of planning for Federico's sporadic attendance, Adam understood that he needed to do his best to support Federico's learning when he did come to school.

Adam was conscious that other teachers had given up on Federico. It wasn't that they had not tried, but that they had tried and failed again and again. Federico was on a short list of students of high concern to the school leaders, and Adam had even heard of one teacher who intentionally tried to provoke students like Federico so that when they crossed the line the school had grounds to expel them. Though it seemed naive, Adam could not fight the feeling that he could have a different relationship with Federico—he was new to the school and the profession, he was the only male ESL teacher, and he shared Federico's love for baseball—what if Federico grew to trust Adam in a way that he had not trusted other teachers?

Federico was seventeen when he left El Salvador and spent at least a year in the US not enrolled in school. The stories about the conditions that drove him to leave his parents and three sisters behind were not entirely clear, but Adam knew about the escalating violent crime in El Salvador and pieced together that Federico fled aggressive gang recruitment efforts. Adam supposed other students knew some of these details as well, as he was beginning to detect divisions among Hispanic students who identified Central Americans as "más thug" (more thug) than those from the Caribbean or elsewhere.

Just as students were getting to work on the group activity, Federico let out a sigh and mumbled something across the room in a low voice. All eyes were on Federico as he and Blanca exchanged what sounded like insults in Spanish. Adam called the class to attention, but to everyone's amusement both students raised their voices and the exchange continued as if Adam were not in the room at all. Federico routinely disrupted Blanca during class activities. Blanca's attendance was only slightly better than Federico's, so their clashes were infrequent, though Adam suspected that Federico's treatment was influencing Blanca's own interest in attending class. Federico glared at Blanca. Blanca turned in her seat to face him, thrust an insult, then swung back around to avoid his gaze. Adam struggled to gain control. He moved to the center of the room, waving his hands, asking for students to "please quiet down," and requesting that they work on expressing themselves in English.

Adam's high school Spanish skills were a distant memory at this point, but some words were coming back to him. He distinctly heard the word for "slut," affirming his suspicions that Federico's taunts were abusive and targeted towards Blanca as the only female in the class. At this, Blanca stood up, pushed her chair in, and stormed out of the room. Federico locked eyes with Adam and asked, still agitated, "you gonna call?". Calling the school's support staff or one of the deans was supposed to be a last resort to handle classroom management issues. Adam considered it a defeat, both professional and personal, each time he hit that button on the classroom wall to call the front office and request assistance. He knew it would not help this time. Federico would settle down. Adam would "write him up" later, documenting the incident and submitting it to the dean as he had at least a half-dozen times before.

At the beginning of the school year, students moved their desks into a circle and Adam talked openly about the value of education in shaping one's future. He was aware of the disparity between his own schooling experiences and theirs. Adam was white and a native English speaker. But he wanted his students to know that he was the first in his family to attend college. It was a lecture he had been honing for some time, knowing he wanted to serve a population that had historically not been granted equitable or inclusive educational opportunities. He also knew many of his students would be the first in their families to complete high school. Drawing on statistics of income disparities across levels of educational attainment, Adam encouraged students to consider pursuing university and to see the role of education in opening up future opportunities. He felt responsible for helping his students understand the bigger picture of inequity and how it mapped onto education. But he was starting to feel ambivalent about this message, which placed unequivocal value on higher education in a way that seemed to undercut conversations about vocational skills or job training that might better align with students' employment opportunities and longer-term interests. Federico had suggested this in some of their conversations, and Adam was beginning to wonder if a student like Federico did not require a different type of motivation to succeed but a different type of education. Immediately after entertaining this thought, Adam worried that he was falling into the trap of conveying lower expectations for a student who did not conform to the norms that traditional U.S. schools demanded.

So much of what Adam had learned in his teaching preparation courses did not seem to apply to his classroom. When would he find the time to author his own curriculum, which would integrate community service and foster meaningful links to the students' home communities? He could not even get all of his students in class on the same day. Surely there was no chance of Federico learning if he was not present, but when he showed up everyone else seemed to suffer. On some days it seemed like the best Adam could do was keep Federico out of trouble.

Problem Statement

Adam's commitments to social justice have always translated into a belief that more and better education, especially for underserved populations, is key to transforming individuals and society, but how can we provide an inclusive, relevant, and appropriate educational experience to students for whom school is not seen as a path to academic or economic success?

Adam's primary goal as an educator has been conveying high expectations for all students' academic achievement and potential. But he was beginning to question the feasibility and utility of "college for all" as the envisioned future for all of his students. Even if formal education provided upward mobility for some individuals in his class, he was uncertain "whether success for all of them was a social possibility: was there, in fact, enough 'success' to go around" (Nygreen, 2013, p. 4)? Nygreen calls for a shift in educational attention from the "achievement gap" to the "consequence gap," where poor, working-class, non-native, and nonwhite students suffer "disproportionate economic consequences of educational underachievement" (p. 171). Linking educational and economic justice, Anyon (2014) cautions, "we have been counting on education to solve the problems of unemployment, joblessness, and poverty for many years. But education did not cause the problems, and education cannot solve them" (p. 5). For this reason, she urges that educational policy expand beyond school walls, into the social, political, and economic systems that create and reproduce inequities. In the case of Adam's students, it seemed that educational policy would need to account for economic justice, the politics of global migration, and the discrimination that so often relegated immigrants to subordinate social positions. How can Adam as an individual teacher enact social justice in his classroom while recognizing the structural inequities within educational systems and practices, as well as the social, political, and economic contexts in which schools are embedded? What tensions underlie the discourse of "college for all," and what harms might there be in conveying higher education as the future aspiration and vehicle for socioeconomic advancement for all students?

Case problems/ Discussion questions

1. How can Adam communicate and demonstrate care towards Federico?
2. How should Adam address the various types of diversity in his class in a way that supports all students?
3. For a number of struggling students, we might ask: What do they need? When do they need it? And why didn't they get it? How

can we apply these questions to Federico?
4. In what ways might Federico's migration experience have contributed to the challenges he faces in school?
5. What kinds of structures, activities, or dialogues could the school put in place to better support students like Federico, as well as teachers like Adam?
6. How can Adam understand and encourage his students' future aspirations and support them in confronting potential challenges to realizing those aspirations?

Teaching Strategies

Consider the intrinsic and extrinsic motivators that can be activated in order to encourage students to "buy in" to their own academic success. Discuss which of these strategies Adam may or may not have tried and how you might approach them in your own classroom context.

Reflect on how your particular school thinks about college-going. How and where are these messages conveyed? To what extent do they serve all students? What alternatives, if any, are presented to pursuing higher education? Consider what kinds of changes could be made at your school level, community level, and national level.

Consider whether learning more about students' prior educational experiences might help inform your understanding of their current dispositions toward school. What kind of information is relevant? How might you gather it?

Investigate what Nygreen (2013) calls the "consequence gap" within the U.S. Explore average salaries amongst those who have attended some high school, completed high school, pursued some postsecondary education, and those who have completed higher education programs. What kinds of disparities emerge? Now explore income disparities sorted by race, parental education, and native/ non-native status. What patterns do you see?

References

Anyon, J. (2014). Radical possibilities: Public policy, urban education, and a new social movement. (2nd ed.) New York: Routledge.

Nygreen, K. (2013). These kids: Identity, agency, and social justice at a last chance high school. Chicago: University of Chicago Press.

Case #27

Hum ... Social Justice? But the School is Doing Well!

Jhonel Morvan

Introduction

A Caucasian Vice-Principal, Mrs. Black, from a very diverse high school in the Greater Toronto Area (GTA), questions the reasons why most Black students are enrolled predominantly in applied, college, or workplace preparation mathematics courses in her school. She uses her experience in issues pertaining to social justice and culturally relevant leadership (Horsford, Grosland, and Gunn, 2011) to convince her colleagues to look at the hard facts. She is met with denial and resistance from some teachers and parents, who even conspire to get her transferred to another school. This case study examines the various school leaders' perspectives, as well as the reactions from teachers and a specific group of students and parents.

Overview

C. W. McArthur Collegiate (CWMC) is a very diverse high school in the Greater Toronto Area (GTA). The half-century old school has been very successful over the last decade or so, at all provincial levels, in its school-run basketball and soccer programs. On the academic side, CWMC offers the International Baccalaureate (IB) as an option to some of its 950 students. Most of its elite athletes are Black students aspiring to get scholarships to, or get recruited to play in, Division I or II college programs in the United States. Every year two or three students realize this dream. On the other hand, the IB program is predominantly taken by White and Asian students and their admission to elite schools in Canada or the Unites States is a regular occurrence.

The school population is as diverse as the city of Toronto, where, according to the newly-released data from Canada's 2016 census, 51.5 per cent of the population say they belong to a visible minority. In 2011, the percentage was 47. CWMC not only gets its students from the neighbouring feeding schools but also from other surrounding areas outside of the school busing limits. However, the teaching staff at CWMC does not reflect the faces of the current student population. In fact, even though 45% of the students are of Caribbean and African descent, less than 10% of the teaching personnel share similar origins. The school administration is mostly of European descent, except for one administrative assistant who is from Mauritius. All the custodians, except for the head of caretaking, Mr. Boisvert, are of African descent.

CWMC's teachers are very proud of their school. The vast majority of them have been on staff for more than 10 years. In most cases, subject matters have been taught by the same set of teachers for years. They have seen different principals come and go, have built great relationships with some specific groups of parents, and have dictated to a large extent the culture of the school. Talking about a principal who wanted to implement some changes five years ago, Mr. Beatty, the history teacher, commented, "he has been here for three years now, his days are basically counted." They have always made it clear that the teachers have each other's backs. The school union representative is also very powerful, and is well acquainted with provincial union representatives.

Mr. Anderson, the Principal, has been at CWMC for close to 5 years. For the most part, he has built great relationships with the staff and the parents. He is considering retiring in one or two years. Mrs. Black, a Caucasian vice-principal with some experience in issues pertaining to social justice and culturally relevant leadership, has been at the school since last year. Earlier in her career, and as a Caucasian person, she had never felt compelled by social justice issues. But after reading *Restacking the Deck: Streaming by Class, Race and Gender in Ontario Schools* by Clandfield, D., Curtis, B., Galabuzi, G., San Vincente, A., Livinstone, D.W., Smaller, H. (2014), she started to think more seriously about social issues in education. At the beginning of her second year at CWMC, she began to question the *status quo*. She noticed, through data analysis for the school improvement plan, that most of the struggling students were Black. As she dug deeper, she also found out that 90% of Black students in mathematics classes were in the applied, college or workplace preparation streams. After struggling with the findings for a while, she decided to engage the rest of the administration in some courageous conversations. Once she convinced the other school administrators that something needed to change, they agreed to meet with the school improvement team. In addition to the Principal and the Vice-Principal, the team consisted of the Guidance Counselor, Mrs. Holmes, the Special Education Resource Teacher (SERT), Ms. Whittaker, the Mathematics Department Head, Mr. Ross, and the Student Success Teacher, Mrs. Applewood. The first meeting went very well, but Ms. Whittaker, Mr. Ross, and Mrs. Applewood were skeptical about Mrs. Black's intentions. In their view, their school was very successful in providing differentiated pathways to the school's diverse clientele.

Two weeks later, the superintendent, Mr. Brown, was invited by the principal to attend the second meeting with the school improvement team. The Vice-Principal set the context for the meeting. She pointed to everyone's moral obligation as educators to offer every student the best path to success. They all agreed that there were urgent equity issues that needed their attention. They spent the first hour or so looking at the data together, and quickly came to the realization that Black and First Nations students were disproportionately represented in special education programs at the school. These students were subjected to higher suspension and expulsion rates, and were more likely to have less access to rigorous courses and programs. Also, their graduation rates, as well as their admissions rates to university programs, were far lower than their Asian or Caucasian peers. These findings justified a call for action from everyone involved.

The improvement team seemed to have a better understanding of the concerns raised by Mrs. Black. As a team, they made the decision to select the most urgent underlying issues in order to better focus their interventions. Among other things, they chose to have the whole school project anchored in the three following pillars:

1. Reducing the 40-point percentage gap between students' achievement in Grade 9 applied and academic math courses;
2. Promoting better representation of the school population in the IB programs and in all academic and pre-university courses from Grade 9 to Grade 12; and
3. Increasing the graduation rates, within 4 years, of racialized and traditionally marginalized groups (Black and First Nations students).

They quickly realized that changes within these priority areas would not happen on their own, nor would they happen quickly, and so they brainstormed about ways forward. The leadership team, including the Supervisory Officer (SO) for CWMC, discussed establishing a more caring school culture. They created a plan to foster more family and community engagement through a more focused leadership style. The school administrators saw it fit to introduce their plan to the school personnel in their upcoming full staff meeting, the second of the year. The plan emphasized the need to hold high expectations, and to ensure access to high-quality curriculum and instruction—mostly in mathematics and science—for all students.

School leaders also discussed the need to allow adequate time for students to learn. They made it clear that appropriate emphasis will be put on differentiated processes that broaden Black and First Nations students' productive engagement with core subject areas. They also made the commitment to make strategic use of human and material resources for the betterment of the school.

After the meeting, Mr. Ross, who is both the mathematics department head and the union representative for CWMC, became very concerned. He decided, informally, to double-check with the SERT and the Student Success Teacher to make sure his worries were shared. Mrs.

Holmes and Mrs. Applewood were on the fence about the plan, but were convinced by Mr. Ross to spread the news that the upcoming changes could have a devastating impact on their school climate. Several informal hallway meetings and phone calls took place in the weeks leading up to the staff meeting. Most teachers made up their mind before they even had a chance to hear what the administration had to say about the new directions. The beginning of a toxic atmosphere started setting in before the staff meeting even occurred.

Once the staff meeting took place, Mrs. Black and Mr. Anderson made a convincing case for the need to change the school culture. They strategically and tactfully used data analysis to try and bring the teachers on board. The reaction from the teaching staff was somewhat mixed. Teachers who had been in the school for less than five years or so were generally supportive of the administration. The more experienced teachers, who had been in the school for longer period of time, were for the most part very hesitant and suspicious. After the meeting, they openly started a rumor that Mrs. Black wanted to change everything in the school because she was positioning herself to replace the principal once he retired. It became clear there was no consensus at the end of the meeting.

The school improvement plan had been launched, but the teaching personnel remained divided. The plan focused on mathematics and science achievement, in addition to course selections and graduation rates for all students. It included promising practices and strategies that were identified by the improvement team. Most teachers were not on board, but the administration still chose to pursue the implementation of their plan. Despite the open and transparent leadership style of the school administrators, they managed to get barely any traction to get the project going. In the midst of it all, some of the most disenfranchised groups of students started complaining about high expectations. They admitted that they did not understand why they had to deal with the added pressure of high expectations. They questioned what was in it for them. They believed they were getting mixed messages from teachers and administrators. Most of these students had become very comfortable with the way they had been treated, and the expectations that had previously been communicated. They had come to accept their realities as the norm.

Small progress was being made early in the second semester, as more and more underserved students were enrolled in high-quality mathematics and science courses. Some students and teachers were concerned that this move may lower the caliber of their courses, and hence the standards of the school. These students, mostly White, were encouraged by a few teachers to talk to their parents about their discomfort. These concerns got to the ears of some prominent parents, who were not too pleased about their kids taking the same classes as some so-called troublemakers. After multiple complaints to the SO, several parents started a push to get Mrs. Black transferred to another school. The superintendent was puzzled by their demand, given his knowledge of the case, and asked to meet with them.

Status Report

Mr. Brown asked the school to set a meeting with the dissenting parents. In addition to the Principal and the Vice-Principal, the school council was invited to join the meeting as well. The school leaders set the tone for the meeting by stating how important student and parent voices are for the whole school community. They offered the parents an opportunity to make their case and explain why they were concerned about the changes. Most of the exchange was very cordial. The leadership seized the opportunity to try to get the parents on board. Using provincial, district, and school data analysis, Mrs. Black made a compelling case for equity and social justice at CWMC. She made it clear that equity will not be at the expense of excellence. The superintendent reassured all the parents that they are all in it for the well-being and successful future of each and every student. Some of the dissidents did not hide their doubt and left the meeting abruptly, visibly unsatisfied.

Questions

1. The Principal seems to be absent in this case study. How could Mr. Anderson play a more important role?
2. How did school administrators handle teachers' concerns?
3. What could school administrators have done to better handle parents' concerns?
4. What should the school leaders have done to better engage students and teachers in the change process in order to take their voices into account?
5. The 2013 revised Ontario Leadership Framework (OLF) states that, "The demographic and contextual diversity in Ontario schools, together with the province's commitment to high levels of student achievement and well-being, have heightened the importance of effective leadership in schools and districts led by leaders who support diverse student needs by providing caring, safe, respectful and engaging learning environments" (p. 5). Reflect on how the educational leaders of CWMC fit the bill relative to the OLF.
6. Talking about effective school leadership, Leithwood, Day, Sammons, Harris, and Hopkins (2006) refer to "four broad categories of practices identified in research summaries: setting directions, developing people, redesigning the organization, and managing the instructional (teaching and learning) programme" (pp. 18-19). How do these categories align with Mrs. Black's actions?
7. One seminal work in the area of inequities in school practices in Ontario is *Restacking the Deck: Streaming by Class, Race and Gender in Ontario Schools (2014)*. Besides streaming, what other issues does this case study raise for you as an educational leader?
8. How do you think school leaders from CWMC understand culturally responsive leadership?
9. What does this case study reveal about relationship building as a means of promoting cultural responsiveness? What could the school administration have done better in terms of engagement and relationship building?

10. What are some of the issues of equity and social justice raised by this case study?
11. What does this case study say about the leadership style of the Superintendent, the Principal, or the Vice-Principal?
12. Edgar Schein in his seminal work on organizational culture and leadership argues for the need to equip individual in organizations to collaborate and work together in very diverse and multicultural settings (Schein & Schein, 2017). Based on the classical work of Edgar Schein on organizational culture and his argument that leadership and culture are fundamentally intertwined, what are some of the mistakes committed by the different stakeholders?

References

Clandfield, D., Curtis, B., Galabuzi, G., San Vincente, A., Livinstone, D.W., Smaller, H. (2014). *Restacking the Deck: Streaming by Class, Gender and Race in Ontario Schools*. Canadian Centre for Policy Alternatives. Ottawa.

Horsford, S., Grosland, T., & Gunn, K. M. (2011). Pedagogy of the personal and professional: Toward a framework for culturally relevant leadership.

Leithwood, K., Day, C., Sammons, P., Harris, A., & Hopkins, D. (2006). *Successful school leadership: What it is and how it influences student learning*. Research Report 800. London, UK: Department for Education.

Schein, E. H., & Schein, P. (2017). *Organizational culture and leadership*. Hoboken, New Jersey: John Wiley and Sons, Inc.

The Institute for Education Leadership (2013). The Ontario leadership framework: *A School and System Leader's Guide to Putting Ontario's Leadership Framework into Action*.

Case #28

Nang Tat's New Life

Troy Boddy

Introduction

Nang Tat, a tall, thin, 13-year-old, male, English as a Second Language speaker (ESOL), arrived in the United States to live with his parents and a younger brother whom he has never met. Nang Tat was left to live with his grandmother as a baby in a small village in China while his mother and father came to the United States to start a business. Upon his arrival, his parents took him to the International Student Office to enroll him in school. It was decided to place him in 5th grade even though he was middle-school age. Nang Tat was an excellent student in his small rural school in China. Nang Tat's transition to living with his family was not an easy one. He felt alone with a family and sibling he did not know, as well as being in a new school where he did not speak the language, know the customs, and was older than the other students.

Overview/Analysis

Principal Hopkins sat at his desk after another busy day running one of the biggest elementary schools in his district. He glanced up to see Mrs. Hernandez, a fifth-grade teacher, and Mr. Axer, an ESOL teacher. Mr. Hopkins could see by the looks on their faces that they had a something to share. Mrs. Hernandez cleared her throat and said, "Nang Tat had a rough first day." Mr. Axer added, "We set him up with a partner who spoke Mandarin, and he told the student that he hated school and he was stupid." Mrs. Hernandez shared how he refused to do any work and would not move from his seat when the class was asked to come to the carpet. Mr. Axer said that after much cajoling he was able to get him to come to his ESOL class. Mr. Axer said he did not interact with the other kids, and when they tried to help him out, he yelled at them. Mr. Hopkins replied, "We need to come up with a plan to make sure that tomorrow is better." "Do you all have any thoughts?" Mrs. Hernandez added, "Maybe you and Mr. Axer can meet him at the door and check in with him before he comes to class." Mr. Hopkins replied, "That might help him to feel more comfortable." Mr. Axer added, "We might want to reach out to Mrs. Chen, the ESOL counselor, to join us so she can translate for us." The team decided to go with the plan and invite Mrs. Chen to join them in the morning.

The team assembled in the morning and waited for Nang Tat to get off the bus. Nang Tat entered the main entrance, totally ignoring his younger brother who was trying to show him the way to his classroom. Upon seeing the team waiting at the entrance, Nang Tat got an angry look on his face and tried to walk past them and go to class. Mrs. Chen asked him to come over in Mandarin several times before he stopped and listened to her. Nang Tat seemed to relax as he heard Mrs. Chen speak to him in his language. She introduced herself to him, and Nang Tat responded. Mrs. Chen asked him if he wanted to get breakfast and talk. Nang nodded his head, and they went into the cafeteria, which was just around the corner; when they emerged Mrs. Chen asked Mr. Hopkins if she could use the conference room to speak with Nang Tat. Mr. Hopkins said of course and walked the two to the conference room. They came back out after about an hour and Mrs. Chen and Mr. Hopkins walked Nang Tat to class. Nang Tat entered the classroom, and Mrs. Hernandez greeted him and communicated to Nang Tat what the class was doing. Mrs. Chen translated the instructions after which Nang Tat reluctantly joined his group.

Mr. Hopkins and Mrs. Chen walked back to the office from the fifth-grade wing. As they walked, Mrs. Chen shared highlights from her conversation. Mrs. Chen said that Nang Tat was very angry about leaving his grandmother to come and live with his parents. To him, his grandmother was the only family he has known, and now he is here in the U.S. living with parents he doesn't know. On top of that he has a younger brother who makes fun of him because he doesn't speak English or know anything about popular American culture. After school, he and his brother go to their parent's restaurant and stay in the office and do their homework. He said they often don't leave for home until very late and then, on top of not wanting to be here, he is tired. He is also older than his classmates and doesn't like being in class with what he calls babies. Mr. Hopkins and Mrs. Chen decided they should reach out to the family to make a connection and share the conversation that Mrs. Chen had with Nang Tat. Mr. Hopkins wondered if they were having similar challenges at home.

Over the next several days Nang Tat's behavior remained the same. Mrs. Hernandez tried her best to win him over. She tried to use visuals to help communicate directions and to see how he was feeling. She could tell Nang Tat was very smart, but he wanted no part of school. The students in the class tried to include him in the activities, but he just ignored them. Mr. Axer used everything he knew about working with newcomers to make him feel welcomed, but nothing was working. Mrs. Chen finally was able to reach Nang Tat's mother. She said she was not surprised by his behavior because they saw the same thing at home. She said she felt like her son hated her. Mrs. Chen set up a time when it was convenient for Nang Tat's mother to come in to meet with us. In the meantime his struggles continued; Nang Tat was sent to the office at least twice a day. Mr. Hopkins had never seen Mrs. Hernandez lose her patience with a student before.

One morning Mr. Hopkins had an idea. He remembered that the keyboard on his tablet could be switched to other languages. He also had a translation program on it for when he traveled out of the country. He remembered that Nang Tat was fluent in reading and writing Mandarin, so he thought he would try to communicate with Nang Tat using this technology. He called Nang Tat down to the office to check in with him. Nang came into the office, and Mr. Hopkins signaled him to sit at the round table that sat in the center of his office. Nang Tat was curious about the tablet.

Mr. Hopkins typed, "How are you today?" The translation program did its thing and translated it into Mandarin. Nang Tat actually smiled. Mr. Hopkins slid the tablet over to Nang Tat, and he typed back, "I am well." Mr. Hopkins asked a few more questions, and let Nang Tat know they wanted to help him and how smart everyone thinks he is.

Finally, a breakthrough. Mr. Hopkins shared his discovery that they can communicate with him with Mrs. Hernandez and Mr. Axer.

Problem Statement

The small step forward was short lived: the next day Mr. Hopkins administrative secretary came rushing in to let him know Mrs. Hernandez had to evacuate the class from the room because Nang Tat was throwing chairs and books. When Mr. Hopkins got to the room, it was in shambles. Nang Tat stood in the corner of the room. He was shaking, and it was evident that he had been crying. Mr. Hopkins wondered what they were going to do to support Nang Tat. He had intentionally placed him in Mrs. Hernandez class because she was able to connect with and teach the most challenging students, but even she was at her wit's end. With the language barrier and the emotional challenges Nang Tat was going through, this was going to be a long road—but they only had until June to help him settle in before he left for middle school.

Case Questions

School systems across the country have elevated the need to demonstrate cultural proficiency in the way in which they interact with students and families.

1. How does the lack of or the demonstration of cultural proficiency affect the ability to know your culture and how it impacts others in order to create a better understanding of people different then you play out in this case?
2. Should the International Student Placement office had placed a

13-year-old in a class with 11-year-olds? What might have been guiding factors in making this decision?
3. With the complexity of Nang Tat's challenges, how should the school prioritize for him?
4. What are some of the missed opportunities the principal, classroom teacher, ESOL teacher, and ESOL counselor could have implemented to better support Nang Tat?
5. In framing the parent meeting with Nang Tat's parents how would you do this in a culturally responsive manner? What are some of the additional questions would be important to ask during the meeting?
6. Nang Tat is two years older than his peers; how could the school support him to create friendships at school?

Teaching Strategies

Everything ESL http://www.everythingesl.net/

English Learner Portal https://englishlearnerportal.teachable.com

National Education Association http://www.nea.org/tools/30402.htm

National Association of Elementary School Principals https://www.naesp.org/communicator-august-2015/5-elements-cultural-proficiency

Colorin Colorado ttp://www.colorincolorado.org/article/social-and-emotional-needs-middle-and-high-school-ells

Center for Applied linguistics http://www.cal.org/what-we-do/projects/newcomer

Case #29

A Question of Gender Dysphoria in a Preschool Age Child

Camille Quinton

This case highlights challenges that arose around gender identity, gender expression, language acquisition, and parental discord.

Overview

Mason lived in a small town of 6,000 people. He was 3 years old when his mother enrolled him in pre-kindergarten. At this time his parents were in the midst of a divorce, and embroiled in a volatile custody battle.

Approximately 10 months later, Mason's mom told school staff that her son wanted to be a girl and to be identified by a female name, and began dressing him in female clothing. Mason's dad disagreed and felt that the mom was pushing her agenda on Mason to bring more attention to herself.

Mason

Mason was registered in the pre-kindergarten program in January. On the registration form, his mom indicated that she had custody of Mason. She indicated that there was a restraining order in place, and provided no contact information for the dad. As per district regulations, the school requested that his mom provide a copy of the custody agreement, which actually showed that custody was shared.

Mason was placed in Mr. Johnson's junior kindergarten classroom with the other 3- and 4-year-old children, and attended two mornings a week. Mr. Johnson was aware that Mason had severe delays in both expressive and receptive language and had experienced some behavioral challenges at his previous preschool. Mason fit in nicely with the other children, and although he did have a few incidents of hitting, yelling and pushing, the behaviors were not anything Mr. Johnson was concerned about. By the end of the third week, Mason had adjusted to the rules and routines of the classroom and was just another kid.

Mason's Individual Program Plan (IPP) transferred with him, and the school called his mom in to review it in early February. To address his language delays the school was requesting permission for speech therapy services. As there was shared custody, consent of both parents was required. When asked for Dad's contact information, Mom stated that she did not have any way to contact him. She then became confrontational, claiming the school did not know her son. She began talking about Mason's behavior, and demanded that the school document and date any incidents so she could "prove to the Crown that Mason needs help due to his dad". The school had nothing to share at that point.

After the school was able to obtain contact information, Dad came in to review the IPP and discuss speech-language supports. He was very supportive of Mason receiving in-school assistance, but expressed concern over additional testing being done, explaining that his "mom was always trying to find something wrong with Mason". He also provided clarification that the restraining order was actually against the mom, rather than the dad as the school had been led to believe. These revelations left school staff wary of the mom's intent.

Over the summer, his dad was given primary custody of Mason. Due to the nature of Dad's work, he was unable to take Mason to school in the morning. The courts determined that Mason would be dropped off at his mother's, and she would be responsible for getting him to school. In September, Mason, now 4, returned to Mr. Johnson's class, attending every morning. Mr. Johnson did not notice any changes in Mason from the previous school year.

At the beginning of October, Mason was unexpectedly absent from school. After a week of unexplained absence, the school contacted Mom. Mom reported that Mason had experienced a breakdown earlier that week, asking when *her penis* fell off and screaming that he wanted to cut off his own penis. Unable to get him to calm down, she took him to the local hospital and had him admitted. She stated that he was sent to the Children's Hospital to be evaluated for *gender dysphoria*. She indicated that he would be absent for another couple of weeks, requesting a meeting prior to his return.

At the meeting, Mason's mom provided a letter from a Pediatric Endocrinologist who specialized in transgendered individuals. It was clearly stated that the letter was being written at the mother's request and that the diagnosis of gender dysphoria **had not been confirmed**. The diagnosis was challenging to make in a child this age and required assessment by mental health experts trained in the area. He summarized that Mom reported that Mason was now saying he wanted to be a female, to have opportunities to play and dress in the role of a female, and to be called Owlette[1]. Key points to support his care were provided. Noticeably absent was the father.

Mason arrived for his first day back wearing a white dress with pants underneath. He asked for a "Mason shirt" so he could change out of the dress. No additional clothes were in his backpack. Over the next month and a half, Mason arrived at school dressed in stereotypically female gender clothes – pinks and purples with hearts, kittens etc. Mason often told school staff that he didn't want to wear the clothes he was sent in; however, despite repeated requests, no male gender clothes were provided by the mother. During this time Mason's choice of name was inconsistent, but as time went on he more consistently chose Owlette.

When it came time to sign the IPP in November, Mason's dad inquired about the clothing Mason wore to school. When told what Mason was wearing, his dad expressed concern that the mom was not allowing Mason to choose which gender of clothes he wanted to wear. He then explained that Mason's official diagnosis was *Unspecified Anxiety Disorder*. As this was not in the original letter, or disclosed by Mom, a new letter of diagnosis was required. Dad signed the consent form that day, but Mom refused, changing her story to say that Mason had never seen the doctor at Children's Hospital.

Around Christmas, Mom told school staff she was scared because the court-ordered psychologist had recommended Mason be called by his birth name and she was scared this might "drive him to harm himself ... that he might try and cut off his penis! The school is supposed to be a safe place, but I guess it's not". She said that she was being portrayed to the courts as "brainwashing and mentally ill." Court-mandated parent counseling also began, and stressed that in order to protect Mason/Owlette's mental health, the parents would need to communicate on issues such as: what name to use when addressing the child; his/her clothing choices; how to respond to anxiety, anger and aggression; and appropriate discipline practices.

By early January, Mason's behavior changed dramatically. He was visibly agitated and began making statements to Mr. Johnson and other school staff such as: "I hate Dad. He's crossed the line. He's bad!"; "The boss says you have to call me Owlette"; "I'm supposed to hate you. You're a liar!" Often he would become aggressive, pushing or hitting the staff members and yelling "My mom told me to scream if you call me Mason".

Throughout that spring, many things happened that caused Mr. Johnson to have doubts as to the validity of *Mason's* desire to be a girl, or whether Mason even understood the difference between genders. Mason always chose typically male costumes during dress up time, even though there were princess and fairy costumes available. On one instance Mason pointed across the room at a male student saying "I know her. I've been to her house before", and shortly after pointed to a female student and said: "I'm scared of him." On a separate occasion, Mason was playing with a pair of anatomically correct dolls. As he opened the diaper to change the male doll, Mason pointed to the penis and, genuinely curious, asked Mr. Johnson, "what's that?"

As the year progressed, the Court became more heavily involved. When unhappy with decisions by the court, Mason's mom garnered the support of the transgender community and took her cause to the media. The case continues unsettled to this day.

Problem Statement

Staff at the school found it challenging to figure out how to best support the student and address the demands from each of the parents. In answering the questions below, consider how your answers may change whether you were the school principal or the classroom teacher.

Discussion Questions

1. Upon learning that the restraining order was against the mom, school staff were forced to reflect on assumptions they had made during their initial conversations with Mom and recognized that they had an impact on early decisions. Reviewing the case as presented:
    a. What biases may have come into play?
    b. How might these have influenced the initial decisions made by school staff?
    c. How would you guide your staff so that they did not fall into a similar bias as the teachers/administrators in the school?
2. At various times throughout this case, red flags were raised as to the authenticity of the mother's reports and intent, as well as whether Mason truly understood the differences between a male and a female. In fact, Mr. Johnson reflected that his impression of Mason's confusion stemmed more from "indoctrination as opposed to self-fulfillment."
    a. Identify these flags and discuss how the school reacted to them.
    b. Did the school respond appropriately? Why/why not?
    c. Were there flags the school missed?
    d. If you were to find yourself in this situation, what might you have done the same as the school, and what might you have done differently? Be prepared to explain your reasoning.
3. School staff found themselves trapped within their mandate to educate the child, the conflicting wishes of the parents, the

parenting specialists, doctors, special interest groups, the political climate of the day, the rulings of the courts, and ultimately the desires of the child. Starting where this story ends, and taking into consideration the stakeholders involved in this case, create a plan to guide the school in moving forward. Ensure you are being culturally and gender sensitive while keeping the best interests of the child in mind.

4. At the beginning of the case, Mason was identified as having severe delays in both expressive (making himself understood) and receptive (understanding what others say) language. In looking back on how this unfolded,
    a. Would Mason have had the language capability to express the thoughts attributed to him? e.g., "I want to cut off my penis."
    b. Would he have been able to understand the questions and requests asked of him? e.g., "Do you want to be a girl or a boy?"

References

American College of Pediatricians. Gender Dysphoria in Children. Aug 2016. Available at: https://www.acpeds.org/the-college-speaks/position-statements/gender-dysphoria-in-children Accessed Jan 21, 2017

American College of Pediatricians – Position Statement -Gender Ideology Harms Children (Jan 2017). Available at: https://www.acpeds.org/the-college-speaks/position-statements/gender-ideology-harms-children Accessed Feb 2, 2017

American Psychiatric Association. What is Gender Dysphoria Feb, 2016. Available at https://www.psychiatry.org/patients-families/gender-dysphoria/what-is-gender-dysphoria Accessed Feb 2, 2017

Definitions Related to Sexual Orientation and Gender Diversity in APA Documents Available at: https://www.apa.org/pi/lgbt/resources/sexuality-definitions.pdf Accessed Feb 2, 2017

Case #30

The Challenges of the Lavendale Juvenile Center

Raymond Tonchen, Jr.

The United States has the largest number of incarcerated children. At Lavendale Juvenile Center, the education and repatriation of these children present unique challenges to the new Principal, David Gurnham.

Lavendale Juvenile Center

At Lavendale, there are nine general education teachers (math, social studies, ELA, art, music, physical education, science, reading, and health), one educational counselor, one administrative assistant, and one superintendent. Teachers have two contacts with students each week, with a third (Fridays) swapped between semesters. Education is year-long, utilizing project-based learning during the summer.

Lavendale is a juvenile lock-up, with comforts few and far between. Students have been adjudicated here. There are reinforced doors, concertina wire, the faculty is searched for contraband (drugs, weapons, cell phones, etc.), and classes are video monitored.

The students mostly come from urban areas and often belong to gangs. The girls are often victims of various forms of sexual assault; they are the survivors. The arrogant toughness is a way to cover up their pain. This locked down 24/7 prison environment represents a *Most Restrictive Environment* (MRE) educationally. Now excluded from society, these students are also excluded from traditional schools.

At Lavendale, students have emotional, psychological, and/or learning impairments, with some on medication. Families are either non-existent or dysfunctional. These kids have become highly manipulative and pathological from over-exposure to family dysfunction, illegal/prescription drugs, and the societal influence of street gangs they belong to. They have been labeled uneducable, delinquents, and criminals by teaching and other staff. It has turned into a systemic bias trading one form of societal dysfunction for another.

There is a maximum of 12 students in a pod, with usually seven out of eight pods in operation. One pod is for isolation. All students have an individual cell. The student population consists of about 65-75 students at any one time, and there is a constant turnover. This represents *three times* the population that is recommended by the Casey Foundation (Mendel, 2011) and Cuomo (Strauss & Stanoch, 2012). There is no grass underfoot or fresh air. Welcome to school.

A New Principal

Meet David Gurnham, M.Ed., a veteran administrator of several urban schools. Like most people, his first taste of an institution such as this is a degree of disbelief. Almost immediately he realizes the bias from the staff as his main obstacle in creating a culture of learning within this highly unique situation. But how is this to be accomplished? Mr. Gurnham is a problem solver but solving this problem might be a formidable undertaking.

Lavendale Staff

Lavendale staff are young to middle-aged persons, but for the most part are young educators. While on one hand they teach, on the other hand the staff refers these students as *"criminals."* Despite their best professional overtures, the teaching staff does not believe that these students will ultimately succeed. It is a false front: a job one may describe as mercenary in nature. Students will not succeed or be rehabilitated; it is a systemic bias.

Donna, who teaches English, states to Mr. Gurnham that the street language and culture is too overwhelming. The math position is open and is being filled by day-substitutes as a long-term substitute for math cannot be found. Jackie, the social studies teacher just runs off busywork papers for them to do, along with giving a short lecture. The PE teacher gets along great with the kids as his class provides stress relief and recreation for the students; however, in the end his bias is the same. Homework (pod work) is mostly stories in the Cloze format with the students copying from each other.

A Pod, where the students stay and have most of their classes (except music), consists of two additional adults and maybe a third; a traveling therapist for group therapy sessions. The adults pretty much stay away from the classroom activities, except for one that has oversight always, *"just in case."* These professionals need to collaborate with teachers, if only on the spot to assist with the lessons. Greater involvement here could make a real difference, but most of them don't hold out hope for the students either. Therefore, between the facility staff and teaching staff we see an institutional bias emerging. The students sense the bias when the teachers teach with their backs to the wall and staff read newspapers. Motivation is low for learning.

Some students have been in the facility several times. Teachers have been stabbed with pencils. There have been psychotic breaks in which the students fight and throw eight-foot tables. And so the bias continues. Despite all of this, national statistics show at least a 50% success rate; not good, but better than the staff attitudes would indicate.

Problem Statement

The challenge comes in changing attitudes and systemic bias towards students and motivating them to learn while demonstrating that someone actually cares about their success. Teachers and other staff label students as *"criminals,"* indicating that they are impossible to rehabilitate and reinclude into society. Students can sense this; it is not a feel-good environment.

If eliminating teacher bias and augmenting student success is to occur, then significant systemic changes are required. At the principal's level there is just not enough authority. David must search out from other sources what is required. Leadership always starts by example and fortunately Mr. Gurnham provides a good one. These students share similar developmental requirements with any other group of students; meeting them, however, is an ongoing challenge. How do we get that baseball or soccer field, with grass underfoot, and stay secure at the same time? Will this make too much of a *"brat camp"* image publicly and politically? How do we change staff attitudes? This will be the hardest sell of all, since David has to change hearts and minds and his sphere of influence is on the teaching staff.

Out of the 70 students that are incarcerated when Gurnham takes the helm, there are many who will fall between the cracks of the system and end up labeled as criminals. These labels further reinforce the limited life changes for students. The students see themselves as they are viewed and labeled as criminals. These labels and staff biases further reinforce the students' negative self-image, perpetuating a cycle of criminal behavior.

As a start, David Gurnham must find small fixes from inside the facility. The challenge becomes three-fold: staff, students, and the facility. The reality is that this is a top-down fix that starts with the state, not a principal. He will have to reorganize somehow, and make changes in small batches. David is not sure where to start.

Case Problems

1. There are significant issues concerning the staff's deficit ideologies and biases towards the students; how might David begin to address these areas in the short and long term? What would these steps be?
2. What are some other barriers that David might encounter when it comes to staff, and how would he address them?
3. How can David begin addressing how the students see themselves, and challenge the deficit ideologies and biases within the institution? What barriers do you envision David will encounter when working the students on this area?

4. What suggestions do you have for David in terms of addressing how the facility resources could support his work with staff and students?

Suggested Reading and Viewing List

Annie E. Casey Foundation. (2015, June 24). Maltreatment of youth in U.S. Juvenile Corrections Facilities: An Update. Retrieved from: http://www.aecf.org/resources/maltreatment-of-youth-in-us-juvenile-corrections-facilities/?gclid=COrVjc_8sc8CFQQbaQod0AAIXw

Cuomo, C. (Reporter), Strauss, E. M. & Stanoch, M. (Producers). ABC News (2012). The Lost Children Behind Bars: Juvenile Corrections Adobe Mountain School, Phoenix, Arizona [Television series documentary]. ABC News PrimeTime. Retrieved from: https://www.youtube.com/watch?v=B8c1LahPSIA

Mendel, R. A. (2011). *No Place for Kids*. Baltimore, MD: The Annie E. Casey Foundation.

Ritchhart, R. (2015). *Creating Cultures of Thinking: The 8Fforces We Must Master to Truly Transform our Schools*. San Francisco, CA: Jossey-Bass.

Turner, J. (2017). General Effects of Music Therapy. *Psychology Encyclopedia*. Retrieved from: http://psychology.jrank.org/pages/435/Music-Therapy.html

References

Annie E. Casey Foundation. (2015, June 24). Maltreatment of Youth in U.S. Juvenile CorrectionFacilities: An Update. Retrieved from: http://www.aecf.org/resources/maltreatment-of-youth-in-us-juvenile-corrections-facilities/?gclid=COrVjc_8sc8CFQQbaQod0AAIXw

Armstrong, P. (2017) Blooms Taxonomy. *Vanderbilt University Center for Teaching*. Retrieved from: https://cft.vanderbilt.edu/guides-sub-pages/blooms-taxonomy/

Cuomo, C. (Reporter), Strauss, E. M. & Stanoch, M. (Producers). ABC News (2012). The Lost Children Behind Bars: Juvenile Corrections Adobe Mountain School, Phoenix, Arizona [Television series documentary]. ABC News PrimeTime. Retrieved from: https://www.youtube.com/watch?v=B8c1LahPSIA

Gabel, S. L. & Connor, D. J. (2014). *Disability and Teaching*. New York: Routledge.

Hattie, J. (2009). *Visible Learning.* New York: Routledge.

Mendel, R. A. (2011). *No Place for Kids.* Baltimore, MD: The Annie E. Casey Foundation.

PEW Charitable Trusts. (2015, April 20). Re-examining Juvenile Incarceration. Retrieved from: http://www.pewtrusts.org/~/media/assets/2015/04/reexamining_juvenile_incarceration.pdf

Postman, N. (1995). *The End of Education.* New York: Knopf.

Postman, N. (1995). The End of Education. In Gabel & Connor. *Disability and teaching.* New York: Routledge.

Public Law No. 94-142. (1975). *Individuals with Disabilities Education Act* (IDEA).

Ritchhart, R. (2015). *Creating Cultures of Thinking: The 8Fforces We Must Master to Truly Transform our Schools.* San Francisco, CA: Jossey-Bass.

Turner, J. (2017). General Effects of Music Therapy. *Psychology Encyclopedia.* Retrieved from: http://psychology.jrank.org/pages/435/Music-Therapy.html

Turuk, M. C. (2008), The Relevance and Implications of Vygotsky's Sociocultural Theory in the Second Language Classroom. *Annual Review of Education, Communication & Language Sciences;* Oct 2008, 5, 244-262

Case #31

The Case of the Service Dog

Adelee J. Penner & Carmen Mombourquette

Introduction

This is a case of a father, Hal Anderson, who is advocating for his two sons, both of whom are diagnosed as being on the autism spectrum. One son, Cody, is in Grade 3 and is very high functioning. The older son, Brody, is in Grade 4 and uses a service dog to provide safety, companionship, and independence. The service dog functions as an *assistive device* to aid him in daily life. Recognizing that Brody was going to attend Grade 5 at a new school in a year's time, the father called Taylor Rider, the principal of the Middle School Brody would be entering. The purpose of the call was to alert Mr. Rider to the fact that his son would be bringing with him his service dog, Charlie.

Mr. Anderson took the time to explain to Mr. Rider that Charlie was trained to respond to commands given by the caregiver or educator, and is necessary to keep him safe. The case also involves a Grade 5 student who has a severe allergy to dog dander. Questions then arise: What happens when the rights of two students collide? How does the Principal respond? Do the rights of one student supersede that of another? Is there a critical role for effective leadership? If so, what is it?

Overview/Analysis

The first day of the new school year arrived and Brody and Charlie were excited to be at Copper Town Middle School. It was also the day that the reality of having a service dog proved to be problematic. Annie, a Grade 5 student with a well-known allergy to dog dander, went into anaphylaxis. A teacher administered an epipen, and Mr. Rider took her to the local hospital. Annie's parents were very concerned about a dog being in school, especially given that they did not have prior knowledge of the arrival of a service animal.

After speaking to Annie's parents, Mr. Rider called Mr. Anderson. Mr. Rider explained to Mr. Anderson that due to the anaphylaxis reaction, Charlie was no longer welcome to attend Copper Town Middle School with Brody.

Mr. Anderson was quite frustrated. He was upset that the school had not taken the year to prepare a plan for the arrival of his child, and that the Principal was taking away independence and the possibility for success from Brody. He contacted the Autism Dog Service to see if he had any legal avenue to force the school to reconsider. A spokesperson directed him to research the Provincial Service Dog Act.

Mr. Anderson contacted Mr. Rider and asked for a meeting. During the meeting, Mr. Anderson explained the Service Dog Act to Mr. Rider. The school had to allow the dog and Brody to attend school together. Mr. Rider and Mr. Anderson talked, and came to an agreement that both felt could work for all involved. The dog and Brody would enter the school using a separate entrance, and the school would ensure that Annie and Brody were not in the same hall at the same time.

Mr. Rider spoke to the teachers about the plan. The teachers felt that Brody and Charlie should be kept to a single hallway to avoid causing any further anaphylaxis for Annie. The consequence of this plan was that Brody could no longer participate in Music, Art, or Physical Education classes, as they were not held in the wing that they planned to keep Brody and Charlie. Brody's homeroom teacher shared that she would like support in dealing with Charlie. As the administration had not created an entry plan or procedures for Charlie, she was left to command the dog, feed him, and take him outside for bathroom breaks. The Principal said that he would look into finding a teacher assistant to support Brody and Charlie.

Upon hearing that Brody's education would become quite limited, Mr. Anderson contacted the Associate Superintendent of Student Services, Mrs. Susan Peptry. Mr. Anderson shared his story, and current concern of Brody not being able to participate in all classes. He maintained that both Brody and Charlie should have access to the whole school.

Mrs. Peptry also received a call from Annie's parents. They were quite frustrated with the whole situation. They felt that Mr. Rider was not doing enough to protect their child. Annie was experiencing increased symptoms due to her exposure to dog dander and regularly needed medical intervention to cope with the situation.

Mrs. Peptry called Mr. Rider to meet and to create an action plan. She was very concerned that the situation had escalated to this point without Mr. Rider bringing her into the loop. When the two met, Mrs. Peptry and Mr. Rider created a plan that they felt could work. There were three parts to the plan:

- The jurisdiction would upgrade the present school ventilation system to an HVAC filtration system.
- The school would move teachers' classrooms to avoid the two students coming into contact with each other.
- The parents would be asked to bring their children into the school in separate entrances from each other to avoid the cross mingling of child and dog dander.

Mrs. Peptry and Mr. Rider shared the plan with both sets of parents. All parties agreed that this was a good plan and compromise. The parents thanked Mrs. Peptry and Mr. Rider for their work. This plan worked for four weeks.

Winter hit Copper Town with a big snowfall. The separate entrances had not been cleared of snow in the morning when the kids were dropped off at school. Rather than have their students try to climb over large snow banks, each set of parents independently decided to have their child enter school by the front door of the school, where the sidewalk had been cleared. This sharing of the front door of the school proceeded for a few weeks, as the parents did not feel that their children should have to walk farther to separate entrances than other children.

Mr. Rider soon began to hear from both sets of parents again. Annie's parents were frustrated that they were relying more and more on medical intervention to help her to be in school. Brody's father, Mr. Anderson, was frustrated that teachers were choosing to restrict Brody and Charlie's movements in the school. The consequence of the new restriction was that Brody could not attend his math or science class, and he was falling behind. This time, after hearing the parents, Mr. Rider chose to meet with the Superintendent, Ms. Arpena Babian. Ms. Babian decided that the next logical step would be to meet with both sets of parents, Mrs. Peptry, Mr. Rider, and the homeroom teachers, together to see if a solution could be found collaboratively. She also had a group come into the school to test the air quality to determine if the new HVAC system was purifying the air.

When the group met a few weeks later, Ms. Babian had carefully prepared an agenda. She decided to start by sharing the results of the air quality test.

"No allergens were found to be in the air of the school," she reported.

"So," she said, "really this seems to be an issue of how we share a learning space. How can we do this peacefully?"

Annie's parents were quite upset and felt that the dog was more accommodated than their child. They shared that they were not interested in compromising in a situation where "clearly a life should take precedent over a dog". They felt that Brody should be moved to another school in the district that already had a few service dogs.

Mr. Anderson was frustrated that the only solution presented was that his child be moved to another school. He shared that the Human Rights Tribunal may see things very differently. He also suggested that perhaps the CBC (Canadian Broadcasting Corporation, national public broadcaster for radio and television) and the Minister of Education might be interested in the case.

Problem Statement

The rights of two children collide. Do the rights of one child supersede those of another? What should/could happen at this point?

Items for Consideration and Discussion

Examine this case from an Educational Leadership perspective. The following questions can be used to guide your discussion and thoughts. Feel free to introduce other issues that you feel speak to the leadership demonstrated in this case study.

1. Comment on the Principal's decision to remove the dog from the school after one day of school. Was this the best decision for the situation? Is it an indicator of how prepared he was to accept the service dog into the learning environment?
2. Should an allergy take precedence over a service dog? What supports exist to help a leader find the answer? Who do you involve in this decision?
3. Should the principal have involved district office staff earlier in the case? When should they be involved? What kinds of decisions should include jurisdictional staff?
4. Can this case be resolved in a manner that benefits both students? If so, how?
5. Was the year lead time provided by Mr. Anderson enough? What could the school have done to prepare for a service dog? Were they ready?

References

Autism in Education. (2011). *Service dogs and children with Autism Spectrum Disorders*. Retrieved from Halifax, NS: http://www.gov.pe.ca/photos/original/eecd_servdogsEn.pdf

Case #32

Indigenous Peoples and Inclusivity in Education

John Roberts

Many Indigenous peoples believe that they are not treated equally with non-Indigenous people in Canada's education system. This case study has as its focus one Indigenous individual who personally feels excluded from having the same educational opportunities as his non-Indigenous peers.

Introduction

Brian Lighthorse is an eighteen-year-old male from an Anishnabe nation in northern Ontario. He recently completed secondary school off reserve after eight years of elementary schooling on reserve. He was bused 20 km each way to the local off-reserve secondary school, and went on to the local community college where he intended to study law enforcement. Due to a teacher's strike, Brian dropped out after a few weeks at the college. He stated that he was feeling "disconnected" from his culture, was not doing well at his part-time, off-reserve job, and felt that he was not adjusting socially to life off reserve when he was at school. He also felt strongly that, as an Indigenous person, he was treated differently by his teachers from non-Indigenous students, and that education in the reserve system had not prepared him for learning past the elementary level. Brian took courses in the Ojibway language in elementary school, but did not feel that these courses contributed to his understanding of his culture.

Background – Indigenous Education

Historically, about two out of every five Indigenous people had not completed a high school education, almost twice the number of non-Indigenous people. Although there is a significant gap in attainment between First Nations students and the general population, somewhat more than 50% of First Nations people now have completed secondary school, a significant increase over ten years ago, but still a considerable distance behind the number of non-indigenous people who have completed high school.

Increases in completion rates may be in part attributed to:
1. the introduction of languages and cultural classes in off-reserve secondary schools,
2. greater awareness and promotion of education by native bands themselves,
3. the development of secondary schools managed by First Nations, and
4. additional qualified Indigenous teachers.

Education, therefore, was being made more inclusive for Indigenous students. However, Indigenous students' enrolment and participation in education lags significantly behind the average Canadian rate.

Overview

Brian was an average student through elementary and secondary school. Having to take his secondary education off reserve didn't seem to have a significant effect on him; he remained an average student (although his marks in math were below average) and maintained friendships with his on-reserve peers. He was active in sports during secondary school, and was named junior athlete of the year after finishing Grade 10. However, many aspects of his life changed after that.

It was at lacrosse that Brian excelled. He had always been an outstanding lacrosse player, and became a member of a junior B on-reserve team when he was 16 years of age. His first two years on the team were marked with a reasonable amount of scoring, but his penalty minutes increased year to year. Then, when he was 18, it seemed as though something significant changed in his life that affected his lacrosse. Penalties became the norm, rather than scoring for his team, and he was ejected from a number of games for misconduct, mainly for arguing with referees and not accepting the way they called the games. He was seen as a team leader by his peers because he always stood up for his teammates, but his assertiveness in putting the team first and being penalized as a result was unacceptable to his coaches.

As he approached graduation from secondary school, he was awarded a partial scholarship to play for a college in the United States. It was obvious to family members that Brian was unenthused about this honour, and in the end Brian turned down the scholarship in order to stay on the reserve and attend a local community college, where he wanted to major in technology. Brian said that he felt "safe" on the reserve. In general he seemed to be ambivalent about the idea of attending college. However, he didn't know what else to do with himself, so he attended for a few weeks until a teacher's strike led him to drop out. Even though he attended for only a few weeks, he was already in danger of being asked to leave the college because of poor academic performance.

He became a manual labourer on his reserve, moved out of his mother's house, and was working irregularly until an injury on the job made it impossible for him to work. Brian feels that his academic problems stemmed from elementary school. Native education is a federal matter (non-native education is administered by the provinces), and many reserves have one or two elementary schools, staffed in large part by non-natives who are neither required in all cases to have teaching qualifications (in Ontario, registration with the Ontario College of Teachers), nor to attend professional development programs with the off-reserve teachers. The on-reserve education system (run in many cases by a tribal education authority made up of non-teachers), to many, lacks the discipline and standards of the provincial system. This is an undocumented opinion, but it is a prevailing opinion among on-reserve Indigenous people, who see themselves as academically lacking when compared to students off reserve.

Coming from a native elementary school "really messed me up a lot," says Brian. "I didn't know as much as I was supposed to about each subject. Teachers have expectations," and they are required to teach to the provincial curriculum in secondary school. Brian states that this happened in almost every class. "I had no idea what they were talking about in class, and the teachers didn't have the time to help me catch up."

Brian cited one example from his Grade 10 math class that stayed with him throughout his secondary school career. One day, he showed up in math class without his math notebook; he forgot it at home because he was doing math homework, and in the rush to catch the bus the notebook was left behind.

He attended math class that day without his notebook. As he walked into the class, his teacher looked at him and asked where his notebook was. Without waiting for an answer, the teacher told him to turn around and find the notebook before he came to class, assuming that the notebook was in his locker or somewhere else easily accessible. Brian told the teacher that the notebook was left at home.

Brian's teacher told him that there was no use coming to class without a notebook, and that if he continued to show attitude, he could go to the office. "I didn't believe that I was being sent to the office just because I didn't have my notebook with me," Brian said. "At least I took the responsibility to show up for class, and all I got for it was to be embarrassed in front of the other students."

The Vice-Principal asked the teacher to give Brian work that he could do on his own, and the teacher gave him worksheets containing material that the class hadn't taken up yet. "This teacher never treated non-native kids like this," said Brian. "It was as if the native kids were being centred out. I felt that the teacher's attitude toward native kids was that they were all lazy and didn't have the right to be in that class with non-indigenous students."

Brian transferred out of that class, but even so he later failed math.

This was not the only example of what Brian saw as exclusive behaviour on the part of the math teacher. In speaking with other Indigenous students, Brian was told that others had dropped this teacher's class because the teacher was rude to them. The others felt that the teacher was blaming the native students for the fact that the teacher had been teaching academic math (university stream) but was being forced to teach applied math (college or workplace stream) for the first time. They felt that this teacher resented it, therefore taking this resentment out on the native students in the applied stream.

Brian explained that there were three "streams" at the secondary level: academic, applied, and locally developed. "Most Indigenous kids go into the applied stream [college- or workplace-bound] because they feel that they aren't good enough to go into the academic [university] stream." The "locally developed" stream "is the equivalent to Grade 7 or 8. It doesn't teach you anything," Brian feels. Parents can elect to have their children go into this stream "just to get them into high school." Students cannot go to college out of this stream.

It was also discovered that Brian's math teacher checked the students' math scores in Grade 9; if the teacher felt that they weren not high enough or that the students were seen as weak in math, they were sent out of the Grade 10 math course. Every one of these students was native.

Case Problems

Teachers, and others involved in Indigenous education, are looking for ways in which to best support Brian and other Indigenous students like him. Consider the following questions. In your answers, discuss how you might approach Brian's situation if you were one of his teachers (non-native and native), his elementary school principal, a college administrator, and a member of the Indigenous community.

- Should there be an increased sensitivity to First Nations customs and learning styles on the part of teachers and staff in the college that Brian attended?
- What would be the advantages or disadvantages of having Brian's elementary school operated by his Anishnabe band, rather than by the federal government?
- How could the number of qualified native teachers be increased?
- Should both Brian's elementary school and college have incorporated First Nations learning and teaching styles into the curriculum? If so, where would the teachers with an understanding of these

learning and teaching styles come from? Should teaching and learning styles of all learners in the Canadian education system be incorporated into the curriculum? If so, how could this be accomplished?

- How can a student's movement from a remote community to a non-Indigenous secondary school or college be facilitated?

- What preparation can be taken for Indigenous students to be prepared for the labour market, either on reserve or off reserve?

- What might be some of the reasons that Brian's behaviour changed as he approached post-secondary education?

- In general, what principles of inclusivity could be incorporated into the secondary school curriculum to meet the needs of the Indigenous learner?

References

Bundled arrows initiative. Mohawk College of Applied Arts and Technology, Hamilton, Ontario. (January 8, 2018). www.mohawkcollege.ca/indigenous-students/bundled-arrows-initiative

Education. (2006). John Roberts. First nations, Inuit and Metis peoples. Toronto: Emond Montgomery.

Elementary and Secondary Education. (2004). Pamela Williamson and John Roberts, First Nations peoples. Toronto: Emond Montgomery.

Key Questions for Educational Leaders. (2015). Darrin Griffiths and John P. Portelli. Burlington, Ontario: Word & Deed Publishing.

The Principal Reader: Narratives of Experience. (2017). Darrin Griffiths and Scott Lowrey. Burlington, Ontario: Word & Deed Publishing.

Case #33

Including Tony

Vernita Mayfield

When Principal Phil Anderson arrived at work that morning, he had an uneasy feeling about the day. He was seldom wrong about this sort of thing. Eight years behind the principal desk at Grady Middle School had taught him to trust his instincts, and today he felt an uncanny urge to head for the hills. Fearlessly, he grabbed his briefcase and headed for the main hallway. "Good morning Terri", he said, greeting the office manager. Terri pursed her lips and spoke with her eyes, motioning for him to enter his office. She followed him quickly and shut the door behind her.

"Terri, what's wrong?", he asked.

"It's Mrs. Bledsoe." She sighed with mild annoyance.

He shrugged, waiting for her to continue.

"She got here first thing this morning ranting about her son. It seems some kids have been teasing him, and she has been threatening to sue everybody in the building if something isn't done about it immediately. Honestly, she's been driving us crazy! She is the most obnoxious..." Her voice trailed off as loud pounding at the door interrupted.

"Mr. Anderson?!!! Mr. A-n-d-e-r-s-o-n!", Mrs. Bledsoe's voice carried through the door like it was paper. " I saw you come in. I need to speak with you at once!" Her fists hit the door like hammers.

"I told you so", Terri mouthed silently.

Phil grabbed the door and swung it open. "Mrs. Bledsoe, you obviously have something very important to share with me, but you needn't bang on the door. I will be with you as soon as I possibly can. In the meantime, Terri is going to show you to the parents lounge. Please enjoy a fresh cup of coffee or tea while you wait. I will come and get you shortly, and I promise it won't be long." Phil smiled sweetly.

Mrs. Bledsoe looked Terri up and down before grunting and waving her by to lead the way. Phil quietly closed the door before leaning against it. "Whew!" He pinched his forehead and tried to think. "If this Bledsoe kid is as crazy as his mom, it's going to be a long day."

"Tony Bledsoe is a seventh grader", explained Fiona. Fiona Taylor was a first-year Assistant Principal who made it a priority to know each of the students at Grady. As they sat in Phil's office behind closed doors, Phil was gathering background knowledge for his conversation with Mrs. Bledsoe.

"His mother's a piece of work", Fiona continued. "*He's* a likeable kid, however. There is something about him I noticed, though."

"What's that?" Phil probed.

Phil's door burst open before she could speak. It was Terri. "Come quick!" she panted, nearly out of breath. "There's a fight down the hall. We're going to need you both!"

"Girls or boys?" asked Fiona as she grabbed her walkie-talkie.

"Both!" yelled Terri.

"Yikes!" Fiona took off running.

"Damn it", Phil muttered, "Call the resource officer, please."

Terri quickly grabbed her phone.

As Phil hurried down the hallway he caught a glimpse of the fighters. What he saw next, however, made him suddenly sprint toward the students. Steve Seay, Grady's star defensive back, drew his fist and landed a whopping punch square in the face of a tall, fragile, young woman, scrambling for her balance. Phil grabbed Steve by the collar. "Stop this now!" he shouted. He glared at Steve with a deliberate look of disgust. "Steve, you know better than this! At Grady, we don't resolve our differences with our fists! But I am especially appalled at what I just witnessed! Steve, how could you hit a girl like that? I know your parents have taught you better than that!"

Steve straightened his shoulders and postured, as an arrogant smirk crept across his lips. "That's no *girl*, Mr. Anderson."

Fiona lifted the fragile frame of the other fighter. As she pulled back the long, dark hair to reveal the lipstick-smeared, mascara-stained face, she met Phil's astonished gaze. "Phil", she said calmly, "this is Tony Bledsoe."

Steve eyed the photos on the wall of the Assistant Principal's office. "I never been in here before", he said glumly.

"I'm sorry your first time is under these circumstances", said Fiona, "but you must understand we cannot allow this kind of behavior at Grady. You're suspended for three days and will need to return with one of your parents. What is their phone number? I need to call them immediately." Fiona delivered the verdict with no emotion.

"What?" shouted Steve. "What about Tony? Does he get suspended too?" Steve stood up, indignant. "He started it – telling everybody he was coming to the game as a cheerleader. We got school pride, you know, and it ain't cheerleaders with beards! So, does this mean I can't play in the game tonight? Coach Dan is going to have a fit! You just wait!" He crossed his arms and sat down defiantly. "He'll be down here in a minute. He and my dad . . . You know my dad, right? He's the school board president. Anyway, he played football with Coach Dan when they were in high school. And if I miss a game on account of that fool, there will be trouble at the school board meeting this month. You just wait!"

"Steve Seay, is that a threat?" Fiona narrowed her eyes and focused them on his.

"Naw, Miss Taylor. I'm just trying to tell you what other folks won't." Steve settled back in his chair. The air was thick with arrogance.

"And what's that?"

"That nobody likes that kid. Not even the teachers. And especially not Coach."

"What do you mean?"

"I mean everybody makes fun of him and nobody cares. The teachers look the other way or pretend not to notice. He's a disgrace to this community and to this school. My dad says he needs to go to one of them special schools for special kids. He told me to knock the hell out of him if he ever put his hands on me. So, when he put his hand on my shoulder this morning and asked me what time the game starts . . .POW!" Steve slammed his fist into his hand for emphasis. "Call my daddy at 545-689-9000. I guarantee he's going to come down here and shake my hand!"

The blood began to drain from Fiona's face.

"Tell me what's going on." Phil Anderson leaned forward in his seat. They were within the sanctuary of the school counselor's office now. Deborah Pace sat beside him, a small notebook in hand. Tony faced them both, his face a smeared blur of cosmetic colors. His dress, draped over his jeans, was torn at the collar and sleeve, and was now stained with blood and mucous.

"They tease me", he began. "They tease me every day."

"Who is *they*?" asked Deborah, the school counselor.

"Everybody. Well, not the girls. I've got lots of girl friends. They comb my hair, and paint my nails and show me how to put on make-up." He gave a half smile and showed them his hands, grinning with pride. "Nice, huh? I guess it's the boys mostly. They call me names. They push me as I walk down the hallway. They push my books off my desk in class. They spit in my food at lunch. They chase me home after school and threaten to beat me up all the time.

"Why do you think they do that?" asked Phil.

"What does it matter?" Tony demanded angrily. "Whatever the reason, they got no right to treat me like that! I can be anyone I want to be!"

Phil winced. "I deserved that."

"Who do you want to be, Tony?" Deborah asked gently.

"I don't know." His head rocked slowly from side to side. "I don't know."

The phone rang. Deborah answered it, then handed it to Phil.

"Yes?"

"It's Mrs. Bledsoe, Phil." Phil could scarcely hear Terri's hushed whisper. "I'm not sure how but she heard about the fight. She's pounding on Jill's desk while calling her attorney. You better get down here now."

Mrs. Bledsoe was pacing in the hallway outside the main office. "Mr. Anderson, where the hell were you when they were beating up my kid?" she demanded. Her face swelled with heat. She was screaming so loud, two teachers poked their heads out of the classroom and stared in curiosity. Phil waved them back into their rooms, but considered momentarily the eerie absence of teachers during the fight.

"Mrs. Bledsoe, come into my office and let's talk."

Tanya Bledsoe followed behind him. "You have kept me waiting for almost an hour!!! I want to talk to Tony. I *knew* this was going to happen. Get Tony in here now! NOW!!! We're going to see my attorney TODAY!!!!!"

Phil opened his office door and motioned for her to step in. He continued to respond calmly even as she continued to yell. "Mrs. Bledsoe, I understand why you are upset. We are all pretty upset at the events that have unfolded, today. Tony is speaking with our school counselor right now. Let's give them a few moments to sort things out while you and I talk about your concerns. I have only been made aware of the teasing today, and it is important to me to resolve your concerns as quickly as possible. We want Tony to be included and respected at school. Will you give us some time to see if we can resolve this today? I believe we can." He handed her a bottle of cold water from the fridge behind his desk.

She took it, yanked off the cap and burst into tears of frustration. Phil pushed a box of tissue toward her and sank into his chair.

"Mr. Anderson, I knew from the moment I was pregnant that I was having a girl. Even when the doctor announced it was a boy, I took one look at Tony and said to myself, 'Naw, he can be whatever he wants to be. I dressed him in girl's clothes from the time he was knee high. There's nothing wrong with that. Everybody has a right to choose what they want to be. So sometimes he wants to act like a boy and sometimes he wants to act like a girl. I told him that's fine. He can do both! He's androgynous. I tell him he can choose to be anything he wants to be any day of the week. But these dagblasted kids at school. They are not going to ever leave him alone. They tease him mercilessly. The older he gets, the worse it has gotten. I can't take this! He's got a right to come to school and learn the same as anybody else! Now, what are you going to do about this? Hmm? How are you going to make sure my child feels included at this school wherever he goes? That YOUR job! And right now, you are failing! You're failing Tony! What is your plan?

Phil Anderson ran his hands through his hair, before folding them under his chin.

Case Questions

- Define Principal Anderson's challenge.
- Prioritize Principal Anderson's immediate next steps.
- How might Principal Anderson frame his subsequent conversations on inclusion with teachers? With students? With parents?
- What are the potential political implications of this matter?
- Who else needs to be notified? When and how should they be notified?
- What legally defensive policies and procedures should be in place to minimize the risk of litigation?
- What can Phil do to keep Tony, and all other students of difference, safe at school?
- What steps should Phil take to create a more inclusive environment at the school?

Case #34

Gay Boys Do Cry:
Homophobia and Victimization in Canadian School Culture

André P. Grace

Introduction

The case below was created using an interview I conducted with Colin (pseudonym) during the summer before he entered Grade 9. Colin's story is a found narrative that stays true to language and expressions he used during the interview. As a self-affirmed gay boy, Colin had experienced homophobia and victimization in schooling, which were most pronounced and persistent during Grade 6. Fortunately, his assets included having a strong and supportive mother, cousins who protected him, and a principal who listened when Colin and his mom discussed the matter with him. While gay boys like Colin have been historically targeted in Canadian schools due to their sexual differences, in contemporary times the *Canadian Charter of Rights and Freedoms* guarantees them equality rights—human and civil—and provides them with individual protection against discrimination in Section 15. Subsection 1 states, "Every individual is equal before and under the law and has the right to the equal protection and equal benefit of the law without discrimination" (Government of Canada, 2018).

Despite Charter accommodation, and its positive incremental impact on educational legislation and policymaking recognizing sexual minorities (and more recently gender minorities), vestiges of a national history of sexual-minority exclusion remain in Canadian schooling (Grace & Wells, 2016). Consequently, forms of violence like homophobic bullying and name-calling continue to be normalized in school culture (Grace, 2015; Taylor & Peter, et al., 2011). Students like Colin, and indeed all sexual- and gender-minority students, warrant protections in schooling that ensure their recognition, respect, accommodation, safety, security, and good health and wellness (Grace, 2015; Grace & Wells, 2016; Taylor & Peter, et al., 2016). When they are below the age of majority, these students are of particular concern because their age impacts how they understand what happens to them, which, in turn, affects how they mediate schooling as visible or stealth students (Grace, 2015).

Colin's Story:
A Perspective Using His Words on Navigating School

Culture as a Gay Male Student

I describe myself as a gay male. All of my family is good with me being gay. They don't have any problem with it because my mom is also a sexual minority. She made it much easier for me because she had already dealt with the issue and any resistance within our extended family. My mom is a strong, passionate, and caring woman. She knows when you're supposed to do something. She can be stern and kind. She's the best. I'm an only child. I have two cousins and they're both supportive. They both have my back.

I thought about being gay when I was younger because you have to think about that. From Kindergarten to Grade 5, I lived a sheltered life. I was protected by my family, especially my girl cousin who supported me and protected me against bullies. Then we moved to a new house, and I went to a new school. Without my cousin, I had no protection. Some people say they have a thick skin. However, when I went into Grade 6, I was skinless. If somebody bullied me, I would cry. I just did not like conflict. I missed my cousin, and there was so much trouble with bullies in my new school. I think they bullied me because they thought I was gay. I felt I was a target and people just judged me. It was mainly two boy bullies. One was in my grade. He didn't physically bully me, but he verbally bullied me quite harshly. The other bully was in Grade 8. His bullying was verbal and very, very physical. Between them, I would be bullied pretty much daily. The older one who was very physical would take me to the field by the school and he would hold me down, or he would push me around the field. Then he would just throw me down and pick me back up, and throw me back down again until I found a way to scurry off. I reached a point where I just couldn't take it anymore, so I told my mom and we went to the principal. I was lucky because the principal listened and helped. He spoke to the bullies. He also spoke to my homeroom teacher and my other teachers. Having them know was effective. By Grade 7, the bullying really stopped. This year I was in Grade 8, and it was a good year. I think it got better because people got to know me. Before I was just a kid on the playground who was probably gay and who liked computers and Pokémon. Once I actually had friends, things turned around. I like to hang out with my friends at the mall.

This fall I am going into Grade 9, and I will be attending a Grade 9-to-12 high school. I don't want to stand out. I want to blend in and be the kind of kid who everybody knows, but nobody knows. Maybe I can just advance and try to be more social until people know who I am as a person. I'm not going to be closed about my sexuality, but I don't think I'll go to a GSA. I know it's a Gay-Straight Alliance, but people will pretty much judge you completely. I want to blend in because I want to get a good footing. I have a beautiful portrait painted of what I want my high school to be like. One of the reasons why I chose this school is because it has law and psychology. I want to get high marks throughout because I need to go to a superb university. I just need to do it. I think about going into law, and then going into politics. I'd love to advance Canada and move it forward in a progressive way, focusing more on healthcare and education.

When I think of schools today, the programs we have that are supposed to help either do a little bit or nothing at all. I remember we had a pink shirt day and we watched a video that had all these kids saying rude, insulting words. One of the words was "faggot." There was no context provided about this video, so it had the exact opposite effect. Almost everybody in the class started saying faggot like the kids in the video. They missed the message. I think we need to focus on finding programs that actually help prevent the problem of homophobia. We also need to provide coping strategies for youth because, while people always say it's good to prevent homophobia, it's going to happen. A lot of the time, teachers only see ten percent of what goes on. When youth don't have coping strategies, that's when we have depression, suicides, and school shootings—because people just can't handle it anymore. Teachers, parents, guardians, and anybody with authority, should be taught to notice mental-health problems. We need to teach people the signs of depression and mental illness.

I would tell teachers: Educate yourself, but educate your students better. Wherever there is education, wherever you can learn, there is always less hate. This is just a little thing, but I had this teacher and she knew I was gay just from hearing things. She should have tried to address issues like gay sexuality with all her students. Instead, when she talked about gay bullying, I felt it was clearly, clearly, directed at me. I knew that everybody was looking at me, so she should have directed the talk at everyone, and not just the gay kid. Everyone should know about these things.

The Problem with Homophobia and Victimization of Gay Boys

In contemporary times we realize that sexual- and gender-minority students comprise a multivariate population, marked by diverse sexualities and gender identities and expressions (Grace, 2015). There is a need to recognize, respect, and accommodate all subgroups making up this population. Of incessant concern, gay males continue to experience violence in physical and symbolic forms as their status quo. Gay boys in school are still victimized by pronounced homophobia in demeaning words and defiling actions (Grace, 2015). For Colin, homophobic bullying not only indelibly marked his schooldays in Grade 6, but it has also impacted how he plans to mediate life in high school. Colin wants high school to work for him, and to lay the groundwork for a future where his goal is to be a lawyer. Sadly, there are subtexts of invisibility and caution in Colin's story that influence how he is planning his move into Grade 9.

Questions for Critically Analyzing Colin's Case

- Colin is a survivor of homophobic bullying and victimization in schooling. What assets enabled him to deal with these experiences that have often led other students toward negative outcomes like truancy, substance abuse, and suicide ideation? What does Colin's story tell us about the importance of having significant adults in young lives?

- Colin just wants to blend in once he enters Grade 9. How might we understand this? Is it a coping mechanism or a survival strategy in the face of homophobia?

- It is vital that school principals and teachers be advocates for gay students like Colin. When working with students across sexual and gender differences, what does it mean for a school principal or teacher to be an advocate? To be vigilant? To be a change agent in school culture? To help vulnerable students to be at promise instead of at risk?

- Gay-Straight alliances have long been viewed as safe social spaces for sexual and gender minority students in schools (Canadian Teachers' Federation, 2006). However, Colin implies in his story that a GSA might not be a safe and welcoming space for him, and that GSA culture is problematic? Develop a communication plan to promote the value and utility of GSAs for students like Colin.

Acknowledgment

I conducted the research informing the case with funding from the Social Sciences and Humanities Research Council of Canada (Council Identification No.: 65592). Participation in the research was voluntary, with those being interviewed assured of anonymity and confidentiality, while being free to withdraw at any time. For participating youth under the age of majority, parents provided written, informed consent. Ethics approval was obtained from the University of Alberta Research Ethics Board.

References

Canadian Teachers' Federation. (2006). Gay-straight student alliance handbook. Ottawa, ON: Author. (Available at https://publications.ctf-fce.ca/en/product/gay-straight-student-alliance-handbook-1/)

Government of Canada. (2018). *Constitution Act, 1982 – Part 1: Canadian Charter of Rights and Freedoms.* Retrieved April 15, 2018 from http://laws-lois.justice.gc.ca/eng/Const/page-15.html

Grace, A. P., (2015). *Growing into resilience: Sexual and gender minority youth in Canada.* Part II with K. Wells. Toronto: University of Toronto Press.

Grace, A. P., & Wells, K. (2016). *Sexual and gender minorities in Canadian education and society (1969-2013): A national handbook for K-12 educators.* Ottawa, ON: Canadian Teachers' Federation. (Published in English & French.)

Taylor, C., Peter, T., Edkins, T., Campbell, C., Émond, G., & Saewyc, E. (2016). *The national inventory of school district interventions in support of LGBTQ student wellbeing: Final report. Vancouver, BC: Stigma and Resilience Among Vulnerable Youth Centre, University of British Columbia. Retrieved April 15, 2018 from* http://www.saravyc.ubc.ca/2016/07/07/announcing-release-of-the-national-inventory-of-school-district-interventions-in-support-of-lgbq-student-wellbeing/

Taylor, C., & Peter, T., with McMinn, T. L., Schachter, K., Beldom, S., Ferry, A., Gross, Z., & Paquin, S. (2011). *Every class in every school: The first national climate survey on homophobia, biphobia, and transphobia in Canadian schools. Final report.* Toronto, ON: Egale Canada Human Rights Trust. Retrieved April 15, 2018 from http://egale.ca/wp-content/uploads/2011/05/EgaleFinalReport-web.pdf

Other Resources

My academic website with resources: https://www.andrepgrace.com

Chief Public Health Officer (CPHO). (2011). *The Chief Public Health Officer's report on the state of public health in Canada 2011: Youth and young adults – life in transition.* Ottawa: Office of the CPHO. (Available at http://www.phac-aspc.gc.ca/cphorsphc-respcacsp/2011/index-eng.php)

Government of Saskatchewan. (2015). *Deepening the discussion: Gender and sexual diversity.* Regina, SK: Saskatchewan Ministry of Education. Retrieved April 15, 2018 from http://publications.gov.sk.ca/documents/11/84995-Deepening%20the%20Discussion_Saskatchewan%20Ministry%20of%20Education%20Oct%202015%20FINAL.pdf

Public Health Agency of Canada (PHAC). (2014). *Questions & answers: Sexual orientation in schools.* Ottawa, ON: Author. (Available at http://www.phac-aspc.gc.ca/std-mts/rp/so-os/index-eng.php)

Case #35

Doing Things Right or Doing the Right Things:
The Case of Inclusion in the Republic of Ireland

Carol-Ann O'Síoráin, Miriam Twomey,
Michael Shevlin, & Conor Mc Guckin,
School of Education, Trinity College Dublin, Ireland

Towards Inclusive Education and the Role of Inclusive Leaders

The move towards inclusion, nationally and internationally, over the past three decades is a socio-political response. Warnock (1978) drew attention to categorization and labeling and its use in justifying placement and provisions for persons with different educational needs. Pedagogical practices were also identified as an important element of successful integration. This raises an important question: if special education in a special school is not the answer, is special education in a mainstream system the answer to historical exclusionary practices?

Norwich (2007) asserts that there is a choice in the ethical decision making of policy makers, teachers, and education systems and structures, positing that the "dilemma" arises in relation to the gaps in the rights-based versus the needs-based dilemma. So, in essence, the central challenge of inclusion is whether we include individuals because every person is entitled to be treated the "same", or do we include and recognise "different needs".

In Ireland, educational inclusion has progressed with the partial enactment of the Education for Person's with Special Educational Needs Act (EPSEN: 2004). The Act "enshrines" in law that that the preferred educational provision for children with Special Educational Needs (SEN) is inclusive education (Day & Travers, 2014). However, as with many educational and social concepts, the daily practice of "inclusive education" is variable across individual educators, children, and schools. A proscriptive and homogenous "top down" approach to the operational delivery of inclusive education would not be welcome. However, Ravet (2011) cautions us to the disconnect between each individual's professional knowledge and their applied practice.

The Case of Inclusion for SEN and Autism

In terms of inclusive education for pupils with SEN and autism in the Republic of Ireland, Shevlin, Kenny, and Loxley (2008) noted that pupils with SEN are now predominately educated in mainstream settings. This is a positive development, and moves us beyond the historical approach where many pupils, especially those with autism, were home-schooled.

There are three main types of SEN provision in Ireland; (i) mainstream classes, (ii) special classes in mainstream schools, and (iii) special schools. Figure 1 (below) illustrates the structure of options available to parents and frontline personnel in the possible educational placement for these children and young people.

In highlighting Ireland's move to inclusive practice, the National Council for Special Education (2013) reported that in the year 2011/2012, just 1% of children with SEN now attending Special Schools. Since the majority of pupils with SEN attend their local mainstream school there is a need to keep a constant research focus on the practices of inclusion for advancing better outcomes for pupils with SEN (McCoy et al., 2014).

Figure 1: Modes of SEN provision in Ireland.

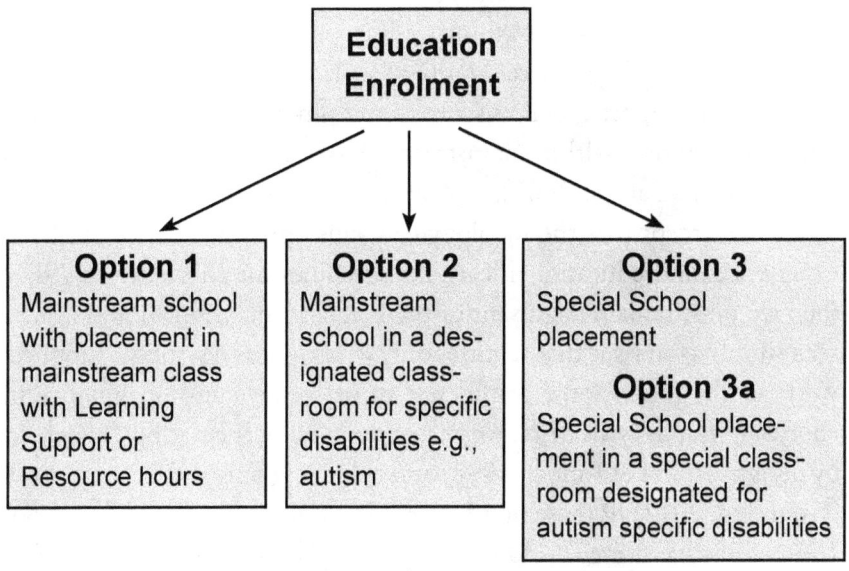

For pupils with autism, the option to be educated alongside their non-SEN peers in the classroom, with access to learning support / resource hours, is now available. Notably, the largest number of pupils with autism (and many with a co-morbid intellectual learning disability) are currently enrolled in mainstream schools, albeit in a segregated autism-specific classroom. However, little is known about the inclusion practices within these settings. Whilst Parsons et al. (2009) called for urgent, focused research in this area nearly 10 years ago, McCoy et al. (2014) reported that little has changed in the intervening years, despite the fact that, by 2014, 60% of "special class provision" in mainstream schools was identified as being specifically for these pupils. Cullinan (2017) reaffirmed these concerns, in that the pupils ". . . did not experience a level of social acceptance on par with their typically developing peers" (p. 34). Finally, for those pupils requiring extensive support, "autism classrooms" have been established in Special Schools. This is not an ideal solution for these pupils as; (i) special schools are predominantly in large urban areas, (ii) they do not have access to non-SEN peers, and (iii) they are further segregated within the special school setting by being enrolled in the autism classroom.

This approach to provision in the Republic of Ireland differs in comparison to the practices in other European countries (e.g., Finland, Germany, Italy, UK) where funding is made available for additional services and supports, such as sensory and physical therapies, to sustain pupils with autism within mainstream classes alongside their non-SEN peers (Autism-Europe, 2007).

If we accept that the ideology of inclusion is to enhance the lived experiences and educational learning outcomes for children with SEN, then we must remain cognisant of the fact that inclusion should not be seen simply as an issue that requires only structural and systemic supports. Without the professional confidence to be creative and imaginative in educating pupils with SEN, we may simply be perpetuating "apartheid by design" (Imrie & Kumar, 1998) and achieving only the "containment" (Goulding, 2012) of these pupils in the built environment of the school. Thus, whilst we strive to "do the right thing" by setting up special classrooms, we should reflect upon whether this will evidence our philosophy of educational and social inclusion.

Case Examples for Inclusive Leaders

We have selected the following two case examples from our research, as they are useful in terms of demonstrating that inclusive leadership may be either formal (e.g., by the school leader) or informal (e.g., by educators). Our goal here is to explore practice that positions itself between a rights-based approach and a needs-based approach. That is, as you read the following examples, the overarching question that we would ask you to consider is:

Is the case an example of "doing things right" . . . or "doing the right things"?

Perhaps before reading the first case, jot down the following questions that may help guide your reading and analysis of the case:

- Who is leading inclusion? What skills are being demonstrated?
- How would you advise the school staff in terms of enhancing the leadership role in this case?
- A hallmark of professional practice is the ability to "self-care" – was 'self-care' evident (were you able to cope with the demands of the workload)?
- Did the teachers work within their remit?
- Is there evidence of safe practice in the case?
- Is anything else required from other people to help the learning-support teacher in a leadership role?
- _____ (can you think of a question?);
- _____ (can you think of a question?)

By seeking these types of answers from the case, you will be in a great position to compile a report of the leadership attributes that are either evident, or missing, from practice.

As you read, Kipling's *six honest serving*-men may help you - their names are Who and What and Why, and When and Where and Which.

Case Example 1

This case example is drawn from Project IRIS, a longitudinal research project exploring inclusive educational practice in Ireland (Rose, Shevlin, Winters, & O'Raw, 2015). This case explores the interview response of 'Mary', a Learning support teacher in a five-teacher, co-educational, rural school in Ireland. Within the Education Act (1998) the mainstream class teacher has overall responsibility for the teaching of all pupils enrolled within their class. Learning support teachers (LST) provide a range of supports, including direct individualised support for the pupil, small-group support, within mainstream class support and consultation with class teachers regarding appropriate interventions to support the pupil who has special educational needs. LST within a rural setting often operate on a peripatetic basis, offering support to a number of schools depending on the level of individual needs within each school. In this instance, Mary, as the local LST, supports pupils and teachers within two neighbouring schools. The role of the LST within the Irish system is to provide additional learning opportunities for learners with a specific SEN, for example dyslexia. There are two levels of support provision within this role; they provide a choice of either in-class support or withdrawal to a small-group or one-to-one setting. In-class support requires a co-teaching partnership and an equal division of roles and responsibilities between the mainstream class teacher and the LST. The increased enrolment of learners with SEN across all categories of need has presented a challenge to a whole-school approach to inclusion and quality provision and outcomes for all learners. Mary's case reflects how increased demands, and the complexity of needs, presented by pupils who have special educational needs impacts on her capacity to deliver appropriate levels of support.

Mary, the support teacher in this rural school, appeared to be overwhelmed by the demands of her expanding role as a co-operating partner to all the mainstream class teachers in providing support to the pupils with SEN. As a LST she is also tasked with providing the professional supports that are needed by the other teachers in the school. Mary suggests that there is a good relationship between the teaching staff and that everyone is committed to their roles and responsibilities. However, she states clearly that her case load of learners with SEN is too large, and she perceives that there are more children in need of her support than she can accommodate.

> "… there are too many children in each group, the numbers are just, it's very difficult then to meet their needs within that, it really is … "

As a partner in a co-teaching capacity, Mary also describes a situation where a possible lack of a leading-for-learning approach within the school compromises the potential for effective, sustainable, co-teaching partnerships. The following reflection indicates that the co-planning and co-practice of this teaching pair is in need of revision for better learner engagement and outcomes.

> "......like in particular in Kevin's room there are so many children in the room, and there are so many needy children in the room, and they're not supported enough, and then I can see that they're frustrated because they're not working at their level at times...."

The lack of a whole-school leadership approach became evident when Mary points out that there had been no whole-school professional development to support and create a systematic model of support, and preparing teachers to work with the pupils who have learning needs was absent. She expands on the challenges and lack of professional conversations when she directs our attention to the lack of shared knowledge about the learner outcomes during school transitions.

> "...so if we think about the transitions between teachers, it's a bit haphazard at the moment."

Mary, in her role as LST, has the responsibility of compiling summative assessment results across the school and building a profile of the learning-support needs of the whole school. It is her responsibility to share this knowledge with her colleagues during whole-school meetings. In the absence of whole-school collegial engagement, vital pupil information was not transferred to the classroom teachers receiving children with SEN into their class. Mary reflects:

> "... they really need to be more shown their actual formal testing and the reports that they've got, and I know I didn't do that in some cases."

While there was multi-disciplinary input to individual education plans [Note: not yet mandatory in Irish schools], there appeared to be little review and reflection, or real engagement with parents, on progress and the development of new targets. The following statement from Mary suggests that there is no structured communications policy relating to the educational partnerships between school and home.

> "No. No, it would be more just me really. And the class teacher, or if sometimes the parent comes or if you feel that

there is something that you need to talk to them about, they would come in, but we wouldn't actually get the whole group back together again to look at them, no."

It is apparent that the school and this support teacher are struggling with the challenges inherent in the support role. However, it is equally apparent that this support teacher has very limited support from school leaders in devising support procedures that ensure whole-school approaches are developed to address transition issues and ongoing review of individual education planning.

So, from this case example, we hope that you can appreciate the complexities that Mary must deal with on a daily basis. In reading the case, and considering your questions, did you get a sense of Mary "doing the right things" or "doing things right"? As researchers and practitioners, we often reflect on cases like this by posing reflexive questions and using "thinking tools" – just as you have done. In addition to the types of questions that you might have considered asking, we tend to pose questions at four different levels:

- Policy - was Mary supported by:
    - national legislation?
    - quasi-legislation (e.g., Department of Education Circular)?
    - school policy?
- Practice:
    - Was Mary responding in a rights-based mode or a needs-based mode?
    - Was she reflective of her own skills and competencies?
    - Has Mary taken ownership of the complex situation in which she has found herself?
- Experience:
    - What adjective would you use to describe Mary's experience?
    - How do you think her role is seen from a class teacher perspective?
    - Was the support for the pupils positive?
- Outcomes:
    - What were the outcomes for Mary, the pupils, the school, the parents, and society?

- Overloaded timetable:
  - How can the school address the timetabling of learning support?
  - What or who may need to be sacrificed for a change to happen?

Case Example 2

Ok – so now that you have had a chance to think about the first case example, this next one is more detailed and complex. Be confident – after getting to this stage of the chapter and having analysed the first case example, you should enjoy the opportunity to analyse the issues related to inclusive leadership that may – or may not – be evident...

This school is positioned in a well-settled farming community in the midlands area of the country, and serves a number of satellite towns / communities that are within driving distance. The school has an "open door" policy to SEN. Three buses are required to transport pupils with SEN from considerable distances to this school. It is a large, vertical (ages 4-12 years), co-educational, primary school that has served generations of families within and beyond its locale. The school is a single-story building that has recently been refurbished and extended to provide suitable accommodation for pupils with SEN, including an autism unit.

There are eighteen pupils with a diagnosis of autism enrolled within an autism unit (3 classrooms). Three teachers are appointed with responsibilities for these pupils and there are ten Special Needs Assistants (SNA) all working within the special education resource team. The principal and two of the unit teachers decided in the school year 2013/2014 to change their approach to the management and function of the 6-9 and 9-12 year autism class groups. They decided to amalgamate these pupils, and to team teach for communication and social skills training only, in effect turning the unit into a "life skills centre". All academic work is prepared and completed by the mainstream class teacher through a differentiated approach.

A differentiated approach to inclusion

The 6- to 12-year-old pupils with autism attend mainstream for all core subjects, and the mainstream teachers collaborate with the two unit teachers to provide insights and direction for future learning and support. The unit is used as a resource for all pupils with communication and social-learning difficulties, not just for pupils with an autism diagnosis. Pupils with autism invite their peers to join them in the unit for both academic and social/play tasks. This means that there is a constant flow of pupils coming and going through the unit. The school also decided to utilise the SNA provision in a different manner. All SNAs are used as learner resources, both in the unit and mainstream. None are attached specifically to the same pupil in any one day (which is the norm in most schools in Ireland, though this is gradually changing). They are constantly moving from class to class and pupil to pupil. Both unit teachers meet each morning with the SNAs and provide detailed timetables and directions for learner support.

Leaders of inclusion

Throughout the observations (N = 27 hours) of teaching and learning in this school, it becomes clear that both teachers have taken a significant leadership role in the functioning and management of the unit, and they have become key facilitators to the effectiveness of this inclusion initiative. In essence they have taken on a transactional leadership role (Bass, 1999; Burns, 1978). They have set up a system that appeals to the better judgment of best practice as a whole school. In order to realise this goal of inclusion, the teachers engage in a high level of preparation and planning to develop what appears to be an "exchange relationship" (Bass, 1999). It is well acknowledged that teaching is challenging, and teaching children with autism is more challenging. To keep the mainstream teachers on board with the project, both of the unit teachers offer a "contingent reward". The mainstream teachers get additional teaching support for all learners and take a shared responsibility for academic and social learning of children enrolled in their classrooms. They also get additional support through the timetabling of Special Needs Assistants (SNA) to support the whole class during academic work tasks. Both of the unit teachers engage in an "management by exception" model (Bass, 1999), in that they do not assume sole responsibility and they value the skills and practices of the class teacher, monitoring from a distance and liaising on planning and team-teaching activities. They schedule all of the movement and deployment of the SNA team and support them in their practice as care givers. The "exception" happens when issues arise that disturb the practice and communications of the team. Both unit teachers are the designated problem-solvers and intervene only to protect the system and the initiative. However, as a pair, they engage in high level planning with each other.

The principal of this school has an administrative role and leads the whole staff, parents, and the Board of Management through a "transformational leadership style" (Bass, 1999; Burns, 1978). He is proactive in encouraging change and supporting creative ideas. Parents have expressed how he has demonstrated care and opened up opportunities for their children with autism; he has also encouraged their full participation in local community activities. He is an active listener, and he has regular meetings with both unit teachers as to the day-to-day workings of the unit and the inclusion timetabling. He seeks to support the whole staff in problem-solving, and takes direction on immediate actions - especially if an issue arises for parents.

Using the "thinking tools" discussed above, consider:

Policy:
- How policy in Case School 2 differs from Case School 1.
- How Case School 2 responds to learner needs locally in light of national and international policy.

Practice:
- How leadership in practice supports quality provision for all learners across the school.
- How collaboration on a number of different levels within the school can generate great flexibility among staff, and build capacity for an integrative approach to inclusion.

Experience:
- How the co-operating partners build quality teaching and learning experiences for the whole staff. Why does this matter?
- Outcomes: The outcomes for learners in this inclusion model.

- How you perceive the outcomes for the parents in this school.

Schedule:

- What/who, if anything or anyone, may have been sacrificed to achieve this inclusion model.

Discussion

The latter case study provides a thesis that inclusion requires team collaboration and collective or "distributive" leadership. As an example of success it might draw us to the belief that it is the role of individual schools to be successful in the implementation of "inclusion" for all learners. However, the success of this school is reliant on the quality of school and community relationships. What would happen with a change of principal or a change of teacher partners? Relationships, and the development of mutual understanding and progressive attitudes to inclusion, are a constant organic feature within a school and it's community. This is well evidenced in Case School 2, where the "transactional" leaders maintain a flexible support and trust their colleagues to make decisions and take risks. Inclusive education is a national priority, but different systems exist within the Irish state and this provides a greater level of diversity to the ideology and practice of inclusion. While it is the responsibility of the state as a whole to function more effectively, schools must be autonomous in achieving quality inclusive practices by thinking globally and acting locally (Booth & Ainscow, 1998). School-wide structures that support the school and community's collective philosophy of inclusion emerge through a collaboration for risk-taking and change-making. Case School 2 is working from a "bottom up" approach. In the instance of Case School 1, a direct result of the harsh realities of the workplace is that the teachers and staff of this school appear to have limited agency, limited opportunities to show leadership, and a lack of control to influence better practice options.. A greater 'top down' approach is needed in this school to implement a reflective workplace audit on "what is/isn't being achieved, and how or why?" This requires capacity-building from the national school support services to enable the school to engage meaningfully with generating a collective ideology and strategic plan for better inclusive practices. To conclude on a positive note, Project IRIS (Rose, Shevlin, Winters, & O'Raw, 2015) and other NCSE research projects have enabled Ireland to re-evaluate the allocation of resources, including staff. Going forward from 2018, schools are required to establish a team approach to SEN provision and support. It is early days in this venture, but the case of Mary will be an important one to follow as rural schools have, as stated earlier, limited resources; this raises the question about whether rural schools will emerge as disadvantaged in the new drive for autonomy and team-led decision making for better inclusive outcomes and practice.

References

Allen, J. (2008). *Rethinking inclusive education: The philosophers of difference in practice.* London: Springer.

Autism-Europe. (2007). *Autism and case law: Protecting the rights to education for children with autism.* Retrieved from http://www.autismeurope.org/files/files/caselaw-uk.pdf

Bass, B. M. (1999). Two decades of research and development in transformational leadership. *European Journal of Work and Organizational Psychology, 8*(1), 9-32.

Booth, T. & Ainscow, M. (Eds) (1998). *From them to us: An international study of inclusion in Education.* London. Routledge.

Burns, J. (1978 / 1982). *Leadership.* New York: Harper Row Publishers.

Centre for Disease Control, (2014). Facts About Autism.

Couper, L. (2015). The road to inclusion for children with autism spectrum disorders. In R. Craven, A. Morin, D. Tracey, P. Parker, & H. F. Zhong (Eds.), *Inclusive education for students with intellectual disabilities.* Charlotte, NC: Information Age Publishing IAP.

Cullinan, E. (2017). Voice of the child - An investigation into the social inclusion of children with autism spectrum disorder in mainstream primary settings. *REACH Journal of Special Needs Education in Ireland, 30*(1), 23-35.

Danforth, S., & Jones, P. (2015). From special education to integration to genuine inclusion. In P. Jones & S. Dansforth (Eds.), *Foundations of inclusive education research (International perspectives on inclusive education* (Vol. 6). Bingley, UK: Emerald Group Publishing.

Day, T., & Travers, J. (Eds.). (2014). *Special and inclusive education: A research perspective*. Oxford: Peter Lang.

Department of Health (2014). *The prevalence of Autism (including Asperger Syndrome) in school age children in Northern Ireland 2014*. Retrieved from Information Analysis Directorate.

Golding, M. M. (2012). Beyond compliance: The importance of group work in the education of children and young people with autism. In S. Powell & R. Jordan (Eds.), *Autism and learning: A guide to good practice*. (2nd Edn.). Oxfordshire, UK: David Fulton Publishers.

Higgins, N., MacArthur, J., & Kelly, B. (2009). Including disabled children at school: is it really as simple as 'a, c, d'? *International Journal of Inclusive Education, 13*(5), 471-487.

Imrie, R., & Kumar, M. (1998). Focusing on disability and access in the built environment. *Disability and Society, 13*(3), 357-374.

McCoy, S., Banks, J., Frawley, D., Watson, D., Shevlin, M., & Smyth, F. (2014). *Understanding Special Class Provision in Ireland. Phase 1: Finding from a national survey of schools* (16). Retrieved from http://www.ncse.ie

NCSE. (2015). *Supporting Students with Autism spectrum Disorder in Schools, Policy Advice*. Retrieved from http://www.ncse.ie

NCSE. (2013) *Choosing A School: A guide for parents and guardians of children and young people with Special Educational Needs*. Retrieved from http://www.ncse.ie

Norwich, B. (2007). *Dilemmas of Difference, Inclusion and Disability: International Perspectives and Future Directions*. London: Taylor and Francis.

Ravet, J. (2011). Inclusive/exclusive? Contradictory perspectives on autism and inclusion: the case for an integrative position. *International Journal of Inclusive Education, 15*(6), 667-682.

Rose, R., Shevlin, M., Winter, E., & O'Raw, P. (2015). *Project IRIS: Inclusive Research in Irish Schools. A longitudinal study of the experiences of and outcomes for pupils with special educational needs (SEN) in Irish schools*. National Council for Special Educational Needs (NCSE): Trim, Co. Meath.

Russell, G., Rogers, L. R., & Ukoumunne, O. C. (2014). Prevalance of Parental Reported ASD and ADHD in the UK: Findings from the Millennium Cohort Study. *Journal of Autism and Developmental Dosorders, 44*(1), 30-41.

Shevlin, M., Kenny, M., & Loxley, A. (2008). A time of transition: Exploring special educational provision in the Republic of Ireland. *Journal of Research in special Educational Needs, 8*(3), 141-152.

Warnock, M. (1978). *Report of the Committee of Enquiry into the Education of Handicapped Children and Young People*. Retrieved from London: http://www.educationengland.org.uk/documents/warnock/warnock1978.html

Case #36

Educator Bias and Judgement and Student Discipline

Bill de la Cruz

This case highlights challenges that arise around discipline disproportionality of black students in K-12 public education.

Overview

Denver Public Schools, (DPS), is located in Denver, Colorado, and is a majority/minority school district. DPS has 92,000 students and over 5000 teachers. 74% of our students identify as students of color and 75% of our teachers are white. Black students in DPS are over-referred for in-school discipline, and are given out-of-school suspensions at 3 times the rate of white students—for the same behaviors. As we look at the data we see that many of these referrals are for subjective behaviors that are rooted in biases and judgments towards black students. The social message and stereotypes of black students in society is driving many of these referrals, and DPS is looking at how to lower these subjective discipline referrals.

DPS is focusing on studying how implicit and explicit biases, coupled with social stereotypes, are affecting the high number of black students referred for suspensions.

In Denver Public Schools, (DPS), 14% of the students are black while only about 4% of the teachers are black. In the fall of 2017 the Superintendent and Board of Education commissioned a report on the experiences of African American educators and students in DPS. The report was titled, "An Examination of Student and Educator Experiences in Denver Public Schools Through the Voices of African American Teachers and Administrators". The report was written by Dr. Sharon Bailey, of Denver Public Schools, and had a number of outcomes. Many issues regarding the discipline of black students surfaced, including the fact that black students are more harshly disciplined than white students — in part, the educators said, because young, white, female teachers seem afraid of them. The Board of Education and Superintendent have publicly admitted that DPS operates in an institutionally biased and racist system that was not designed to educate the diversity of students in our classrooms. Admitting that this is our construct of education is only a first step in addressing the inequities of discipline disproportionality. Currently, teachers are ill equipped to address implicit and explicit bias issues in the classrooms, and discipline issues with black students quickly digress into racial issues. Racial conversations are very challenging, because as soon as someone is told their behavior, language, or interaction is racist the conversation moves to one person defending themselves about not being racist and the other person justifying why they believe the other person is racist.

This turns into a lose/lose conversation, and the relationship is impacted in a negative manner. During observations and assessment of teacher practices by senior team teacher leads, the racial impacts of teacher interactions is the most challenging conversation. In terms of suspensions, the district has suspended fewer African-American boys than eight years ago, yet African-American boys are still more likely to be suspended than white boys. This disproportionate trend also holds true in the expulsion of African-American boys (DPS, African-American and Black Student Outcomes in the Denver Public Schools, 2015).

Despite these indicators of progress, African-American students remain at the bottom of the ladders of student achievement and opportunity in the district. Within the Denver Plan 2020, there are specific goals related to diversity, equity, and inclusion, as well as closing achievement and opportunity gaps. However, without a strong and intentional focus on these elements of the plan, and targeted initiatives focused on

African-American students, equity and progress will remain elusive.

Despite policies and practices like restorative justice, the discipline matrix, and reductions in the number of African-American students suspended or expelled, African-American students remain disproportionately impacted. Participants observed that staffs are still struggling with discipline, and there's not enough support for the effective implementation of restorative justice. Additionally, the discipline matrix is viewed by some as too cumbersome.

Study participants shared that many of the young, female, Anglo teachers and administrators, who comprise the disproportionate majority of the DPS workforce, fear African-American students. "I think some of our teachers are afraid of African-American males. Because of this, these teachers just kick African-American males out of the classrooms. One day I counted six different African-American males just hanging out in the hallway because they were kicked out of class. I went to the principal about this. I think the principal wants to help but does not know how." (P15T). The following is a quote from a participant in the study regarding the impacts of white teachers' discipline approaches to black students. "African-American students are suffering a great deal. I don't think the teachers of other races are interested in really helping our students, so it becomes a situation where the acting-out behavior takes over to get the attention they so desperately want." (P22T)

DPS has started to take some action to address these issues by requiring teachers new to the district to take 4 hours of culturally responsive practic and bias awareness training. This is built into their onboarding experience, and is required if you are new to DPS, whether you are a teacher just out of college or have been teaching for many years. The challenge is that these new teachers do not always go back into schools where the culturally responsive practices and bias awareness protocols are standard practice. The district is also moving towards a process called choice and autonomy, where the school is the focus of change and all professional development must be invited in by the leadership team.

With this process, it is challenging to require and mandate that culturally responsive and bias awareness training be implemented in the schools. There are also quite a few approaches to the discipline process, including restorative practices, no nonsense nurturing, multi-tiered system of supports, as well as other approaches to discipline referrals. Like many school districts, the approach to solving the discipline issues comes in the form of a program-driven approach. The idea being that there is a program out there that will shift our biases and judgment and positively impact discipline-behavioral outcomes.

However, the reality is that over the past 50 years there has been no program that achieved this goal. If the approach to discipline disproportionality is not in programs then it must be about people, and the question becomes, "How do we invest more in the relationships between teachers and students"? In a recent similarity study conducted by Harvard, researchers were looking at what changed in the classroom when a teacher and student had a known relational similarity.

The finding of this study showed that, for the students who had a known similarity with the teacher, performance went up and discipline issues went down. As Gehlbach notes, "Additional analyses led to an interesting, albeit, more speculative finding." When looking at students who are often well-served in schools (White and Asian) in comparison to historically underserved students (Black and Latino), the "analyses suggest that the intervention was most effective in helping teachers connect with the historically underserved students. On average, the achievement gap between the well-served and underserved students at this school is reduced by over 60 percent, as measured by course grades."

As DPS embarks on a multi-year approach to shifting the negative impacts of over-referring black students to in-school and out-of-school suspension, many of these findings play an important role. As DPS explores the impact of bias awareness, coupled with culturally responsive practices and protocols, there will have to be a shift in professional development and the value of relationships. DPS is still struggling with what to require in a school district of choice and autonomy, and will continue to work to find the balance between assessment and relationships between teachers and students.

Problem Statement

In a culture driven by test-assessment, where we teach to the test, how do teachers and administrators make time to facilitate relational leadership between teachers and students. In answering the questions below, consider how your answers may change whether you were the school principal or the classroom teacher.

Questions

- Upon learning that biases and judgments were adding to the high number of discipline referrals for black students, teachers were not sure how to uncover those biases. Teachers and administrators were asked to reflect on the biases and judgments assumptions they have when assessing the behaviors of black students compared with similar behaviors by white students. Reviewing the case as presented:
    a. What biases and judgments may have come into play?
    b. How might these biases have influenced the overreferral of black students to discipline by school staff?
    c. How would you guide professional development of staff so that they became aware of discipline biases and judgments of black students?

- In DPS there are multiple practices and approaches to shift discipline behavior and referrals in the classroom. Many of these approaches are not designed from the relational approach between teacher and student. Teachers are not trained about how to bring vulnerability-based stories into the classroom. Without these tools, teachers do not know or understand the student's story. This lack of understanding is prevalent in the black teacher's quote we saw above.
    a. How would you evaluate the impact of a programmatic approach, and the effectiveness of programs in shifting and reducing discipline referrals for black students?

b. What is the balance between an assessment-driven culture and building relationships with students?
　　c. What was the level of your own training on culturally-responsive teaching and bias awareness?
　　d. If you are teaching in a classroom with students whom you do not reflect you , how do you heighten your self-awareness of your own biases and judgments? Be prepared to explain your process.

- School staff find themselves in a mandate where they are assessed based on test scores. Schools are judged and rated based on the outcomes of these tests, and families pick schools based on test scores. If you are a school leader, how would you restructure professional development to address the balance between assessments and relationships between teachers and students?

- Many teachers in this case study talk about the importance of relationship, and understood the impacts of bias and judgment in relationships with black students. In the DPS African American study there is an acknowledgement that white teachers are not prepared in teacher colleges to teach the diversity of students in classrooms today.
　　a. As a building leader how prepared are you to have conversations about your own biases and judgments towards students, staff, and families who are different from you?
　　b. As a teacher how will you advocate for a shift to a balanced approach to assessment and relationships in the classroom and school building?
　　c. In an assessment-driven culture what does 'relationships matter' really mean?

References

Asmar, M. 2016, *One Way Denver Public Schools is addressing race and culture in the classrooms.* Retrieved from: https://www.chalkbeat.org/posts/co/2016/08/12/one-way-denver-public-schools-is-addressing-race-and-culture-in-the-classroom/

Asmar, M, 2016, *Acknowledging institutional racism, Denver Public Schools details response to black educators' concerns* retrieved from: https://www.chalkbeat.org/posts/co/2016/10/03/acknowledging-institutional-racism-denver-public-schools-details-response-to-black-educators-concerns/

Bailey, S. 2017, *An Examination of Student and Educator Experiences in Denver Public Schools Through the Voices of African American Teachers and Administrators* retrieved from: https://celt.dpsk12.org/wp-content/uploads/sites/52/Dr.-Bailey-Report-FULL-2.pdf

Boasberg, T, 2016 *Empowerment and Equity: Schools as the Unit of Change,* retrieved from: http://board.dpsk12.org/2016/10/07/empowerment-and-equity-schools-as-the-unit-of-change/

H. Gehlbach, M. Brinkwirth, A. King, L. Hsu, J. McIntrye, T. Rogers, 2014, *Creating Birds of Similar Studies* retrieved from: http://panorama-www.s3.amazonaws.com/research/similarity.pdf

Case #37

Stacey Is Not Attending School

Debbie Donsky & Darrin Griffiths

Stonehouse Elementary School is a kindergarten to Grade 8 school located in a large urban area. There are approximately 440 students and 29 staff members, many of whom have been at the school longer than ten years. The school has a reputation of being the gem of the District, as standardized test scores have always been high, so high that a number of national media outlets did stories on the school in June 2016. The school principal, Todd Boyd, is known for his laser-like focus on quantitative statistics and pursuit of excellent on the district's standardized tests. Principal Boyd had been at Stonehouse for eight years, and prided himself on narrowing the focus of all staff to defining success as being directly linked to the outcomes of those tests. Principal Boyd was promoted in July 2016 to a district school position and a new principal, Shelagh Fenton, was hired to begin at Stonehouse for September 2016. Fenton, an experienced principal herself, is excited about starting at the gem of the district, but has heard from colleagues that Stonehouse has some major challenges in terms of addressing students' needs.

During her first week in her new role, Principal Fenton begins to better understand what her colleagues meant. The school operated much like an efficient factory, or manufacturing plant, based on rules and regulations outlined by Dr. Boyd: no talking in the hallways; detention for being late—or any transgressions against the rules and regulations—takes place after school in the library, where students work on literacy and numeracy practice sheets; and few teams or activities take place during the lunches or after school except for an activity here or there that is championed by an individual staff member. The students seemed to be compliant, but there did not seem to be joy or excitement with any of the school participants, including the staff.

A parent, Ms. Davis, came on the second day of that first week wanting to speak with Principal Fenton. Principal Fenton welcomed her into her office and Ms. Davis began sharing about her daughter, Stacey. Stacey, who is in grade seven this year, hardly attended last year due to severe anxiety that is heightened when she arrives at school. Stacey started at Stonehouse School in grade six, and after the first couple of days started dreading and resisting going to school. Mom acknowledged that when Stacy was in grade five she was diagnosed with generalized anxiety disorder by a psychiatrist who felt that using non-medicinal solutions (such as cognitive behaviour therapy, mindfulness and meditative practices) was best at the time. This diagnosis was combined with her previous educational assessment in which she was determined to have a non-verbal learning disability. Both assessments concluded that Stacey would need differentiated support in school in order for her to be successful. In grade five Stacey attended school on a regular basis; she felt very anxious throughout the day, especially when there were assessments and tests for which she required more time and differentiated instruction and assessment. Mom continues by saying that she brought the doctor's note and recommendations for supporting Stacey when they first came to Stonehouse in September 2015. Principal Boyd was too busy to meet with her, but indicated that if Stacey was anxious at Stonehouse it would only be from changing schools, and that she soon would be fine "as the Stonehouse rules and regulations and programs work for everyone". Principal Boyd had been given the doctor's letter, but neither he nor any other person from the school contacted mom about it. Stacey started resisting going to school in the third week of grade six and it became more and more difficult for mom to get her to school. Mom requested meetings with the school, and the only response she got back was that Stacey could have support from the school district with regard to instruction at home, four hours per week. Mom pursued that option in January 2016 after Stacey stopped attending altogether.

Now in September 2016, Mom is hopeful that with a new principal Stacey's needs will be addressed by the school. Principal Fenton thanked Mom for the meeting and told her she would contact her in a couple of days with some information. After Stacey's mom left the office, one of the school secretaries remarked that there are fourteen other students on home instruction. Principal Fenton was shocked to hear this number; home instruction is a rare occurrence in elementary schools, unless there is a physical reason why the student cannot attend school. Principal Fenton spoke with the grade seven teacher, Mr. Rolph, who is supposed to be Stacey's teacher this year. Mr. Rolph said that "he is not a big believer in this anxiety stuff, and most of the time people use it as an excuse not to work or follow the rules." Principal Fenton then met with Patricia Cole, the special education support teacher [SERT], who mentioned that for the past number of years she had been directed to support the students who were doing well on the standardized tests with little to no differentiation, and to provide very little support for the students who require extensive support. Ms. Cole hopes that Principal Fenton's arrival will mean an end to this over-reliance and focus on standardized testing.

It is 5:00 p.m. on Thursday of the first week of school, and Principal Fenton is feeling overwhelmed about the challenges and issues she has uncovered in her first couple of days; she does not know how or where to proceed.

Case Problems

- What questions do you have in this scenario?
- What are the key issues that Principal Fenton will have to address with students, staff, and community?
- What district and local supports can Principal Fenton access? Who would be the first contact? What will be the considerations for the plan going forward?
- Knowing that the previous principal was promoted to a district-level position, what questions might you have about how and why he was promoted? In what ways might Principal Fenton feel vulnerable

given this reality?
- What professional learning might be needed for staff?
- What support is needed with parents and community?
- How might Principal Fenton begin to build a mentally-healthy school community? Policies? Programs?

Teaching Strategies

- Making learning relevant and authentic to the students' experiences and interests can have a profound impact on student achievement and wellbeing. Seek opportunities for learning that has real world connection, is inquiry based, and culturally relevant and responsive.

- Bringing parents and community into the learning of their children is proven to have a positive impact. Building strong connections between home and school, while supporting a mentally-healthy school community is key to student achievement and wellbeing. Find ways to engage community in this dialogue for school wide change, as well as goal setting with families to improve connection between home and school. Ensuring that your school environment is welcoming is a key way to begin to connect with parents, families, and community.

- Incorporating mindfulness and physical activity will improve student and staff wellbeing. Create opportunities for quiet spaces, reflection rooms, outdoor and land-based learning, and culturally relevant and responsive learning.

Resources

Carney, Patrick and Parr, Michelann (2014). *"Resilient, Active, and Flourishing: Supporting Positive Mental Health and Well-Being in School Communities"* from *What Works? Research into Practice*, Toronto: Queen's Printer for Ontario.

Douglas, Ann (2015). *Parenting through the Storm*. Toronto: Harper Collins Publishers Ltd.

Jennings, Patricia A (2018). *The Trauma-Sensitive Classroom: Building Resilience with Compassionate.* Teaching. New York: WW Norton, Inc.

Ontario Ministry of Education (2014). *Culturally Responsive Pedagogy Towards Equity and Inclusivity in Ontario Schools.* Queen's Printer for Ontario.

Ontario Ministry of Education (2014). *Foundations for a Healthy School Promoting well-being is part of Ontario's Achieving Excellence vision.* Queen's Printer for Ontario.

Reilly, Nadja (2015) *Anxiety and Depression in the Classroom: A Teacher's Guide to Fostering Self-Regulation in Young Students.* New York: WW Norton, Inc.

Tranter, David, Carson, Lori, & Boland, Tom (2018) *The Third Path: A Relationship Based Approach to Student Well-Being and Achievement.* Nelson.

Case #38

Including Samir:
Resistance to Inclusion - how to help school communities embrace integration, and moderate/severe disabilities

DeLacy Ganley & Samara Suafo'a

Introduction

Introducing Samir

Samir is an eleven year old boy in Grade 6. An above average reader who is gifted with numbers, Samir does suitably well academically (mostly As and Bs). His teachers say he could easily earn top marks if he put greater effort into being more organized and if he took more pride in his work.

He finds the most joy in the non-academic aspects of his school day: recess, PE, lunch. He sees himself as a "scholar athlete."

Samir is involved in a number of afterschool sports: sometimes soccer, sometimes baseball, sometimes basketball…and occasionally, when the seasons overlap, all three. Practices run about two hours a day, and there are typically two to three games on the weekend. Samir's mother says that when Samir doesn't get this high level of activity that he gets crabby and has trouble falling to sleep at night at a reasonable hour.

Samir's typical demeanor is cheerful, helpful, and kind. His teachers often pair him with shy peers for group activities because they seem to come out of their shell around him. His teachers notice that he often looks out for others. Once, when a teacher assigned the students in the class to print some pictures off the internet for homework, he made two sets, knowing the girl who sat next to him was homeless, bobbling between a motel and the car, and wouldn't be able to do the assignment. In the morning, he slipped her a set of photos with no fanfare. She grinned, and he winked. It is this easy-going nature that has made him well liked by his peers.

Introducing Walnut Elementary & Jackson Elementary

Walnut Elementary is a PreK-Grade 6 public school in Southern California that serves approximately 700 students. As is typical for public schools of its kind in the area, the student-to-teacher ratio is 32:1. Approximately 40% of the students are English Language Learners and about 55% are on reduced-cost lunch.

Sharing a campus with Walnut Elementary is Jackson Elementary, a PreK-Grade 6 public school that serves a small, unique population: approximately 70 - 80 students who have physical disabilities and/or health impairments [i.e., cerebral palsy, traumatic brain injury (TBI), muscular dystrophy, spina bifida, brittle bone disease, and autism with secondary physical impairments, etc.]. The vast majority of these students use wheelchairs and/or walkers, and many require feeding tubes. Their teachers have an educational specialist credential (typically moderate/sever) with an added authorization in orthopedic impairment (OI). In the classrooms serving the students with physical disabilities and/or health impairments, there is a high ratio of adults to children (5:1).

Although they've shared a campus for 40+ years, students and staff of these two schools have historically had little interaction with each other. In fact, they often didn't even see each other as each school had its own space, its own office, its own entrance.

A new school: Walnut Jackson Elementary

Samir attended Walnut Elementary since Grade K. On his first day of Grade 6 (his last year in elementary), Samir learned that a change had happened over the summer: Walnut and Jackson had merged into a single school, and he now was a student of Walnut Jackson Elementary.

The change caught Samir by surprise.

According to informal campus scuttlebutt, the "district's master plan" from the get-go (i.e., from fifty years ago) was for there to be a single school on the site. Nobody on campus could tell you why the original plan wasn't followed and what led to two separate schools co-existing on the same campus for so long. Equally vague, though, was the motivation for the two schools to suddenly be merged. At the end of last year, it was announced that the long-time principal from Jackson was retiring, and the principal from Walnut was being promoted to a different district-level position. At the time, the assumption among the schools' parents and students was that two new principals would be hired. Nobody had expected to return to one merged entity.

When staff is asked why the schools had merged, a concise and static answer is provided: "This was always the idea, always the plan... isn't it great that it is becoming a reality? We are finally one school!"

The biggest public cheerleader for the merger has been the new principal. Much earlier in her career, before transferring to a different district, she had worked as a primary teacher at Walnut. As such, although she has ties to the school, few current families or personnel knew her. On opening day, she explained that it was always "her dream" to see the schools unified. She didn't provide any detail about why she liked the idea of merging the schools but her enthusiasm and commitment to the idea was publicly evident. On Day 1 of the new year, she beamed as she cut the new-school ribbon with pomp.

Re-Norming Walnut Jackson Elementary

In recognition of being a single school, Walnut Jackson adopted a new motto: TEAM (Together Everyone Achieves More). Also, the school logo was changed to a mash-up of the prior two mascots: the tail of an alligator (previously the mascot of Walnut) and the tail of a whale (previously the mascot of Jackson).

Although officially one school, the students are still separate from each other for their instructional day. The former students of Jackson, for example, are still with the same teachers as before in the same cluster of classrooms on the south side of campus. Likewise, the composition and location of the "Walnut classes" have not changed. (Almost all of the students and staff continue to self-identify as being from "Jackson" or from "Walnut." Similarly, areas of campus are still referred to as "up on the Walnut side" or "down by Jackson.")

In the non-instructional parts of the day, the students have increased contact with each other. Assemblies are joint affairs and there are now common spaces shared by both student groups, including the cafeteria, library, multipurpose room, and the outside lunch area. Once a week the various students of Walnut Jackson gather on the blacktop for morning announcements and recognition awards (the favorite being the weekly 'I caught you doing something good' award which is celebrated by the awardees running—or rolling—through a high-five line.)

Student council is another combined activity. There are now two school presidents, two vice-presidents, two treasurers, and two secretaries, with a representative for each office coming from both student populations. These student officers meet to weigh-in on campus-wide issues. Morning announcements are done by the two presidents in tandem.

The "Walnut" and "Jackson" students have the most regular contact with each other at lunch and at recess. At lunch, the students are told to "file in," filling one table at a time as they arrive. This has led to Walnut students and Jackson students (and their aides) being interspersed at the same tables. After lunch, the students head to the playground for recess. The principal has put strict rules in place to make the recess area safe for all students. It is now "illegal" to do anything on the playground that might jostle students who are in wheelchairs, using walkers or are otherwise unstable on their feet.

Problem Statement

In the last three months Samir has started bellyaching about going to school. He now drags himself out of bed saying, "I'm only going because you won't let me go to afterschool sports if I don't go to school."

Samir doesn't voice his frustrations in public. At home his complaints to his family revolve around:

Recess.

- "The new principal stands out there and watches us. She says we might knock down one of the Jackson kids. She makes sure nobody runs, even when there aren't Jackson students on the blacktop."
- "We can't play *real* basketball anymore. We can't steal the ball. We can't keep score. We are all just standing there on the court and occasionally throwing the ball at the hoop. Yawn."

Lunch.

- "We can't pick who we sit next to or save seats, so I can't sit with my friends. When I have to sit next to a Jackson kid I get grossed out. Their food spills out of their mouth and flies everywhere. It lands on my food …"
- "It's not fun to sit next to a Jackson kid at lunch…They can't talk and eat at the same time or they will choke, so we just sit there. Boring."
- "One of the kids sitting next to at lunch me pooped in his diaper. I had to sit there like nothing happened. I felt trapped."

Morning Announcements.

- "I can't understand morning announcements. Half of them are done by the Jackson president, and I can't understand what he says. Nobody can. So we just sit there bored." (The assessment that the announcements done by the Jackson students over the loudspeaker are typically unrecognizable is not hyperbolic.)

Plans are being changed (read "made less attractive" for Samir) because of the Jackson students.

- "Darcy said that the new principal is going to tear down the handball court because the Jackson kids can't play handball. I love handball! There is going to be nothing to do at recess!"
- "We were going to go to the pool for our Grade 6 graduation picnic but now we can't go there because they don't have ramps for the Jackson students. So it's just going to be at school. That sucks!" Samir's teacher has told Samir's parents that she has seen an "attitude

change" in Samir. She doesn't like the subtle eyerolls or huffs. She misses the helpful student whose positive nature, humor and popularity could buoy the group. He seems restless and edgy, particularly coming in from lunch and recess.

Samir's mother has mused to her colleagues, "The 'be empathetic,' 'be kind,' 'imagine if that was you' pitch just isn't working." At first, Samir's mom explains, she was really disappointed in his new (negative, impatient) attitude but more and more she is seeing how the situation isn't set up to meet her son's needs. She wonders if he is so crabby because he isn't allowed to "blow off steam" during after-lunch recess. Samir's mother is a teacher educator who has spent her professional life supporting inclusive, socially just learning environments that promote educational excellence and equity. The situation with Samir is making her reexamine many core beliefs. Maybe, she wonders silently, inclusivity all the time isn't really that great?

Case Problems

Discuss the following:
1. Lately Samir feels like his contact with the Jackson students (and the degree to which he needs to accommodate them and their unique needs) is "too much," that he is being asked to sacrifice and adjust "too much." Is his perception at all valid? Why or why not?
2. Identify various factors that might be linked to Samir's "restless edginess" and his (new) negative attitudes toward school.
3. How is the school's need to keep the Jackson students safe at recess at odds with Samir's need to be physical? Is there a way to balance the needs of both…and to still maintain the spirit of inclusivity?
4. One of the school's goals is to "help our students develop sound character and understand the responsibilities that go along with living in a democracy." Through the lens of this situation, how is this goal being met? How is it not being met? Support your answer.
5. How does one define inclusivity in this context? Are kids being exclusionary if they are playing a rigorous game of soccer that

isn't likely to be played or enjoyed by a peer who only has limited control of his body and must use a motorized wheelchair?

6. Currently, students at Walnut Jackson Elementary are being forced to sit next to each other at lunch. There is no "self-selection." How might things be different if kids were allowed to sit anywhere they want? When answering, take into account the work of Echols and Graham (2013). They found that youth have a natural proclivity toward "homophily;" that is, youth tend to form friendships with other children that they perceive to be "like" them in some way, be it in terms of academic achievement, or in their place in the social pecking order of the class, or in terms of some other factor.

7. Talk about the pros and cons of "forced integration." How does "forced interaction" feel fundamentally different to the parties involved than "self-initiated interaction?" Does "forced interaction" speed up (or slow down?) segregation? If you can, cite examples from history (i.e., America's civil right's movement, racial segregation, religious factions, etc.).

8. What should Samir's parents do? Where is the sweet spot between telling Samir to "suck it up" and validating his experience? Role play the conversation that Samir's parent should have with Samir.

9. Up until this point Samir has not voiced his frustration in a public place. But, let's say that he complains at school. What would you say to him (if anything) if you were his teacher? Would you contact his parents, and, if so, what would you say? And, switching perspectives, what would you say (if anything) if you were the principal and overheard Samir complaining? Role play these conversations.

10. Discuss the situation through the lens of privilege. How is Samir privileged? How is his response indicative of privilege? Do you think Samir sees himself as being privileged? In the context of Walnut Jackson, does simply not having a physical or learning challenge automatically make someone privileged?

11. Discuss the juxtaposition or interplay between *exclusivity* and *personal boundaries*. Where is the line between setting a personal

boundary and being non-inclusive? Where is the line between setting a personal boundary and being prejudicial? In an inclusive world, is it "okay" for someone with privilege to set personal boundaries? Is it okay for Samir to say he doesn't want to eat next to someone who is going to the bathroom in his pants? And, from what you can see from this limited case study, are students at Walnut Jackson Elementary allowed to set personal boundaries? How much agency does Samir have in the situation?

12. The change to one school was sudden. There was no community dialogue. Likewise, there was no orientation program once the merger had happened. Would an "orientation* program" have helped? If you think it would be helpful, articulate what an effective orientation program would involve; sketch out the components of an ideal orientation program. If you don't think an orientation would be helpful, articulate why. (*Orientations are often thought of as an event at the *beginning* of the year. Might an on-going program be more valuable? How are schools that are strapped for budget –and who have a limited number of days when they can expect families to be on campus– afford to have a program that spans the academic year?)

13. Identify evidence that suggests Samir has a history of being an ally to those who might be/feel disenfranchised or on the outs. In the long run, do you think Samir's recent experiences at Walnut Jackson will cultivate or erode Samir's proclivity to being an ally for others? Are we at risk of losing an ally...or might we have already lost him as an ally? What can be done to help Samir develop a genuine feeling of support/ally-ship for his peers?

14. Samir's mother, an educator who has built her professional career on promoting high quality teaching in the name of social justice, finds herself reexamining some of her core beliefs regarding inclusion. In an environment where one strives to embrace "research-based practice," is there space for personal experience? Does being a parent as well as an educator enhance Samir's mother's perspective or does it just muddle the issues with personal bias?

Relevant Resources & References

Ainscow, M., Howes, A., Farrell, P., & Frankham, J. (2003). Making sense of the development of inclusive practices. *European Journal of Special Needs Education, 18*(2), 227–242. https://doi.org/10.1080/0885625032000079005

Boyd, B., Seo, S., Ryndak, D. L., Fisher, D. (2005). Inclusive Education for Students with Severe Disabilities in the United States. Inclusive and Supportive Education Congress. Lecture

Brown, F., & Snell, M. E. (2006). *Instruction of students with severe disabilities* (6th ed.). Columbus, OH: Pearson

Burstein, N., Sears, S., Wilcoxen, A., Cabello, B., & Spagna, M. (2004). Moving toward inclusive practices. *Remedial and Special Education, 25*(2), 104–116.

Dyson, A., Gallannaugh, F., & Millward, A. (2003). Making space in the standards agenda: developing inclusive practices in schools. *European Educational Research Journal, 2*(2), 228–244.

Echols, L., & Graham, S. (2013). Birds of a different feather: How do cross-ethnic friends flock together? *Merrill-Palmer Quarterly, 59*(4), 461-488.

Freire, S., & César, M. (2003). Inclusive ideals/inclusive practices: how far is a dream from reality? Five comparative case studies. *European Journal of Special Needs Education, 18*(3), 341–354. https://doi.org/10.1080/0885625032000120224

IRIS Center & its web-based resources. https://iris.peabody.vanderbilt.edu/ and https://iris.peabody.vanderbilt.edu/iris-resource-locator/.

Katz, J., Mirenda, P. (2002). Including students with developmental disabilities in general education classrooms: Educational benefits. International Journal of Special Education, 17(2), 14-24.

King-Sears, M. E., & Cummings, C. S. (1996). Inclusive practices of classroom teachers. *Remedial and Special Education, 17*(4), 217–225.

Palacio, R.J. (2012). *Wonder*. New York: Random House.

Riehl, C.J. (2009). The Principal's Role in Creating Inclusive Schools for Diverse Students: A

Review of Normative, Empirical, and Critical Literature on the Practice of Educational Administration. Volume: 189 issue: 1-2, page(s): 183-197. https://doi.org/10.1177/0022057409189001-213.

Villa, R. A., Thousand, J. S., Nevin, A., & Liston, A. (2005). Successful inclusive practices in middle and secondary schools. *American Secondary Education*, 33–50.

Case #39

Navigating Religion, Creed, and Accommodation

Hiren Mistry

Introduction

Mr. Budwal, Principal at Maplegate PS, receives an email from parents of a Grade 1 child in his school. They ask for exemptions from classes that teach their son to identify body parts, including genitalia, using correct terminology. Ever since this became embedded as an expectation in the Healthy Living strand of the revised Grade 1 Health and Physical Education Curriculum, Mr. Budwal has received many of these exemption requests. In the email they ask that the school accommodate their son because they prefer to teach him the anatomically correct terms when they deem it "to be appropriate".

Principal Budwal invites the parents in for a meeting, which takes place the following morning. He respectfully asks the parents to clarify why they are asking for an exemption. Principal Budwal is aware that he is able to make exemptions due to sincerely held religious beliefs, though, based on what he was told recently at a religious accommodation workshop sponsored by the Board, he cannot if personal preference is the reason. The parents respond that it is their "personal choice", and felt that it was "their right" as parents to decide. They explain that the cultural values of their "tradition" place great importance on protecting the modesty of children, and that this is something they want to continue to uphold at home. The parents make no mention of a sacred text, nor the authority of a religious leader. They end the conversation with the following comment, "We hope you respect our personal choice in this matter, Principal Budwal. Our traditions mean a lot to us".

Principal Budwal returns to his desk and wonders out loud if the parents' request for exemption is due to personal preference, or if the request qualifies as a sincerely held religious or creed belief. To Budwal, their explanation sounds like something in between. He thumbs through two documents in front of him: the board approved Religious Accommodation Guidelines and a copy of the revised Ontario Human Rights Commission *Policy on the prevention of discrimination based on Creed* (2015). He groans, and then calls the Board's Equity Officer. "I just wish the answer was clear, and the process more straightforward", Budwal exclaims. "Who am I to judge if a request is personal preference, or a sincere religious belief? And...what is 'creed' anyway? I am a principal, not a lawyer or religious studies professor!"

Recent literature in legal scholarship that recasts religious-freedom cases as "cross cultural encounters" provides some clues about the importance of relationship and context building to support inclusive school practices for religious accommodation[1] Harold Kislowicz (2014) argues that there is a huge gap, in most cases, between the cultural and institutional worlds of judges and litigants. This observation often applies similarly to encounters between parents and administrators. Like judges, school principals have a long institutional involvement with the technical norms of schooling. When they make their decisions, they think and act in terms of the conventions of the school administration and leadership culture, using the "rules and symbols of those cultures" (2014, p. 149) in making their judgments. This forms the cultural world they occupy. In contrast, prior to a request for religious accommodation, families have a specific meaning attached to the belief or practice under review. Their practices are mostly unfamiliar to school principals and learning about such practices would not be featured in any dimension of their leadership

---

1 Benjamin Berger writes "the meeting of law and religion is not a juridical or technical problem but, rather, an instance of cross-cultural encounter" (2008, p. 246)

education. In order for families to 'translate' their practices and beliefs in the office of a school principal, they must "communicate across a cultural boundary" (p. 150) with administrators who are entrusted to come to a fair and equitable decision. It is not exactly an equitable or neutral context of communication. There are many opportunities, however, for principals to humanize conversations with them, especially when the conversations are about religion, creed and personal values.

Honest and open conversations about religion, creed, and family values requires that some horizon of shared understanding and trust exist. Yet if a principal's first substantial communication with a parent is their request for religious accommodation, then it is reasonable to assume that the conversation takes place across two, partially adversarial, solitudes. What sort of cross-cultural understandings are missing—and need unearthing—leading up to this request? In Principal Budwal's case, the family shares with him their stance on modesty. What is not clear is what exactly they are concerned about with regard to the curriculum and learning environment. It is also not entirely clear to Budwal what the family means by 'tradition' and 'values'. In other words, Principal Budwal requires more context and information to understand what exactly is eliciting the exemption request.

Problem Statement

Principal Budwal does not know what to do and needs support to reach an equitable and socially just decision.

Case Questions

1. Why is Principal Budwal so frustrated? On one hand, he has a professional duty to respond to the parent's request for exemption, while on the other hand Budwal is aware that students can only be exempted from classes that teach the correct name of body parts if there is a demonstrated conflict with a family's religious beliefs and values. This means, of course, that Budwal needs to make a series of difficult assessments: What counts as

religion or creed in this case, and others like it?

- How does a principal determine sincerity of belief?
- What is the difference between religion and creed, and how does a principal assess this?

2. What guides a principal's decision making process? In this scenario, it would be advisable for Principal Budwal to ask a series of self-reflective questions:

- What do I think I know about this family, their needs, worries, strengths, values?
- What opportunities as a school leader have I created to regularly engage with this family and this student in positive and inviting ways?
- What do I know about the family's social networks and community contexts? Have I made conscious attempts to build trust and relationships with this network?
- What is *my* understanding of religion, creed, secularism, and human rights? How does my situatedness impact how I engage and understand the religious accommodation requests of families who I perceive are different to 'my traditions' and 'my values'?

These questions speak to the larger challenge of how a principal can navigate the competing interests of freedom of religion and received understandings of secularism in public schools. For many school leaders, scenarios like this are some of the most challenging to manage in the context of inclusive leadership, because their decisions can get easily caught up in the messy, decontextualized, and often polarizing, public debates about religion, religious values, and their place in public education.

3. How would you develop leadership capacities to achieve equity and inclusion for diverse families in the context of increased religion and creed diversity in public schools? The following areas of focus are offered for consideration.

Define and Differentiate

There is often a gap between paper policy, teacher practice, and public understanding of learning and teaching in the classroom. When families ask for exemptions or accommodations to classroom practice, how do principals avoid situations where teachers and families get involved in terse exchanges about 'my religions values' versus 'my professional judgment'?

A useful place to turn to is curriculum documents themselves. In most cases, what is outlined are the broad knowledge and skills students are expected to learn. In an age when most curriculum documents embed the practice of differentiation of choice and assessment, a teacher can choose to engage student learning in a variety of ways. This should be based on what they know about the student's interests and prior learning, as well as deep knowledge of the curriculum. As a principal, there are a number of questions to consider that could sidestep polarizing debates about religion, and get closer to the source—whether real or perceived—of the family's concern.

- What is the family's understanding of the learning that will take place in the classroom, that has them concerned about their religious or creed values?
- How does the curriculum document describe the broad knowledge and skills students are expected to demonstrate, and does the teacher have an opportunity to describe the differentiated ways that learning can take place in the classroom?
- Are there opportunities for families to work with the classroom teacher to co-construct curricular accommodations that balance curriculum standards and their professed religious values?

When leaders construct opportunities for families and teachers to understand each other's context, practices, and intentions, religion and creed avoid being framed as monoliths—or as antagonistic to secularism.

However, this requires that principals become conscious of their own understanding of religion and creed, and their own potential biases about families who they perceive are from religious, creed or cultural traditions that are different to their own.

Unlearn Religion: Develop Religious Literacy

Diane L. Moore, Professor at the Harvard Divinity School, notes that "One of the most troubling and urgent consequences of religious illiteracy is that it often fuels prejudice and antagonism, thereby hindering efforts aimed at promoting respect for pluralism, peaceful coexistence, and cooperative endeavors in local, national, and global arenas" (2007). To counter prejudice and antagonism, it is important for principals, and other school leaders, to become conscious of what they think about religion, to learn strategies to understand traditions and practices that are different to their own, and to unlearn the ways in which public discourse harmfully frames religion—and those who are religious—as monoliths and monsters.

As a way into religious literacy, principals should consider the following questions and ideas:

- **Understand religious identity:** Consider ways in which belief, practice, experience, and social/cultural contexts contribute to religious identity formation of the families and students that cross your path. When you consider these different dimensions of religious identity, what nuances or perspectives are revealed to you that you would ordinarily miss?

- **Develop Religious Perspective**: Consider the ways in which students understand religion, both in terms of their experience of diversity within specific religious traditions and in relation to different dispositions to religion (e.g., atheism, agnosticism, orthodoxy, etc.). No one is 'just a Hindu', 'just Muslim', 'just Jewish'. When we pay attention to regional diversity, family traditions, and dispositions to religion, we are encouraged to understand that identities are fluid and complex.

- **Understand Intersectionality:** Consider the ways in which the religious identities of students and families are connected to diverse social identities (gender, sexuality, race etc.), socio-economic factors (immigration, class, etc.), and socio-historical factors (colonialism, war, etc.). Individuals are never just one identity. Intersectionality provokes us to consider student identity beyond 'a single story' (Adichie, 2009).

Consider Creed

Creed is a prohibited ground of discrimination under the Ontario *Human Rights Code*. While creed was one the original grounds of discrimination when the Ontario Human Rights Code became law in 1962, its social meaning and interpretation in case law has changed over time (OHRC, 2012). As of 1996, the OHRC *Policy on creed and the accommodation of religious observances* interprets the word "creed" to mean "religious creed" or "religion", and specifically excludes non-religious or political beliefs. Since then, public understanding of what religion can mean has broadened to include more secular or ethical world views. In addition, the received understanding of the legitimate form of religion has shifted from the 'group', or communal, context, to greater emphasis on the agency of the individual to live by their subject experience of religion or creed (Beaman, 2011).

In December, 2015, the OHRC released the long-anticipated update to the 1996 policy entitled *Policy on preventing discrimination based on Creed*. The most notable change in the updated policy is a redefinition of creed and religion. I refer to the 2015 definition as 'open' to distinguish it from the 'broad' but restricted 1996 definition. This open definition hinges on two features, or concepts, particularly relevant for administrators faced with the responsibility of engaging in religious accommodation.

1. The idea that creed is a shared feature of *human* culture, rather than the expression of exclusively *religious* cultures. This notion recognizes, amongst other things, non-religious belief systems (or, 'conscience') as a dimension of creed (such as atheism). It

makes it possible for individuals with overarching political or philosophical belief systems to receive creed protection under the Code, where creed is an element of their discriminatory treatment.

2. The idea that creed should not be equated with an 'ideal type'. This idea encourages individuals and organizations to consider the behaviour of individuals as conceivably based in creed—even if the behaviours in question do not 'look like' or 'sound like' creed upon first interaction. This call to suspend judgment is to counter assumptions that the only legitimate religion and creed expressions are derivations of an ideal type based on, as the 2015 Creed policy explains, 'western' or 'mainstream' biases (p. 21). This change is applaudable for supporting the fundamental Charter principle of equality rights, as well as the historical liberal social justice roots of federal and provincial diversity policies (Joshee & Sinfield, 2010). Nevertheless, the authors of the OHRC Creed policy appear to recognize the challenge of distinguishing creed from other aspects of human culture, given that creed is no longer equated exclusively with religion. The 2015 OHRC Creed policy therefore offers the following criteria to guide such assessments. It states that creed:

- Is sincerely, freely, and deeply held;
- Is integrally linked to a person's identity, self-definition, and fulfillment;
- Is a particular and comprehensive, overarching system of belief that governs one's conduct and practices;
- Addresses ultimate questions of human existence, including ideas about life, purpose, death, and the existence or non-existence of a Creator and/or a higher or different order of existence; and
- Has some 'nexus' or connection to an organization or community that professes a shared system of belief (OHRC, 2015, p. 2).

From this list, the place and importance of belief is central to the first four guiding criteria. According to the OHRC criteria, a belief is a creed belief, rather than an ordinary or mundane belief, if it is 'sincerely' held and holds a profound significance to informing a person's existential place and purpose in the world. A creed belief, therefore, substantially informs an individual's dreams, desires, and motivations. In this formulation, it allegedly serves as a crucial link between understanding the interior and exterior of an individual.

Conclusion

Reframing school administrators as cross-cultural communicators, and religious accommodation as cross-cultural encounters, has strong potential for fulfilling the OHRC's mandate for preventing discrimination based on creed. This case study has aimed to stimulate questions, and point to some equity-leadership strategies available to administrators to ensure inclusion for diverse students and families who approach schools with religious accommodation requests.

References

Adichie CN. (2009) *The Danger of a Single Story*. TED Talk. Retrieved from: https://www.ted.com/talks/chimamanda_adichie_the_danger_of_a_single_story

Creed case law review. (2012). Retrieved from http://www.ohrc.on.ca/en/creed-case-law-review

Berger, B (2008) "The Cultural Limits of Legal Tolerance" (2008) 21:2 Can JL & Jur 245 at 246

Joshee, R & Sinfield, I (2010). The Canadian Multicultural Education Policy Web: Lessons to 'Learn, Pitfalls to Avoid Multicultural Education Review Vol. 2, No. 1, pp. 55-75

Kislowicz, H (2014). Faithful translations? Cross-cultural communication in Canadian religious freedom litigation. *Osgood Hall Law Journal* 52.1. pp 141-189.

Moore, D. L. (2007). *Overcoming religious illiteracy: A cultural studies approach to the study of religion in secondary education*. New York: Palgrave Macmillan

Policy on creed and the accommodation of religious observances. Retrieved from http://www.ohrc.on.ca/sites/default/files/attachments/Policy_on_creed_and_the_accommodation_of_religious_observances.pdf

Policy on Preventing discrimination based on creed. (2015). Retrieved from http://www.ohrc.on.ca/en/policy-preventing-discrimination-based-creed

Resources to support further learning

Balagangadhara, S.N (1994) *The Heathen in His Blindness: Asia, the West and the Dynamic of Religion.* E.J Brill: Leiden.

Creed, freedom of religion and human rights – Special issue of Diversity Magazine (2012). Volume 9:3. Summer.

Jackson, R (2004) *Rethinking Religious Education and Plurality: Issues in Diversity and Pedagogy.* London: Routledge.

Afterword

Difference, Diversity, and Inclusive Education: Seeing Difference Differently, and Doing Different Things

Denise Armstrong

Issues related to diversity, inclusion, and worthiness have been at the core of human interactions for centuries, resulting in the pervasive belief that some individuals and groups are more human than others. Over time, these ideals have been reproduced and entrenched in institutional structures and practices to ensure that dominant group members automatically receive privileges because of their presumed superiority. Conversely, individuals and groups who do not possess these desirable traits and identities are marginalized and pathologized as different. This conflation of difference and inferiority has historically spawned and justified ongoing systems of domination and oppression, ranging from segregation to slavery, apartheid, and even mass genocide. In many countries, challenges to these—and current—atrocities, and their negative impacts, have motivated human rights legislation, equity and anti-racist policies, and changes to attitudes about the positive aspects of diversity. Indeed, it is not unusual in today's world for businesses, educational institutions, and other organizations to tout difference and diversity as important commodities, and to configure their brands and mission statements to reflect these ideals.

However, after reading the cases in this volume, I was reminded that, in spite of discursive turns, well intended laws, actions, and equity proclamations, many of us are not comfortable with individuals who do not belong to our in-group. Human beings prefer and trust individuals and groups who think, talk, and look like us. Discomfort around including diversity becomes further refracted in multicultural environments where differences in physical and mental ability, race, religion, socioeconomic standing, gender orientation, etc. are the norm. Since educational institutions mirror societal patterns and prejudices, educators advertently and inadvertently translate racist, sexist, and classist prejudices into practices. While sad, it is not surprising that these patterns are reflected in schools, and that they impact students negatively throughout their academic and social lives. Progress has been slow, and authentic inclusion remains a distant dream for many.

The case studies in this volume bring to life important issues about inclusive education and leadership in a broad spectrum of countries and educational contexts. They also span a range of international boundaries (e.g., Canada, the US, UK, and Australia) and educational contexts (ranging from pre-school to higher education), confirming the global and organizational reach of these issues. The contributors describe daily issues of inclusion and exclusion which encompass, but are not limited to religion, race, gender, mental health, intellectual disabilities, and class. Each case delves beneath the surface to reveal the nuanced and complex dynamics that occur between people and organizations when 'difference' is manipulated to maintain the status quo. The cases reflect the struggles disenfranchised individuals face, confirming the endemic and enduring nature of discrimination and exclusion. Using real life examples to illustrate the issues facing students, staff, administrators, caregivers, and communities, the case narratives are chosen to portray different viewpoints and to illuminate how interlocking systems of oppression reinforce hegemonic Whiteness, heteronormativity, and patriarchy. Exposure to these varied and competing perspectives encourages readers to problem-solve issues related to inclusive leadership, and develops awareness of the need for institutional and individual self-examination and morally transformative action.

Reading these case studies also evoked memories of the successes and challenges I have experienced during my varied roles as a teacher, school administrator, and university professor who is committed to equity, social justice, and inclusionary practice. As I reflected on my praxis, I realized that many of challenges I experienced have been related to individual and institutional beliefs about difference and diversity, particularly where individual and institutional power were used to exclude and oppress "othered" individuals. I vividly recall a time when I placed a recently arrived Grade 9 student with refugee status in a compulsory math class. Although the student had scored highly on the school's pre-placement math tests, this math teacher refused to allow her in the class and rudely ordered her to return to the Guidance Office. When challenged, he argued that it was too late to join his class because he had already started a new unit. When I explained that the student was legally required to be registered in school, and there was no other math class available, he replied "Those parents need to figure out that if they want their kids to succeed, they should bring them into the country before September when school starts." I tried explaining that people who are fleeing war-torn countries have little control or choice about when they are allowed in a country, but he just didn't get it! In the end, with the help of the Vice-Principal, I was able to convince the teacher to allow the student to stay in the Math class due to our legal obligation to provide students under 16 years of age with a complete timetable. The defining lesson for me at that moment was that, in spite of our school's location in an economically-deprived area, and our espoused commitment to supporting our diverse immigrant population, not everyone saw diversity and inclusion as I did.

Developing a Critical Consciousness and Conscience

Over the years, I have come to realize that diversity and inclusion are ambiguous and contested terms, meaning different things to different people. Through this, and similar discriminatory incidents, I have learned that being an inclusive leader means understanding different perceptions of difference, how individual and institutional mind frames influence our responses to diversity, and how these can be changed in order to create inclusive environments. I now know that inclusive leaders need to know the range of perspectives on difference and diversity—and their historical genesis—in order to contextualize their praxis. Consequently, when teaching and mentoring organizational leaders, I emphasize the importance of position, perspective, and values, and I expose them to a range of ethical decision-making and frameworks that help them develop awareness of potential responses to difference and diversity. For example, students are introduced to a variety of frameworks, including Steinberg and Kincheloe's (2009) typology of the five common positions taken on diversity and multiculturalism; they are (a) *conservative/ monoculturalists*, (b) *liberal*, (c) *pluralist*, (d) *left-essential*, and (e) *critical diversity and multiculturalism*. I also invite students to position themselves physically in the classroom according to their ideological perspective, and to discuss their views on inclusion, diversity, and difference with like-minded students. They are then asked to debate with groups who hold different viewpoints regarding how to include difference and diversity. When analyzing assigned class readings, students are required to determine the different authors explicit and latent biases and values and to surface their own. These, and related activities, help current and potential educational leaders deconstruct how individuals and institutions respond to diversity based on implicit ideologies, and how sanctions and support vary depending on power, politics, and persuasion.

Students also become aware that issues of difference and diversity are not new, and acknowledge their responsibility to develop historical and social conscience and consciousness. Helen Harper's (1997) analysis of how difference is treated and produced in Ontario provides a useful overview of how educational organizations respond when confronted with the responsibility to "meet the needs of populations that are racially, culturally, and linguistically diverse, to confront gender, racial, and economic disparity and discrimination, to create classrooms in which there is mutual respect and social harmony, and at the same time establish some sense of a cohesive identity" (p. 192). Using an historical perspective, Harper documents five ways in which dominant groups respond to difference and diversity. These include: (a) *suppressing difference* through aggressive assimilation to ensure that Indigenous peoples and immigrants conformed to "Anglo-Saxon and Western ideals (p. 194); (b) *insisting on difference* through separation and segregation of women, Blacks and the mentally challenged based on notions of innate genetic and biological difference and academic ability to ensure maintenance of stereotypical identities, British bloodlines, and "cultural superiority" (p. 196); (c) *denying difference* by insisting on equal treatment for all based on meritocracy as opposed to identity; (d) *inviting difference* by encouraging Canadian cultural pluralism using cultural celebrations of food, festivals, and folklore; and (e) *critiquing difference* by interrogating how racial, ethnocultural, and gender identities are produced as (ab)normal through school curricula, policies, and practices.

I also encourage students to develop awareness of their own—and other—identities through a variety of different activities. One introductory activity asks them to draw a series of circles, and to identify three different identities that are core to how they define themselves. They are then asked to reflect on the countertypes and stereotypes associated with one of their identities, as well as a time when they were proud of one, or ashamed of one, of their identities. Students are then asked to share their responses with a partner. What the class finds interesting about this activity is discovering their similarities to others whom they assumed to be different. Students from non-dominant backgrounds often speak at length about their gendered and racialized identities, while White, male students typically report that this is the first time they reflected on their identities. During our debriefing activity we explore our feelings about the exercise, and raise critical questions about difference and diversity. Some of the common questions raised that are germane to improving our critical literacy can be used to extend the case studies in this volume. What do we mean by diversity? How do individual, institutional, and societal structures impact constructions of difference and diversity? How are diversity and difference produced and treated in schools and other organizations? What role does identity play in understanding and interacting with difference? How is power implicated in this process? What are the barriers to effective administration in diverse schools? What are the possibilities for effective and inclusive schools? How can educators organize and administer schools to support inclusion?

Embracing, Engaging, and Enrolling Difference

The Ontario's Equity and Inclusion Strategy (2014) defines equitable and inclusive schooling as an educational approach that honours and respects students' individuality and intersecting identities and asks all school, families and community members to contribute and participate in education. This implementation and policy guideline further states that,

> "Equity and inclusive education aims to understand, identify, address, and eliminate the biases, barriers, and power dynamics that limit students' prospects for learning, growing, and fully contributing to society. Barriers may be related to sex, sexual orientation, gender identity, gender expression, race, ethnic origin, religion, socio-economic background, physical or mental ability, or other factors...These barriers and biases, whether overt or subtle, intentional or unintentional, need to be identified and addressed" (p. 8).

It also describes inclusion as an ongoing process that requires schools and districts to monitor procedures, policies, and practices, to avoid marginalization and underachievement. For most educators, this appears to be a daunting task. Even those of us who are committed to inclusive leadership may ask, "How can I possibly do this with all of the other administrative and teaching tasks I am accountable for?" We may also point to a lack of many things – time, resources, money, staff, and so on. During my career, I have been privileged to research effective leaders who continue to build inclusive environments in disadvantaged communities in spite of these challenges. When asked to share how they achieve inclusion and equity goals, they provided the responses below; they are amalgamated under four dominant themes:

Relationship Building: Inclusive leaders recognize the impossibility of changing schools on their own, and they work collaboratively with their communities to change perspectives about alienating and discriminatory structures in educational and other societal institutions. In addition to modelling inclusive leadership, they engage in ongoing communication and collaboration with a wide variety of individuals and groups inside their school and district, and within the larger community. They see difference and similarity as important assets, and they intentionally encourage formal and informal leadership by sharing power with others. They consistently send out positive invitations to both supporters and detractors in order to build common ground to support sustainable change. Interacting with different viewpoints, strategizing, and learning how to access relevant resources and navigate political environments are crucial. They also believe that engaging in critical dialogues can surface contradictions that develop awareness of differences and similarities and stimulate thought and action.

Deep and Continuous Learning and Improvement: Inclusive leaders are committed to ongoing learning and improvement for themselves and others. In addition to honing their own self-awareness by critically and honestly examining their beliefs and values, they develop a deep and wide variety of knowledge of the people, programmes, policies, practices, politics, facilities, and finances in order to improve schools. Regular assessments of personal and professional practice and the school environment are conducted to make sure that they are "walking the talk" of equity and inclusion. In addition, they include their communities in generating equity and inclusion audits, and use the data to stimulate critical and courageous dialogue about inclusion and exclusion of various groups, and then subsequent positive action.

Standing Up and Standing Tall for Inclusive Values: These leaders believe that authentically including difference and diversity are an integral part of their professional and ethical responsibilities. They recognize the social and psychological damage that inequitable practices and structures create, and they are not afraid to interrogate and challenge them. When confronting physical, social, and emotional violence (e.g., bullying, sexism, racism, homophobia, religious persecution, etc.), they draw on personal values and organizational policies and work individually and collectively to motivate change.

Caring for Self and Others: Inclusive leaders recognize the social, emotional, and professional tolls associated with challenging hegemonic structures and developing support networks. In addition to coaching and mentoring other invitational leaders, they engage in self-care by seeking out safe spaces where they are supported by colleagues, friends, and family, and intentionally focus on the positives.

Finally, the teaching notes associated with the case studies stimulate thought by providing sociopolitical and historical context, and contradict established notions of equity and inequity. They provide awareness of the presenting and underlying issues, opportunity to reflect on and examine different world views, assume different viewpoints, and pursue related areas of research. They also use critical literacy to deconstruct the role the hegemony plays, and how hidden curriculum of education is used to devalue difference. Participants are also encouraged to explore policies, laws, databases, and resources that can be used to facilitate critical conversations along with proactive and interventive approaches and strategies. By digging deeper, readers can develop new conceptual frames and solutions and translate their new insights into inclusive action. I am hopeful that reading and exploring these issues will create inclusive mindsets, which allow us not only to see difference differently but also to act in different ways for our common good.

References

Harper, H. (1997). Difference and diversity in Ontario schooling. *Canadian Journal of Education, 22*(2), 192-206 Retrieved from: http://www.cssescee.ca/CJE/

Ontario Ministry of Education (2014). Equity and inclusive education in Ontario schools: Guidelines for policy development and implementation. Retrieved from: http://www.edu.gov.on.ca/eng/policyfunding/inclusiveguide.pdf

Steinberg, S, & Kincheloe, J. (2009). Smoke and mirrors: More than one way to be diverse and multicultural. In S. R. Steinberg (Ed.)Diversity and multiculturalism: A reader (pp. 3–22). New York: Peter Lang.

Contributors

Denise Armstrong is a Professor of Administration and Leadership at Brock University. She has worked in K–20 institutions in Canada and the Caribbean in a variety of teaching and administrative roles. Her research focuses on personal, professional, and organizational dynamics, with particular emphasis on administrative transitions, the vice-principalship, and social justice. She has also published extensively in the areas of middle management and leadership, identity construction, micropolitics, and ethics.

Michelle Bellino is an Assistant Professor at the University of Michigan School of Education and Co-Director of the Conflict and Peace Initiative. Her research centers on history education and youth civic development in conflict-affected contexts, examining young people's understandings of historical injustice, civic agency, and social belonging. She is the author of *Youth in Postwar Guatemala: Education and Civic Identity in Transition* (Rutgers University Press) and co-editor (with J. H. Williams) of *(Re)Constructing Memory: Education, Identity, and Conflict* (Sense Publishers).

Diane Linder Berman has been teaching middle and high school mathematics for 27 years as well as math education and inclusion through CUNY for the past 15 years. She became an advocate for inclusion for her son, who has been successfully included since Kindergarten. Her experiences parenting and navigating the world of special education are the inspiration for her writing. Her latest book, co-authored with David J. Connor, is *A Child, a School, a Community: A Tale of Inclusive Education*. She currently teaches High School mathematics at the Stafford Technical Center in Rutland, Vermont.

Troy Boddy is the director of Professional Learning and Equity Initiatives for Montgomery County Public Schools in Rockville, Maryland. Boddy has served as an acting director of School Support and Improvement, elementary school principal, and assistant principal, and is a multi-age teacher of grades K–3. In his current role, he leads system-wide professional learning with a particular focus on equity and cultural proficiency for a school district serving 161,546 students.

Ira Bogotch is Professor of Educational Leadership at Florida Atlantic University. For two decades, he has focused on leadership for social justice, writing journal articles, book chapters, and co-editing the *International Handbook of Educational Leadership and Social (In)Justice*. He is no stranger to Word & Deed, the publisher of this volume, having written a chapter for *Key Questions for Educational Leaders*. He is studying school integration of Syrian newcomers in both Canada (Ontario) and Germany (North Rhein-Westphalia). He periodically expresses his gratitude to others in the field of educational leadership in his blog: https://ibogotchblog.wordpress.com/about/

Sara Bogotch is a traveling Speech Language Pathologist for EBS Healthcare. Her travels have included a year-long residency in pediatrics, treating children with autism and other challenges, and a school year split between Washington State and Hawaii. She is driven by a passion for working with children, assisting in their curiosity, discovery, and problem solving. With a Bachelor's degree in Education from Florida Gulf Coast University and a Masters' degree in Speech-Language Pathology from the University of Florida, she strives to support children in their language development.

Kathleen M. Brown, EdD, is Professor of Educational Leadership and Policy at the University of North Carolina, Chapel Hill. As a scholar-practitioner, her research focuses on effective, site-based servant leadership that connects theory, practice, and issues of social justice in breaking down walls and building a unified profession of culturally aware educators working toward equitable schooling for all. Dr. Brown approaches education from an ethic of social care and works toward changing the metaphor of schools from hierarchical bureaucracies to nurturing communities.

Lynn Butler-Kisber, B.Ed, M.Ed (McGill), EdD (Harvard), is a Professor of Education at McGill University. Her work includes leadership, multiliteracies, professional development, and qualitative research methodologies with a particular interest in arts-based methodologies, especially visual and poetic inquiry. She focuses on issues of marginalization, equity, and social justice and is the founding and current editor of *LEARNing Landscapes*, a peer-reviewed, open-access online journal. The second edition of her book *Qualitative Inquiry: Thematic, Narrative and Arts-Based Perspectives* will be available in spring 2018 (Sage).

Suzanne Carrington is a Professor and Assistant Dean (Research) of the Faculty of Education at Queensland University of Technology, Australia, and has published in international journals in the areas of education for students with disabilities; inclusive culture, policy, and practice; and teaching/professional development for inclusive education. She leads a number of research and consultancy programs in schools to develop a more inclusive approach to education for children with disabilities and is the Program Director of Program 2: Enhancing Learning and Teaching for the Cooperative Research Centre for Living with Autism. See http://www.autismcrc.com.au/

Sveta Davé Chakravarty started her career in education with a PhD in Germanic Languages and Literatures and taught in US universities for 10 years before immersing herself in school transformation initiatives in public systems of education in India. With a deep commitment to equity and excellence in education, Sveta was a founding member of the Dil Se Campaign for the non-custodial care and education of street-children in 2005, a collaborative initiative of the Delhi Government and the Centre for Equity Studies. She was also a Founding Director of The Ferdinand Centre in 2014.

Dr. Linda Chmiliar is an Associate Professor at Athabasca University in Canada. She coordinates a Diploma in Inclusive Education, an after-degree for teachers and other education professionals that focuses on the skills and knowledge required to teach in inclusive classrooms. Her current research focuses on the use of mobile technologies to support the learning of children with diverse learning needs.

Cam Cobb is an Associate Professor at the University of Windsor. His research focuses on social justice, parental engagement, and narrativity and the arts. His work has been published in such journals and books as *Per la filosofia*, *Cinema: Journal of Philosophy and the Moving Image*, *British Journal of Special Education*, *International Journal of Inclusive Education*, *International Journal of Bilingual Education and Bilingualism*, and *Hemingway and Italy: Twenty-First Century Perspectives*. Later this year, his first music biography will be published, entitled *What's Purple and Lives in the Ocean? The Moby Grape Story* (Jawbone Press).

David J. Connor has worked in the field of education for 30 years as a high school classroom teacher, professional regional development specialist, teacher coach, and full time professor. He has focused on the topic of inclusion throughout his career and is the author of numerous publications. His latest book is *Contemplating Dis/Ability in Schools and Society: A Life in Education* (Lexington Books). See https://hunter-cuny.academia.edu/DavidJConnor

Bill de la Cruz is an inspiring leader who has been guiding individuals and groups through the process of personal transformation as a mediator and workshop leader for 30 years. As Director of Equity and Inclusion for Denver Public Schools, he has developed his programs and workshops to help individuals and groups build self-awareness, enhance relationships, and help foster positive, sustainable personal growth. Bill has been on his own personal growth journey for more than 40 years, which inspired him to develop specific practices designed to help create positive, lasting change.

Dr. Jenn de Lugt is an Assistant Professor in Inclusive Education at the University of Regina. Her research interests are the mental health of students and supporting those with emotional and behavioural challenges in inclusive classrooms and schools. She is currently investigating ways in which educative school-based mental health programs can foster open dialogue, reduce stigma, and enhance understandings of mental health concerns of children and youth. Dr. de Lugt's most recent project was an investigation of school-related anxiety experienced by high school students. Her doctoral work at Queen's University focused on the relationship between mental health and academic struggle, particularly in learning to read.

Cindy Diehl-Yang has worked in various capacities in the field of educational reform for 20 years. She was the founder of the Associated Colleges of Illinois' Center for Success in High-Need Schools and was most recently the Director of the Center for Educational Transformation at the University of Northern Iowa. She is the Vice President for Education at VGM Group and is the parent of a child with multiple learning disabilities.

Debbie Donsky is a Student Achievement Officer at the Ministry of Education in Ontario, supporting professional learning for leaders. She has been an elementary principal and teacher for 25 years and has been sketchnoting for about two years as a way to share her thinking. Debbie has an EdD from the Ontario Institute for Studies in Education (OISE) at the University of Toronto and recently did a TEDx talk called "Reclaiming Space" on the marginalization and discrimination faced by fat people. She illustrated and co-authored *Milo's Adventures* (see http://familyisaboutlove.com/our-book/) and has published in other books and professional journals. See www.debbiedonsky.com.

Melissa K. Driver, Ph.D. is an assistant professor in the Inclusive Education Department of the Bagwell College of Education at Kennesaw State University. Dr. Driver's research interests include equitable education for culturally and linguistically diverse students, teacher preparation and ongoing support, and early mathematics interventions. As a former teacher, Dr. Driver co-taught in inclusive elementary and secondary settings and coordinated her school's special education program. In addition to her classroom teaching, Dr. Driver has extensive experience coaching pre-service and novice special education teachers. She is passionate about pursuing innovative methods to prepare and support new teachers to teach all students effectively.

DeLacy Ganley, PhD, was bitten by the teaching bug after volunteering in college to teach English to farm laborers in Tacoma, Washington. She went on to teach college-level English and later high school ESL. In 2003, Ganley earned a PhD from Claremont Graduate University where she researched social capital theory, teacher quality, and how highly effective teachers impact the educational trajectory of historically marginalized students. In 2003, she became Co-Director of CGU's Department of Teacher Education, becoming its Director in 2012. Ganley is currently the interim dean of CGU's School of Educational Studies.

Louise Gazeley, PGCE, MA, DPhil, is a Senior Lecturer in Education in the School of Education and Social Work at the University of Sussex, England. Her research focuses on the intersection of social with educational (dis)advantage and disciplinary exclusion. Louise led a study to identify good practice in reducing inequalities in rates of school exclusion for the Office of the Children's Commissioner for England, which fed into their two-year national enquiry into school exclusions. Louise continues to utilise her professional role to support the development of fairer, more inclusive approaches to education at all levels.

Christopher M. Gilham, PhD, is an Assistant Professor at St. Francis Xavier University. He teaches graduate and undergraduate courses in mental health, inclusion, and qualitative research approaches. His current research projects are focussed on adolescent girls' developmental assets and on mental health literacy for high school and post-secondary students. Previous to this work, Chris was a public school educator and consultant.

André P. Grace, PhD, is Canada Research Chair in Sexual and Gender Minority Studies (Tier 1) in the Faculty of Education, University of Alberta. His research focuses on sexual and gender minority youth and young adults, and includes interests in resilience, comprehensive health education, and educational and social policy studies. For more information, visit his academic website https://www.andrepgrace.com and his community website http://chewproject.ca. His email is andre.grace@ualberta.ca.

Barb Hamilton, B.Sc, B.Ed, M.Ed, works for Calgary Catholic School District. Barb is a passionate educator, working to support student learning in a variety of contexts. She has spent the past several years as a school-based administrator, recently returning to the classroom to support students with various mental health diagnoses in a specialized program. Her current educational interests include nature-based learning, student empowerment, and inclusion.

Bud Harrelson is a PhD student in Education at the University of North Carolina, Chapel Hill, researching creating safe and welcoming environments for LGBTQ students, educators, and parents/guardians. Specifically, Bud researches how school districts go about adding sexual orientation and gender identity to their employee non-discrimination policies and how schools of Education prepare principals and superintendents to meet the needs of LGBTQ people. Prior to returning to school full-time, Bud served as a director of school improvement. He has worked with students from pre-K–12 as a teacher, curriculum facilitator, school leader, academic coach, and gifted and talented program director.

William B. Harvey is Distinguished Scholar at the American Association for Access, Equity and Diversity in Washington, DC. During a career of more than four decades, he has held faculty and administrative positions at nine colleges and universities. He has also served as Vice President and Director of the Center for Advancement of Racial and Ethnic Equity at the American Council on Education, the major coordinating body for the nation's colleges and universities, and as the founding president of the National Association of Diversity Officers in Higher Education.

Lindsay Kwock Hu, EdD, is the key assessment coordinator at the University of Southern California Rossier School of Education researching how teacher educators and preservice teachers are influenced in their preparation programs. Recently, she developed a K–8 problem-based curriculum for a non-profit organization where students analyzed the sociopolitical implications of an environmental disaster in their low-income neighborhood using higher order cognitive skills, including reading and writing, as a means to question and challenge status quo. She has worked as a P–12 educator, a literacy coach, and a professor of education, working to close the opportunity gap for historically marginalized students.

Karleen Pendleton Jiménez is a writer, filmmaker, and associate professor of education at Trent University in Ontario, Canada. She is interested in power, identities, bodies, and stories. She has written three books: *Are You a Boy or a Girl?* (2000), *How to Get a Girl Pregnant* (2011), and *Tomboys and Other Gender Heroes: Confessions from the Classroom* (2016). Her journal articles include "Latina Landscape: Queer Toronto," and "'I love Barbies ... I am a Boy': Gender Happiness for Social Justice Education." Karleen is also the screenwriter for the award-winning animation short *Tomboy*.

Vernita Mayfield is a former primary school teacher and secondary school administrator. She also coordinated state-wide programs for increasing educational opportunities for historically underserved students. Vernita teaches pre-service principals, consults, trains leaders, and develops course curriculum for public agencies. She is also a frequent presenter for ASCD and is completing her first book for them. She holds a PhD in Educational Leadership from the University of Colorado, an EdS in Educational Administration from the University of Colorado, and an MBA from the University of California, San Bernardino. See Vernita@Leadervationlearning.com or follow her on Twitter at @DrVMayfield.

Philip McAdoo, EdD, graduated from the University of Pennsylvania. An original Coca-Cola Scholar, accomplished actor (an original cast member of *The Lion King* on Broadway), youth coordinator, teacher, and program developer, Philip was recognized for his work with inner city youth on the Oprah Winfrey Show. As Director of Diversity, he launched a speaker series, coordinated global education trips, and advocated for access to education. Philip and his partner helped to introduce and advocate for *The Every Child Deserves a Family Act* and the rights of same-sex couples. He is a proud father and little league coach.

Conor Mc Guckin, PhD, is Assistant Professor of Educational Psychology in the School of Education, Trinity College Dublin, Ireland. Conor convenes the Inclusion in Education and Society Research Group and is the founding editor of the *International Journal of Inclusion in Education and Society*. Conor is a Chartered Psychologist and an Associate Fellow of both the British Psychological Society (BPS) and the Psychological Society of Ireland (PSI) and researches psychology applied to educational policy and practices, bully/victim problems among children and adults, and special and inclusive education. Conor is also a Chartered Scientist with the UK Science Council.

Shashi Mendiratta is a Founding Director of The Ferdinand Centre for Education for Social Justice. She was for many years the principal of a school with children from all sections of society, and has for the past decade supported educators teaching children who formerly lived on the streets of Delhi. She has been engaged with the capacity-building of educators of the government school system who serve special needs children, through leadership and management development, curriculum development, and implementation support. A seasoned educator and researcher with 35 years of education experience, Shashi is always learning.

Hiren Mistry is an educator committed to equity and cultural and religious/creed diversity. Hiren has over 15 years of experience as a classroom teacher and school board Equity and Inclusion Coordinator, connecting human rights theory to practice. In addition, Hiren has worked in higher education, with community groups and non-profit organizations. He is a former seconded lecturer at York University (Faculty of Education), and is completing his doctorate in Higher Education and Leadership at the University of Toronto (Ontario Institute for Studies in Education) focusing on the intersection of policy, religious diversity, and school leadership.

Carmen P. Mombourquette, EdD, is an Associate Professor of Education specializing in Educational Leadership at the University of Lethbridge. For many years he was an elementary, junior high school, and high school principal in Alberta and Ontario. He is the co-author of *Enacting Alberta School Leaders' Professional Practice Competencies: A Toolkit*.

Jhonel Morvan, a statistician and economist in a former life, was a math teacher and department head for many years before becoming an Education Officer at the Ontario Ministry of Education. He holds a Master's degree in Educational Administration from the University of Ottawa, an Honor Specialist in mathematics from York University, and both Principal's Qualifications. He is pursuing his PhD in Educational Leadership and Policy Studies at Brock University. His research focuses on school leadership, inclusion, equity in mathematics, mathematics achievement of racial minorities, and teacher expectations.

Divya Murali is Program Lead at The Ferdinand Centre. She is Guest Faculty at Ambedkar University Delhi and was previously Teaching Assistant at the Delhi School of Economics. A social anthropologist by training and educationist by vocation, she develops and facilitates such courses and workshops on understanding society and power, gender, exclusion, and state and citizenship. She has been working on developing 21st century curriculum with multiple stakeholders and making positive interventions in the quality of education at the school and college levels. Her research areas are inclusive education, education policy and development, and inequality and social justice.

Carol-Ann O'Síoráin, PhD, is a lecturer in Special Education/Autism in St. Angela's College, Sligo (National University of Galway), Ireland. Carol-Ann's research focuses on special and inclusive pedagogy, supporting learners with intellectual disabilities, the voice and role of parents in education, and the role of play and playfulness in advancing communication and access to learning. Carol-Ann has held many roles in relation to special education needs (SEN), notably with the Government of Ireland and as President of the Irish Association of Teachers in Special Education.

Eleni Oikonomidoy, PhD, is Associate Professor of Multicultural Education at the University of Nevada, Reno. She teaches classes for both pre-service and in-service teachers and is affiliated with the Masters and Doctoral strands in Equity and Diversity in Education. Her research focuses on the social and academic integration of newcomer students, globalization, culture and education, and culturally responsive practice.

Nicholas J. Pace serves as professor and chair of the Department of Educational Administration at the University of Nebraska-Lincoln. The former social worker, teacher, coach, and principal has written four books on principalship and received the 2010 recipient of the Iowa Friend of Civil Rights Award.

Carl Parsons is a Visiting Professor in Social Inclusion Studies at the University of Greenwich in London, UK. He has a degree in Sociology from the London School of Economics and a PhD in Curriculum Studies from the University of Leeds. He was Professor of Education at Canterbury Christ Church University from 1998–2010. His research interests include poverty, exclusion, marginalized groups, and other equality issues in education. His research has been funded by the World Health Organization (*The Health Promoting School: Policy, Research and Practice*, RoutledgeFalmer, 2002) and the UK Department for Education (Children excluded from primary school, 2001; On Track, 2003; Minority ethnic exclusions, 2005).

Adelee Penner, BHEc, B.Ed, M.Ed, works for Alberta Education improving student learning and teaching through supporting system leaders, administrators, and teachers. Adelee is a passionate and dedicated educator working to support continuous improvement throughout the province. Adelee currently has leadership roles supporting Hutterite and Rural Education. Adelee spent many years as a teacher and administrator in high schools in Alberta and Manitoba.

Nathan Phipps is the Managing Director of the University of Michigan School of Education's Center for Education Design, Evaluation, and Research (CEDER). He has worked for nearly a decade in professional development and as a secondary educator. He taught history, ESL, and technology in Boston Public Schools before joining the University of Michigan School of Education.

Bobbie Plough, former superintendent for three California school districts, is an Associate Professor in the Department of Educational Leadership, College of Education and Allied Studies, California State University East Bay, and the Director of the Center for Research, Equity and Community Engagement (CRECE), a collaborative effort with school districts to research and implement meaningful and sustainable change in K–12 education.

Brad J. Porfilio, PhD, is the Associate Dean of Research and Programs and a Full Professor at Seattle University. His research interests and expertise include urban education, gender and technology, cultural studies, neoliberalism and schooling, and transformative education.

Camille Quinton is the Director of Inclusive Education for a rural school division in Alberta, Canada. She has a Master's degree in Educational Leadership and a graduate diploma in Educational Psychology. As a former Resource Room teacher, principal, and district Student Services Consultant, her educational career has been focused on "inclusive leadership" and supporting all students in the classroom. In additional to her work in the K–12 system, she also developed and moderated an online course, "An Introduction to Disabilities in the Classroom," for the therapy assistant program at a local college. This is her first publication.

Dr. John Roberts is a Metis who has been active in Indigenous affairs in Canada for over 26 years. He was founder and president for 11 years of the Canadian Metis Council, a national organization with over 10,000 members. He was also Director of Education and Governor, region 9, for the Ontario Coalition of Indigenous People. Dr. Roberts retired from Mohawk College as a Professor of Language Studies and Manager of the Aboriginal Education program. Since retiring, he has worked as an occasional teacher with the Hamilton Board of Education. Dr. Roberts has written or contributed to 30 textbooks on communications, law enforcement, and Aboriginal education, along with numerous journal articles.

Diane Ryndak, PhD, is Professor and Chair of the Department of Specialized Education Services at The University of North Carolina at Greensboro. Her work focuses on teacher and doctoral level preparation for meeting the complex needs of students with significant intellectual and other disabilities, working with school districts to facilitate sustainable support systems to improve outcomes for all students. She has served multiple terms on the Executive Board for TASH; is on several editorial boards for professional journals; and has completed Fulbright Research related to inclusive education in Poland, where she continues to collaborate.

Michael Shevlin, PhD, is Professor in Inclusive Education in the School of Education, Trinity College Dublin, Ireland. He was a secondary teacher for 17 years before becoming a lecturer. Michael has developed a number of inclusive education programmes within initial teacher education and continuing professional development. He has researched widely on inclusive education with a strong focus on establishing inclusive learning environments and facilitating pupil voice within schools. He is Director of the Trinity Centre for People with Intellectual Disabilities, which offers a transition-to-employment education programme for young people with intellectual disabilities.

Steve Sider, PhD, is an Associate Professor in the Faculty of Education at Wilfrid Laurier University in Waterloo, Canada, and was a school administrator, special education teacher, and classroom teacher for 15 years. He teaches courses in special education, school leadership, and global education and researches educational leadership in international contexts. Recent publications include a co-edited book that provides comparative and international perspectives on education as well as articles in *International Studies in Educational Administration*, *Canadian Journal of Education*, and *Comparative and International Education*. He is also involved in school leadership and special education training and research in Haiti.

Lynne Sommerstein, M.Ed., has been an educator at Buffalo State College in the Exceptional Education Department for 21 years. She is a consultant to school districts on inclusion, curriculum modification, and friendship facilitation for students with developmental disabilities. She is also a trained lay advocate and leader in the field of supported full inclusion in schools and communities. She is founder and co-advisor to the Buffalo State Chapter of Best Buddies, founder of the SUNY Buffalo State College Based Transition Program for students with developmental disabilities, and a recipient of the Muriel Howard and the Buffalo State President's Awards for the promotion of Equity and Diversity.

Nan Stevens, EdD, began her teaching career supporting marginalized youth within the inner city of Toronto, Canada. Nan also worked for 10 years with the Vancouver School District, teaching street-involved youth and adults who returned to high school. When Nan gave birth to a son with a severe developmental disability and autism, students with exceptional needs became her life's work. Nan has worked as a teacher educator at Thompson Rivers University in Kamloops, British Columbia, since 2001, completing her EdD in 2017. Her commitment to those with exceptional needs aligns well with her social justice advocacy.

Dr. C. Darius Stonebanks, BFA, MA.Ed (Concordia University), PhD (McGill University), teaches at Bishop's University's School of Education and McGill University's Department of Integrated Studies in Education. Having worked in schools, from Pre-K to CEGEP, his teaching focuses heavily on bringing theory into practice and he has been awarded several teaching awards. He has authored *James Bay Cree and Higher Education: Issues of Identity and Culture Shock* and co-edited *Teaching Against Islamophobia* and the award-winning *Muslim Voices in Schools*. Dr. Stonebanks' recent research has included rural Malawi and the secular nature of Canadian public schools.

Samara Suafo'a, MA, is a Special Education and GATE Coordinator in southern California. Over her 20 year career in special education, she has worked as a K–12 special day class teacher, resource teacher, district leader, and school-site coordinator. Suafo'a earned a B.Ed in Elementary

Education from Linfield College, an M.Ed in Special Education with an emphasis on students with Moderate–Severe Disabilities from the California State University at Dominguez Hills, and is a student in the Urban Leadership PhD program at Claremont Graduate University. Aside from being a full-time educator and student, Suafo'a is the mother of two sons.

Raymond Tonchen, Jr., is a proud Viking from Walled Lake, Michigan. He has a Master's in educational leadership from Wayne State University in Detroit and a BSc in Music and Social Studies from Oakland University. Ray is a veteran of the Army's special bands program, playing trumpet and as a composer, writing musical compositions about the Patton legacy. He also spent 20 years in law enforcement. As an educator, he has taught in a juvenile lockup. Ray lifts, rides horses, is a scuba instructor and cave diver, and heads an educational non-profit for scuba diving programs in schools.

Miriam Twomey, PhD, works in the field of Early Intervention, Autism, and Intellectual and Neurodevelopmental disabilities. Miriam completed her M.Litt in Research and Doctoral Degrees at the School of Education, Trinity College Dublin, Ireland. Miriam leads the Masters in Education (Early Intervention) programme, designed to provide post-graduate study for those wishing to develop knowledge and experience working with young children with disabilities in the 0–6 age group. Miriam acts as Academic Advisor on commissioned National research projects and is a member of international and national research in the areas of Early Intervention, Inclusion, and Education for students with Intellectual Disabilities.

Jane Vanelli is an experienced teacher in inclusive education and leads an inclusion program at a large metropolitan state secondary school in Australia. Jane has completed Masters level study in education and her educational philosophy involves inclusive practices to support lifelong learning, providing equity in educational opportunities for students with disabilities, and transitioning students to post-schooling pathways that match their interests and abilities. She has partnered with Queensland

University of Technology in Service-Learning projects to support pre-service teachers in learning more about inclusion and she has worked collaboratively with researchers from the Cooperative Research Centre for Living with Autism.

Robert E. White is Associate Professor in the Faculty of Education at St. Francis Xavier University in Nova Scotia, Canada. His research focuses on diversity and inclusion in education, globalization, critical pedagogy, and leadership. His most recent publications include *Democracy and Its Discontents* (2015), and *Qualitative Research in the Postmodern Era* (2012), for which he won the American Educational Studies Association's Critic's Choice Book Award. In 2013, Robert won the President's Research Award. He is Associate Editor of the *International Journal of Leadership in Education*.

About the Editors:

Darrin Griffiths has worked as an educator in urban elementary schools for more than 25 years in the roles of teacher, vice-principal, and principal. He is also a Senior Lecturer at Niagara University and an in-demand conference speaker and session facilitator. Griffiths earned his Doctorate in Education from OISE/University of Toronto with a specific focus on urban school leadership and inclusion. His first book, *The Principals of Inclusion: Practical Strategies to Grow Inclusion in Urban Schools*, is used in many schools and districts as a foundational piece in the quest for genuine inclusion of all students. He has also co-authored and edited several books that relate directly to issues of equity and social justice in education. Griffiths lives with his family in Burlington, Ontario, and he is the principal of an elementary school in the Hamilton-Wentworth District School Board.

James Ryan is a professor in the Department of Leadership, Higher and Adult Education at the Ontario Institute for Studies in Education of the University of Toronto. He has been a teacher and administrator in schools in northern Canada. His interests are reflected in recent publications and current research activities. They include, among others, the administration of schools with diverse school populations; leadership; inclusion, social justice, and equity; micropolitics and leadership; philosophy and theory in educational administration; research methods; social, critical, and postmodern theory; and various organizational approaches to schooling. His books include *Race and Ethnicity in Multiethnic Schools*, *Leading Diverse Schools*, *Inclusive Leadership*, and *Struggling for Inclusion: Educational Leadership in a Neo-Liberal World*. Jim's latest book is an edited volume with Denise Armstrong entitled *Working With/out the System: Leadership, Micropolitics and Social Justice*.

www.ingramcontent.com/pod-product-compliance
Lightning Source LLC
Chambersburg PA
CBHW050551170426
43201CB00011B/1657